DATE DUE

2 2 1982			
1986 Mahoney			
RECD		MAR 04 RECD	
1 8 2003			
LCS.14 5-26-98 #26		Vernon Area PLD	
		JUL 0 1 RECD	
DEC 0 6 2003		RECD NOV 1 8 2003	
DEC 07 2015			

COUPLE
THERAPY

COUPLE THERAPY

Frank Bockus, Ph.D.

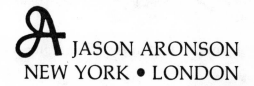 JASON ARONSON
NEW YORK • LONDON

Copyright © 1980 by Jason Aronson, Inc.

ISBN: 0-87668-412-6

Library of Congress Catalog Number 80-66920

Manufactured in the United States of America

to Alice and Keith

Contents

Foreword

As we move into the last two decades of this century, there appears to be an explosion in relational tentativeness—witness the spiraling increase in the divorce rate. Understandably enough, there is a concurrent interest in promoting the viability of marriage and other couple relationships. Family therapy, sex therapy, and couple therapy represent attempts at curbing, and possibly lessening, this epidemic of relational, often family-based unhappiness. The epidemic affects all of us and bodes ill for present and future generations.

The marital couple is quite different from other couple relationships. When couples marry and become parents, they become conduits between the generations with implications far beyond their awareness. As conduits, parents transmit, apart from the biological genetic code, relational patterns, behavior patterns, and cultural patterns from their forebears to their children. This conduit role exists beyond any consciousness of intent.

Various kinds of family-based therapies have evolved. However different their conceptual underpinnings, each converges on the goal of improving the functioning of the family unit. Every kind of family therapy recognizes that each physical, emotional or social symptom in a patient may derive from a maladaption of the extended or nuclear family unit. Treatment is thus conceptualized as directed toward the entire family, aiming at the reduction of both symptoms and family dysfunction.

The family systems perspective is currently the most popular point of view in family and couple therapy. The systems perspective accepts the paradoxical nature of the human being existing both as a whole unto him/herself and at the same time as part of a greater whole, e.g. a family.

Among the array of family therapy theoreticians currently in vogue are Murray Bowen, Jay Haley, Ivan Boszormenyi-Nagy, and Virginia Satir. Bowen's principal contribution to the systems approach has been his focus on a person's differentiation from his family of origin as the critical factor in leading to a sense of self. Haley's structural approach emphasizes hierarchy: he views parents as placed in a position to take responsibility in order to assist disengagement from their children. Boszormenyi-Nagy take a contextual approach. He underscores the sense of accountability a family member has in generating a climate that is trust-inducing. Thus he recognizes an ethical dynamic within a psychodynamic context. Finally, Satir's approach has considered the reenforcement of mutual positive feelings to be critically important.

One of the major problems in the field of family and couple therapy is the notable gap between an experience and its conceptualization in words. Credibility gaps in families are disquieting, principally because there is a presumption that people hearing summaries of experiences will be able to understand immediately the nature of the experience referred to. Unfortunately, this is seldom the case.

Couple Therapy by Frank Bockus is an exciting attempt at bridging this gap between experience and concepts. Whenever possible, Bockus presents experiential examples to accompany the concepts he uses to talk about relationships. This permits the reader a more active perspective on the material presented. The author seems to recognize that for the human being there are two basic modes of acquiring and accumulating information—the rhetorical, via language, and the experiential. It seems that with the mass proliferation of language-related information there has been a concurrent denigration of the importance of experience. The use of metaphor and symbols has been an attempt, however imperfect, at bridging the gap between language and experience.

Couple Therapy is prsented in a spirit of a "sustained attitude of tentativeness," that paradoxical trait necessary to expedite discovery and emergent selfhood. This tentativeness is expressed throughout in the recurrent distillation of seemingly diverse therapeutic orientations into a sensible and well-integrated blend. Bockus's journey, from his theoretical introduction straight through to the glossary and annotated bibliography, is amazingly cogent and masterfully paced.

To meet the needs of our clients, many of us have begun to use the best of each model to bring about the dynamic change and emotional growth needed in systems and individuals. Such an integration allows us to avoid becoming therapeutic machines, and thereby ineffectual, as well as to grow and develop along with our clients. Frank Bockus's book is more than timely—it is superbly sensitive to the present needs of the family therapy community.

Norman L. Paul, M.D.

Introduction

THE NO-MAN'S LAND

The field of marital therapy appears to be in a state of teeming and productive disarray. There are behavioral therapies, psychodynamic therapies, and systems therapies, as well as client-centered therapies, gestalt therapies, transactional analysis, and a host of other approaches.

Within any one of these many orientations, moreover, there are wide divergencies in perspective and procedure. In the systems framework, to cite but one instance, there are structural approaches emphasizing spatial metaphors and relationship boundaries, communications approaches stressing feedback loops, and approaches that focus on individuation within the undifferentiated family ego mass. While one systems therapist, therefore, attends to unfinished differentiation from the family of origin and to the fusions and conflicts thereby precipitated, another will have nothing to do with such extrinsic and historical matters and fixes his or her gaze selectively and deliberately on present symptoms, rigid interaction patterns, and unclear relationship involvements. The one will send clients back into their families for face-to-face encounters with significant other persons. The second will observe and interrupt reified interaction patterns in the present and trust that the resulting change will lead to a more open relationship for the couple.

When one looks beyond the confines of a single orientation, the heterogeneity of the field becomes even more evident. Psychodynamic therapy, like the intergenerational systems approach, pays primary attention to the fusions and projections that occur in couple interaction, but it goes on to an extensive exploration of the subject-object relations, the displacements, and the symbolic enactments that go into the making of such diffuse interpersonal states.

Transactional analysis envisions systems of yet another order. The therapist of this persuasion focuses on the first-order experiences and existential decisions made by one or both partners during the life history and then reenacted in repetitive scripts that strip the relationship of its spontaneity and originality. The behaviorist, like the structural and communications systems therapist, selectively attends to observable and measurable action outputs and inputs that are contingently reenforced. Deliberately not attended to are any intrapersonal or historical experiences underlying observable behavior.

Yet in the midst of all this fundamental and seemingly irreconcilable diversity there are countless similarities, including a number of ironic surprises that can go unheeded in the onrush of systems purity. The behaviorist, for example, after making observations, charting baselines, and specifying objectives of intervention, but prior to the shaping of new actions through intermittent reenforcement, often deliberately creates situations that enable the couple to practice the new behaviors. Such modeling, role playing, and anticipatory learning have all the earmarks of the rehearsal that appears in gestalt and experiential therapy, from which behaviorism supposedly sharply differs. Or again, the mounting recognition of the role of cognition in contemporary behavioral therapy marks a watershed in that approach. For this development opens the theoretical door for projection, symbolic interaction, and other forms of subjective assignment to play a role in the observation and interpretation of actions and events. The recognition of an enlarged function of cognition, therefore, appears to draw the behavioral orientation ever closer to the psychodynamic perspective, and these are a twain that, according to purists in both camps, can never meet.

Other parallels, too, can be hastily overlooked. In the final analysis, the repetitive interaction sequences of psychodynamic therapy, like the scripts of transactional analysis, are as much systems as are the reenforcement patterns of the behaviorist and the cybernetic loops of the communicationist. They differ from the latter in being organized at such very general and comprehensive levels that they encompass the total system of primary and secondary patterns of interaction.

The directives of the strategic therapist, who purports to have nothing to do with the past or the unconscious, are designed to bring about change in part through the client's spontaneous opposition to the prescription. Such a process shows surprising similarities to the dynamics of transference and resistance in the psychoanalytic approach.

The structural or brief therapist, to examine another surprising parallel easily slurred over, uses tasks and metaphors as analogues for relationship boundaries, and frequently intervenes by using both in sessions and homework. Such analogical thinking introduces the principle of correspondence into marital therapy: something stands for something else. The psychodynamic or experiential therapist likewise makes use of analogues, and differs from the structural or the brief approach primarily in the depth to which such symbols are pursued and explored. Thus, if an overt task can stand for, probe, and restructure an enmeshed family triangle, cannot that same triadic process also represent a family projection pattern which in turn represents a marital fusion or conflict, which represents a breakdown in individuation on the part of one or both partners, which represents an intergenerational transmission network from the family of origin? These deeper dimensions of the analogue are associated with and disclose some of the antecedent elements of marital interaction observed by therapists of psychodynamic or experiential persuasion.

These and other striking points of similarity suggest that the time has come for the field of marital therapy to move into new and relatively uncharted domains of theory and practice, into the no-man's land lying between the salients of the existing major orientations. In the present state of the field the plight of both novice and experienced therapist is understandable. New knowledge and methods pour forth from colleagues with whose approach one is identified or sympathetic, and staying abreast is very demanding. In this rather frantic situation it seems wasteful, unproductive, and even threatening to pause for a methodological examination of the basic premises, conceptual frameworks, speculations, and mind-sets that underlie one's perspective. It seems impossible to broaden one's orientation by making an effort to understand and perhaps incorporate the views and procedures of another therapeutic system, especially one supposedly counterpointed against one's own.

Yet the field cannot develop to the fullest unless the area between theoretical salients is explored and the findings made known and useful. One aspect of this new inquiry will be an ongoing methodological examination of the basic assumptions and mind-sets underlying the major approaches. Each therapeutic system, like any other branch of scientific and professional endeavor, rests on a set of paradigms that are partly or wholly unproven.

Another avenue of investigation will consist of a continuing vigorous conversation among exponents of different orientations. While critically reconsidering one's own position, one will also be required to have it exposed to the questions, suggestions, doubts, disagreements, and critiques of others. Needless to say, the climate of this professionally risky and stressful journey cannot be one of wasteful argumentation over rightness and wrongness. Nor can it be the fruitless game of making and breaking theoretical straw men.

In the give-and-take of this new search, issues can be more fully thrashed out. Parallels and similarities can be acknowledged and thus become the basis for a more integrated theory and practice. By the same token, the nature of the remaining disagreements and contrasts can be further clarified, allowing a sharper focus on problems for research.

There are those who are already traversing this virgin domain— therapists who make their own breakthroughts in theory and practice, but who also blend the approaches of others into a unified system. Their work usually lies outside the classifications that are presently appearing in the literature, defying categorization in the pigeonholes of systems purity and often appearing as after-thoughts or postscripts. Such orientations are often referred to as eclectic or as a melange of systems. An integrated approach does not have to be a grab bag of techniques to be applied willy-nilly, if that is the pejorative connotation of a "melange of systems."

In the present development of the field such therapies are

sometimes called experiential. To affix this label is, perhaps unfortunately, to add yet another compartment to an already overcrowded matrix of approaches. The appellation "experiential" is becoming one more part of the mental habitat in which the profession lives. So be it. Labels, as has been suggested here, can obscure deeper parallels and similarities among therapies, but they also provide a technical shorthand which serves to facilitate the rapid exchange of information and viewpoints.

The marital therapy expounded in this volume is grounded in the major existing approaches, but it charts new territory, moving into the no-man's land lying between them. It results both from a critical examination of the basic assumptions and conceptual frameworks inherent in different therapies and from an exploration of common themes as well as areas of real and seemingly irreconcilable difference.

A therapy is presented here which views couple interaction as a complex and deep process whose many elements and levels require intervention using a variety of methods. Systematically integrated in this approach are features of client-centered, communication, gestalt, object relations, sculpting, structural, systems, transactional, and other frameworks.

In the basic model, therapy is viewed as an interaction field in which the couple enact problematic situations. The therapist then uses this evolving field of interaction for gathering information, for recognizing patterns, and for direct and immediate intervention. When one or both of the partners spontaneously displace experience from another time and place into the field, that past environment can then be replicated, its overlap with the present clarified, and its fusions disrupted. Operating throughout with a sustained attitude of tentativeness, the therapist facilitates discovery—the sudden reframings and the unexpected outcomes that so often accompany genuine change.

MAPPING THE TERRITORY

In each chapter of the volume a particular therapeutic function or modality is examined as it is practiced in the experiential, or

integrated, approach. Extensive case material and therapist commentary follow the opening theoretical discussion and demonstrate its implementation. A critique concludes each chapter and
compares and contrasts the experiential approach to the task with
that of other therapies.

In chapter one, "The Interaction Field," procedures used by the
experiential therapist in gathering and sorting information are
examined. The heart of the material examined in this section is a
conceptual model, the interaction field, whose components provide
the therapist a mental framework to use in tracing and organizing
information as it pours forth. With this mental screen the therapist
can conduct an ongoing content analysis of a couple's interaction as
the interview evolves. Data acquired can be cross-referenced, thus
empirically grounding the therapist's clinical inferences.

The model recognizes and allows for the overlap of interaction
fields. Interaction originating in one time and place—for example,
the family of origin—can be displaced into a contemporary field,
where it can be maladaptive. Such overlap between fields can occur
through subject-object assignments, fusions, and consequent symbolic reenactments.

Case examples are presented, affording a look at the utilization
of the conceptual model and its related procedures of clinical
content analysis. A lengthy case is presented, consisting of a
checkup interview with an engaged couple who are just beginning
to experience stress in their relationship. A verbatim record of the
session is provided along with the therapist's detailed commentary
on the application of the conceptual framework in ongoing clinical
analysis. The case material also allows a detailed look at the process
of relationship formation and the relationship's development toward conflict.

This chapter focuses on the conventional therapeutic function of
assessment. In the critique appearing at the end of the chapter,
therapy systems are compared and contrasted with respect to their
orientations to this task. A distinction is drawn between digital and
analogical approaches. The former preestablishes what will be
considered relevant information in the course of therapy. The
analogical view recognizes both the presence of many levels in a
couple's interaction and the fact that levels are interconnected in

such a way that symbols operating at one level are intertwined with and can represent those functioning at another. The experiential therapist approaches data-gathering with a controlled but sustained tentativeness, allowing for the sudden and unexpected disclosure or reframing of information previously hidden or distorted.

In most chapters of the volume, the experiential approach to a particular therapeutic function will be presented first, followed by a comparison of that orientation with other systems. The aim here is to further the theoretical conversation advocated earlier.

Chapter two, "Patterns," examines the progression from the gathering of information to its organization into configurations useful for defining problems, setting goals, and designing interventions. The therapist works toward a meaningful understanding of the pattern of a couple's interaction and the levels within it. That pattern, for the experientialist, is made up of intrapersonal and interpersonal facets interlocked in a complex fashion. Moreover, the pattern consists of both overt and covert elements, the former manifested in observable communication and reenforcement sequences, the latter disclosed in displacement and symbolic interaction. The therapist seeks to conceptualize as cogently as possible the entire pattern of interaction—the unified combination of events, levels, and sequences.

Within this general conception the therapist identifies, in concert with the couple, those points where the greatest stress exists. Parts of the pattern that seem less critical than others can be dropped from immediate attention. The therapist determines which forms of intervention offer the best chance for long-term change. Those facets of the relationship where the risk of therapeutic intervention outweighs the potential gain are isolated. Where disruptions have to be made, the therapist clarifies the risks to be taken and the value choices to be made.

In the case reviewed in this chapter the patterning process is demonstrated for the couple whose checkup interview is reported in chapter one. The parallels recognized between past and present fields of interaction are cited as evidence of displacement. Potential problems and intervention goals connected with this deep structure are delineated, as are problems regarding the surface structure of the couple's interaction. Description of an intrusion-rejection pattern concludes the case material in this chapter.

Interventions are directed at the couple's communication process, and in the critique which follows, alternative intervention designs are evaluated for their appropriateness and their associated risks and rewards.

Chapter three, "The Enactment," is based on material drawn from a second therapy interview with the same couple. The case example demonstrates methods used in experiential therapy for the creation and replication of fields of interaction. Using a variety of procedures drawn from sculpting, gestalt, psychodrama, communications, and systems approaches, the therapist works with the client in simulating an anticipated social situation in the family of origin. The material demonstrates the therapist's use of this enactment for direct and immediate explorations of the interaction field, for formulating patterns, and for making tactical interventions.

The critique ending the chapter discusses the way change is viewed by the experiential therapist, and it relates that perspective to the case example and to other systems of marital therapy.

Chapter four, "The Narrow Passage," examines the use of dreams in marital and family therapy. This material is predicated on the assumption that many of the gains made by an earlier depth psychology are still therapeutically useful. The dream is viewed as a spontaneous production, from the depths of the individual client, of an interaction field in which he or she is immersed.

This chapter demonstrates how dream symbols are used in enacting that field, again taking procedures from a variety of therapy systems. Behind this work with dreams is the belief that fantasy material affords access analogically to intense emotions, impasses, attitudes, and decisions that may be influencing the client's interaction within the field. This deeper experience, therefore, can provide the corrective for perspectives afforded and limited by the surface structure. The value of the simulation in clarifying interpersonal boundaries is shown.

Chapter five, "The Experiential Group," extends the methods of experiential therapy into the setting of the multiple-couples group. The participation of group members in the creation and unfolding of an enactment and in the collective learning that emanates from it are demonstrated. The dynamics of change in such groups are delineated, drawing extensively on the findings of multiple-family therapy and on procedures of cross-encounter.

The final chapter, "The Teachable Moment," shows how experiential methods can be used in the making of the therapist. No attempt is made here to discuss a whole training program; instead, the workings and amelioration of one dimension of displacement are treated. It is the thesis of this approach that displacement, when it occurs in the therapeutic system, signals a most valuable opportunity to teach, leading to personal and professional growth. An enactment of the interaction field represented in the therapeutic system is demonstrated in a case example with a trainee. Again, a range of methods is employed.

The concluding critique discusses experiential approaches to training in general, showing ways in which the experientialist both concurs with and departs from two broad and contrasting orientations. This critique, then, provides a useful summary of experiential therapy and its place within the ongoing development of the field.

Viewing the marital relationship as a complex process of interlocking intrapersonal and interpersonal forces operating at many different levels, experiential therapy can be quite flexible in its approach to couples. It can intervene at the surface structure when that strategy seems indicated, and it can intervene in the deep structure when that seems appropriate. All couples do not have to be met with the same set of methods. Instead, the therapist meets each couple idiographically, in terms of their patterns and needs, and draws from an extensive repertoire of procedures. Experiential therapy is an integrated approach.

Chapter 1

The Interaction Field

The primary characteristic of a session of marital therapy is the rapid outpouring of enormous quantities of information. Gathering and sorting that data in order to understand a couple's interaction is one of the most important therapeutic functions.

The actions on which marital therapy focuses make up a complex process that seems to defy precise definition. The therapist must strive to order this process with respect to both its broad configurations and its moment-by-moment sequences. Other therapeutic tasks presuppose and constantly relate back to this never-ending process.

This chapter will present a conceptual model—the interaction field—and its use as a frame of reference in gathering and sorting information, making observations, eliciting information, and making inferences concerning a couple's interaction.

The model will first be reviewed in outline, together with procedures followed by the therapist in applying it during a therapy session. Then a case example will be presented, and the use of the conceptual model will be demonstrated. This case material consists of a verbatim transcript of an interview, accompanied by detailed therapist commentary. The chapter concludes with a critique comparing the experiential approach to information gathering with those of other systems of marital therapy.

THE CONCEPTUAL MODEL

The interaction field is like a stage upon which a drama is played out, a drama in which the experiential therapist can perceive the couple's relationship pattern and intervene in it. In a given unit of interaction the therapist attempts to keep several interrelated aspects in view simultaneously:

1. The cast of characters
2. The attributes of the environment
3. The stimuli with which the environment confronts the characters
4. The responses of the characters to these stimuli
5. The stimuli which the characters impose on one another
6. The reciprocal responses of the characters to these stimuli
7. The development of various themes of interaction
8. The outcomes of the interaction, especially points of transition or impasse

In the model all of these elements are viewed as foci within a field of interactive forces (Henry 1956). It should be kept in mind that regarding these various elements as foci is abstract and arbitrary; it is useful only for locating the source of action or the emphasis in the field at some moment. Furthermore, concepts like *stimulus* and *response* make arbitrary divisions within the field; the interaction, as we shall see, is always reciprocal.

The Unit of Interaction

One of the first things for the therapist to notice during a session is a shift in attention or focus. Sometimes such a shift is instigated by one of the partners, sometimes by the therapist, but the result is that for a certain period of time the interaction involves a particular overt concern. The topic may be a decision, an issue, an unresolved relationship, a lingering conflict, a particular time or place, a transitional period, a situation.

The block of material that centers around that concern is considered a unit of interaction, to which the therapist applies the conceptual model. In the exchanges within that unit the therapist begins to formulate the cast of characters, their reciprocal actions, the themes of their interactions, and the outcomes.

In the example which follows there are several units of interaction, each with relatively distinct boundaries. The first of these units concerns the couple's recollection of their interaction leading up to a concrete decision on whether to do a relationship checkup. This block of data, then, allows the therapist to investigate the partners' interaction during times of negotiation. The unit is bounded by the beginning and the conclusion of their recall.

As the case material unfolds, the therapist delineates other units of interaction. The couple's remembrances of their earliest encounters reveals their interaction during the formative period of their relationship. The male partner's review of his relationship with his mother sheds light on his family of origin and on some of the interpersonal models afforded him by his early experience. The female partner's recall of her relationship with her father, along with her memories of his relationship with her stepmother, discloses information about her childhood family and its relationship patterns. One of the last units of interaction in the example involves times of disagreement between the partners, revealing their interaction during conflict.

Other units of interaction appear in case materials presented in other chapters. For example, the material in chapter two consists of an enactment of an encounter between the male partner and his mother. Here, the extensive use of the conceptual model in recreating a field of interaction, in exploring and tracing information, in recognizing patterns, and in intervening in the partner's transition towards greater individuation is demonstrated. Chapter four presents an enactment of a dream, which makes up a unit of interaction. In chapter five an extensive unit of interaction occurs in a young woman's enactment, during a couples group, of an encounter within her family of origin. As the unit unfolds, the therapist uses the model of the interaction field in helping her replicate that encounter, move through it, and make the changes it calls for. In the final chapter a unit of interaction concerns a therapy student's anticipated encounter with his client in a session.

The Cast of Characters

The cast of characters is the set of persons whose actions figure in the unit of interaction. That cast changes from unit to unit, and sometimes even within a unit.

Of course, the couple themselves appear most frequently, but by no means exclusively. In the primary case example the cast consists primarily of the male partner and his mother, but his father and his maternal grandparents appear briefly. The female partner and her father are the main cast in another unit, but her stepmother, her mother (though deceased), and her boyfriends during her adolescent years also appear. In a later unit a client's nuclear family of origin makes up the cast.

The Attributes of the Environment

The attributes of the environment in which the characters interact consists principally of both the details and the general properties of the physical situation. Often, this aspect of the model is not mentioned in the unit, or it does not appear with sufficient intensity, frequency, or duration to be of any significance in elucidating the interaction field. At other times, the environment is highly consequential.

In one unit in the primary case, during a time when the partners are recalling their earliest encounters, a physical object, a telephone, appears prominently in the interaction field. College classrooms and the female partner's dormitory room are also mentioned in that same unit.

A telephone is significant in another unit in the example, in the interaction between the male partner and his mother. Also mentioned briefly but significantly here are his childhood home and the neighboring residence of his mother's parents. An environment made up chiefly of the female partner's home and her father's place of business appears in her exploration of her family of origin.

Environmental Stimuli

The environmental stimuli consist of forces that physical objects and situations exert upon persons in the case. Here, too, this element of the model may have no bearing in an interaction unit, especially where the focus is on interpersonal processes. Thus, when our case couple discuss their handling of interpersonal conflict, that issue may be disconnected from physical place.

In another field of interaction, however, the physical environment may have more effect on the persons involved. For the female partner in our principal case, her father's long working hours, coupled with her mother's absence through death, resulted in a highly disengaged model of interpersonal interaction. Her father's unavailability demonstrates that environmental attributes can also include the absence of certain elements.

For the male partner in our chief case, his early college environment is characterized, as he remembers it, by the lack of certain qualities that he had come to take for granted in his family of origin. The deficiencies of the new milieu forced him to adapt, thus inducing a personal transition toward greater autonomy and self-reliance.

Responses to Environment

The responses of characters to environmental stimuli are actions taken in reply to the physical milieu. The therapist focuses on the reception and interpretation of environmental stimuli. The therapist considers what emotions are evoked, what is intended in a reciprocal response, what is anticipated as a consequence of that action, and what is finally done.

In our major example the female partner responds to her father's chronic absence by developing both autonomy and self-sufficiency and a covert wish for closeness. In another unit of interaction, the male partner responds to his early college environment by developing greater self-reliance. The general nature of the male partner's childhood home, as he depicts it in another interaction unit, is a well-defined structure of regular and dependable times and expectations, to which he made a positive and strongly dependent response. In a later chapter, part of the interaction field is two different worship services. The therapist traces the male partner's responses to these alternating situations.

Persons and their environments are foci in a dynamic field. Distinctions between forces "within" a person and those "outside" are useful in locating action or emphasis at a given time. The environment is "inside" a person when his or her thoughts, feelings, and actions refer to people, events, objects, and places in the field of interaction. Conversely, a person is "in" the environment in the actions he or she does.

Interpersonal interaction is also a continuous, reciprocal process. A person responds to an action according to an interpretation of it and anticipates a response. This interactional sequence occurs in a continuous field of involvement.

Actions of Characters on One Another

The stimulus action that one person exerts on others during an interaction unit is his or her total and developing output within the dynamic field. The term *total*, is used here to cover the variety of ways a person can represent his or her experience (Bandler and Grinder 1976) to others. Information is presented using words, phrases, and sentences, as well as tone and volume of voice and tempo and rhythm of speech. Facial expressions and body posture present visual information. Physical movement enhances visual information: the pointed and wagging finger, the shaking foot, the hug, the tear, the glance away from the field of action.

As Bandler and Grinder have shown, messages can be sent through one or a combination of these channels. Messages can be congruent, reflecting integrated action, or incongruent, reflecting mixed communications to others. Incongruent verbal messages can contain deletions, distortions, or denials of some portions of the sender's experience. When such incongruity is occurring, other auditory or visual channels often represent the nonverbal elements of experience.

The term *developing*, applied to a person's stimulus output, refers to his or her changing output as the interaction progresses. In the principal example presented in this chapter, considerable time and attention are directed to tracing the gradual unfolding of each partner's action as reciprocal exchanges evolve.

Reciprocal Responses

The reciprocal response of a character to the stimuli of others focuses on a person's total inner experience during a unit of interaction. A partner internally processes the events that are occurring within a dynamic field in which he or she is immersed.

In their concept of the awareness wheel, Miller, Nunnally, and Wackman (1975) have formulated a framework for viewing individual process during an instance of interpersonal communication. These components, sensing, interpreting, feeling, intending, and acting, are useful categories for tracing intrapersonal experience.

These concepts, though dynamic, cannot fully capture the depth or spontaneous quality of inner life. Experience takes the form of instantaneous and rapidly changing constellations, some portions of which lie outside awareness. The therapist apprehends these shifting elements after the fact—after the experience itself. Still, the concepts are useful in understanding a partner's intrapersonal experience.

Sensing. In sensing, an individual receives raw information concerning the actions of the partner, or of others, in a unit of interaction.

Raw information from others in the dynamic field can be received by means of several channels, some auditory, some visual. One can hear words, voice tones, volume levels, and speech tempos that strike the sense of hearing. Body postures and movements, gestures, facial expressions, and breathing visually transmit the actions of others to the receiver.

Interpreting. Interpreting is in many respects the predominant element in intrapersonal process. A person forms images and meanings out of raw information. Interpretation is sorting out and ordering the diversity of raw sensory inputs from others in an interaction event.

Interpretation is especially difficult when the diverse channels through which others represent themselves are incongruent with one another. When verbal content contains deletions or distortions, interpretation becomes more problematic. Interpretation of mixed auditory and visual messages requires much effort. The probability of mounting anxiety and misunderstanding is increased.

On the other hand, interpretation can help a person to understand accurately the actions of others in the field. Information can be made progressively more concrete and specific. This tends to diminish anxiety and increase the likelihood of mutual understanding. Through the acceptance and clarification of each discrete channel of information, auditory and visual, all elements of experience can be encompassed in assigning meaning to the actions of others. An intended message can become a message heard, seen, and properly interpreted. Whether messages are shared accurately or not, an individual responds to events in the field according to the interpretations that he or she assigns to them.

Feeling. Feelings go along with an interpretation and form part of the response to them. Feelings are the specific emotional states associated with a person's interpretations of events in the field of interaction. An action of the partner, interpreted one way, generates one set of emotions. Interpreted another way the same action can evoke an entirely different emotional state.

As an interaction unit evolves, the experiential therapist pays attention to both the range and the intensity of each partner's emotions. The range can vary over a wide span. Mixed emotions can be experienced simultaneously. In the primary case to follow, for example, the male partner experiences alternating feelings of anxiety, dependency, guilt, resentment, and anger during times of conflict with his fiancee. Simultaneously, the female partner experiences a series of feelings: protective nurture, frustration, self-denial, estrangement, anger, and self-deprecation. The couple's relationship builds to a high pitch of anxiety during these moments. An intense emotional impasse or interaction bind is created, blocking any further movement toward resolution of the issue at hand.

Intending. Intention, as I use it, refers mainly to a purpose or result that motivates a partner toward some eventual action in the field. It refers also to the desired outcome. Like feeling, this element of experience is highly specific, reflecting a purpose or course of action closely tied to specific interpretations and emotions. The intention behind an action often lies outside awareness and is not consciously determined.

Acting. The concept of acting refers to a person's total stimulus output within a dynamic event. A partner, as we saw earlier, transmits his or her immediate response to others through many auditory and visual channels. Acting refers to words, phrases, voice tones and levels, rates of speech, facial expressions, body postures, gestures and other movements which represent internal experience. Action can be integrated, so that messages in different channels are congruent and matching. Or it can be incongruent, in which case transmissions become crossed and mixed. Such incongruent action can once again set the stage for rising anxiety and misunderstanding.

Themes of Interaction

Interaction themes are the dominant motifs in a particular set of exchanges among characters. In one unit in our principal case the dominant theme of interaction between the male partner and his mother is enmeshment and overinvolvement. Between the female partner and her father, in another unit, the dominant theme of interaction is disengagement and interpersonal distance. Such motifs are useful for defining the basic interpersonal models in each partner's family of origin.

Themes can also illuminate major interaction patterns. Thus in our chief case the couple's decision-making process has the theme of irresolute and incomplete action. She hints and he hesitates. This repeated interaction theme sheds light on the couple's inability to disagree in ways that preserve both their separateness and their togetherness.

Principal themes of interaction can evolve towards greater complexity in a given unit, or from one unit to another. Thus, the male partner's overinvolvement with his mother in one unit changes to the issue of individuation in another unit. In a unit focusing on the couple's handling of disagreement, the theme evolves from irresolute caution to outright conflict, with name-calling by the male partner and self-deprecating behavior by the female.

Unfolding themes within units, or between units, enable the therapist to trace the transitions and the impasses in relationship phases. For the male partner, the theme of enmeshment with his maternal parent in one unit evolves to a quest for greater autonomy and differentiation of self in another unit. Within one unit the theme of interaction between the female partner and her father shifts from the motif of disengagement to the wish for closeness and greater involvement with him.

Outcomes

The tracing of interaction outcomes can shed light on the present state, the transitions, or the impasses in relationships. In one unit in our primary case, the male partner's overinvolvement with his mother and his development of greater autonomy, produce the outcome of an interactional impasse. Seeking to make a transition from diffusion to individuation in his relationship with his parent, he experiences an interpersonal and intrapersonal bind. Feeling guilty and disloyal if he individuates, and resentful and unfulfilled if he does not, he faces intense anxiety which remains unresolved. The transition remains unfinished.

For the couple in the principal case, times of decision making and disagreement often result in unsatisfactory outcomes. For the female partner, having to squelch her wishes and being unable to assert her wants openly leaves her feeling frustrated and resentful. For the male partner, unwilling accommodation to his fiancee's initiatives leaves him feeling nullified and resentful. These unresolved interactions result in an even more unsatisfactory outcome—outright conflict.

Times of disagreement thus confront this couple with interaction binds which they cannot effectively transcend to their mutual satisfaction. They remain unable to be both separate and united, both individual and mutual.

DISPLACEMENT

Sometimes, while tracing a unit of interaction, the therapist witnesses the intrusion of material which originates in another field—from some different time and place, or from a different cast of characters. Experience arising from a past set of relationships spontaneously erupts into the present. Rising as if by natural impulse, without forethought or premeditation, patterns learned in some past milieu encroach on the present. An overlap or displacement occurs between one interaction field and another.

The Slip of Speech

One signal of such displacement is the slip of speech. In this occurrence a partner inadvertently expresses some element of his or her experience that previously remained out of awareness, or which he or she wanted to keep concealed. Paradoxically, an incongruent action is involuntarily rendered congruent. Though unintended, experience is represented accurately. The partner says, in the slip, what he or she really means.

In displacement an individual inadvertantly addresses the partner as someone else. A spontaneous happening, the event usually takes the speaker by surprise. It may be regarded as only an accident—which may be the case. For the experiential therapist, however, the occurrence is noted as a possible projection into the present of something which properly belongs to another relationship.

To illustrate, the therapist, tracing one couple's interaction, has observed a recurring theme of conflict around a frequently repeated incident. The husband, a professional man, often arrives home in the evening at erratic times. The wife has striven for years to plan the family dinner around his unpredictable return. For this couple the problem, which might seem easily solved to an outsider, usually ends in the same outcome. The husband feels harassed and pushed by his wife to change his behavior, which he refuses to do. The wife feels guilty when her husband is excluded from family mealtime, but she also resents his refusal to change.

On another occasion, the husband describes an oft-repeated sequence of interactions between himself and his mother during his adolescent years. The dominant theme of interaction is the mother's pushing and his covert resistance. Caught up in considerable emotional intensity toward his partner, the husband blurts out, "Like I said to my moth—uh . . . my wife." The slip takes both partners by surprise. The therapist notes it as evidence for a possible displacement. The hypothesis is generated that the speaker appears to be symbolically reenacting events and themes that have taken place previously, in another relationship. The underlying dynamics of a displacement process such as this will be examined more fully in chapter two.

Key Words

The use of certain words by one of the partners is often a sign of displacement (Goulding 1972). Terms and phrases such as *should, ought, must, have to,* and *need to* creep into a person's conversation. While describing his or her actions in a given situation, an individual's use of such words can reflect a foreordained response in the interaction at hand. The person seems constrained to relate according to assumptions or expectations that have been imposed on present events.

For example, a young woman and her husband are in therapy for sexual concerns. The present issue for her is his insistent demand for sex at times when she is disinterested and unresponsive. For him, the issue is her lack of response and initiative. Pressed by his urgings, she becomes either stiff and restrained, feeling guilty for her refusal, or she complies with his insistence, feeling compelled and angry.

In therapy sessions she frequently makes comments like, "I *should* be more responsive. I *should* be more willing to play the wife's role."

Hearing these words, the therapist conjectures a possible displacement. "What do you mean by 'I should'?" he asks, probing for further evidence.

"Well, I just know that a wife *should* meet her husband's needs," she replies. Her tone suggests that the assumption is self-evident, as though declaring, "everybody knows that."

"Where did you learn that?" asks the therapist.

"I don't know," she replies, smiling, "I just grew up believing that. I just learned it," she says, shrugging her shoulders. At this point, she has spontaneously gone into her past, in a vague, nondescript way.

Wanting to explore the origins of the bind she is placing on herself in the sexual relationship, the therapist inquires specifically, "From whom?"

"I don't know," she replies.

With that, the therapist asks her to get up and stand facing her chair, about four feet in front of it. He then tells her to be someone who is telling her how she *should* relate to her husband. This enactment is intended to help identify some earlier interaction field in which she acquired her inhibiting sexual responses. In her enactment of the fantasized figure imposing the *shoulds* on her, the therapist hopes to discover the original interaction field that is being displaced into the present. If the tracing of those earlier patterns discloses the presence of incomplete or unresolved relationships from the past, the therapist might focus on those unfinished tasks as a means of preventing their maladaptive intrusion into the present.

To the therapist's directive she retorts, "I don't want to do that. I don't like to play those kinds of games," she continues. She looks strained, as if feeling guilty about not complying, but also very determined not to follow the direction.

The therapist, having encountered a similar reluctance to enact in other clients, is at first inclined to be firm and to encourage her to go through with the task. Then, it suddenly strikes him that a displacement is taking place right now, in his own interaction with her. She is being urged to do something against her own wishes, and she is experiencing both culpability and resolve. It is as if she is reexperiencing with the therapist interactions that have taken place between herself and her husband and perhaps between herself and someone else, in her past.

Choosing to use this displacement as a vehicle for intervention, the therapist accommodates her resistance. "I can see that you're feeling compelled right now," he says. "And I don't want to force you to do something you don't really want to do." Using the present interaction and the inferred displacement as a metaphor, the therapist uses himself to relieve the pressure on her and indirectly to provide a model of accommodation for the husband. Since the therapist's original directive was experienced by her as a displaced analogue for the husband's sexual demands, his pulling back can also show the husband a way of adjusting to her feelings and wishes.

Therapist and client return to their seats. She says apologetically, her body in a supplicant posture, "I hope I didn't offend you or hurt your feelings." The displacement continues in the present and provides the therapist with a means for identifying the original interactions out of which it emerged. On the basis of the wife's interaction with him, the therapist hypothesizes that avoiding hurting or disappointing others is a preeminent concern for her. In fact, her interaction bind can be framed as a seemingly unavoidable ambivalence between inflicting pain on herself, through compliance with their wishes, or on others, through noncompliance.

Continuing therapy with this client revealed the origins of her displaced *shoulds* and her constrained interaction with the therapist. Her elementary school years were filled with frequent incestuous contacts with her father, whose feelings she did not want to hurt. But his molestings produced in her a wide range of emotions, including fear, guilt, shame, and anger. Her feelings towards her mother, who she came to see *should* have been her father's sexual companion, opens up yet another domain whose excavation is not germane to the present topic.

Symbolic Reenactment

The symbolic and usually covert reenactment of relationship patterns from the family of origin, or some other source, is yet another way that past fields of interaction trespass on the present. Relationship themes that occurred in the past are repeated in symbolically meaningful present interactions (Boszormenyi-Nagy 1965).

A young woman, in this example, is in therapy with multiple presenting problems. She is estranged from her husband, who is involved with another woman and wants a divorce. Functioning as a single parent is confusing and overwhelming. She perceives her son as quite helpless and in need of considerable attention and guidance. She fears that he may even be manifesting some signs of minimum brain dysfunction. She is unsure, therefore, about discipline—how much to expect of the child on one hand, how lenient to be in the face of a possible mental handicap, on the other.

In one particular session she is expressing considerable perplexity about how to interpret her husband's actions and their implications for the marriage. Tracing her confused image of the husband, the therapist wants to clarify the connection between her interpretations and her possible response. He places a chair in front of her as a symbolic stand-in for the husband.

"I'm going to feed you a sentence as though you are saying this to Bob (a pseudonym to conceal identity)," he tells her. "If the statement makes contact with your experience, if it expresses your thoughts and feelings, you can own it as a message to your husband," he continues.

"If I could just be sure that you're really all together right now, acting with integrity, I could quit hoping," says the therapist doubling for her. "But I'm not sure you really know what you're doing or that you're really all put together," he continues. "Is that where you're coming from?" he asks her.

"Um hum," she responds, nodding her acceptance of the message. "I think if I knew he absolutely . . . positively . . . that he was all together . . .," she says choppily.

Looking once more toward the stand-in for the husband, the therapist develops the simulated interaction further, "I see you as doing things and not really knowing what you're doing, not really acting in an integrated manner. I see you as sort of . . . what's the word?" he says to her, soliciting from her the appropriate word for the image she has assigned to the husband.

"Confused," she provides the missing trait. "And mixed-up," she adds.

The therapist infers that the underlying theme here is her intent to make sure that her confused and mixed-up husband knows what he is doing during the current separation. Probing this inference about the interaction theme, the therapist asks, "Where did you get the idea that it is your responsibility to make sure that somebody like your husband is really functioning and doing what he's doing without being confused—that you have to be sure that he stays together?"

"I don't know," she answers.

"Have you ever had anybody in your life who lived with that attitude toward someone else?" the probe continues.

"Sure," she replies, with a kind of obvious smile.

"Who?" asks the therapist.

"My mother," she responds.

"Toward whom?" inquires the therapist.

"Toward my father," she replies.

Realizing that there is an overlap between a past interaction field

(between her father and mother) and the present one between the
client and her husband, the therapist wishes to explore her parental model. In order to bring that past model into the present and give
it the impact of immediacy, the therapist creates a fantasized
dialogue between her mother and father. "I want you to put your
father over here," he tells her, pulling up a second chair to stand in
for her father. "And I want you to role play your mother. Role play,
her and talk to her husband," he adds.

"That's difficult," she replies. "I could explain it . . ." The wish to
talk about her parental model rather than acting it, the therapist
infers, is a form of avoidance, of flight from emotional intensity.

"What are their names?" asks the therapist.

"Sam and Martha," she answers (again, pseudonyms).

"Martha," says the therapist to his client, addressing her in her
assigned role and thus reinstating her in it, "tell Sam how you see
him."

"My father is trying to fix the tractor," she sets the stage.

"All right," the therapist acknowledges.

"And it's totally out of Mother's realm of authority," she elaborates.

The therapist, noting that this last remark is really the client's
interpretation of her mother's actions, interrupts her. "Let me
interrupt you briefly," he says to her. "Is this what you just said to
your mother? 'Mother, you're overstepping your boundary. And
you. . . .'"

"Yeah," she acknowledges, as if realizing this thought for the
first time.

"You're encroaching on Dad's turf," the therapist continues,
developing the theme of the parents' interaction. "Mom, you're all
over the place. You're being responsible for everything," he adds.
"Let Dad fix his own tractor."

"That's right," she concurs. "But Mother is always there."

"Do you know anybody else like that?" asks the therapist,
assuming that the maternal model from the past could well be
imitated by the client in the present.

"Me," she responds.

"She was your model," the therapist observes.

"Oh, definitely," she exclaims, "That's what Bob told me for

seven years. 'You're just like your mother,' he has said many times
. . . . But Mother is Mother, and I know a lot of her has rubbed off on
me."

Imitating her mother's actions, the client has imposed them onto
her relationship with her husband, and is continuing to do so in the
present separation. For her, the present is a symbolic reenactment
of the past.

Later in that session, and in subsequent interviews as well, the
client manifested the same interaction pattern with her son. She
hovered, and he responded with helplessness and apathy. She
realized that she acted toward her son with far more nurture and
care than he really required.

A metaphor was introduced into the therapy with her and her
son, one which richly expressed a pattern which spanned three
generations. The son was increasingly allowed and encouraged to
"fix his own tractor."

The dynamics of symbolic reenactment will be treated at length
in the following chapter. Consisting of a complex pattern of
intrapersonal and interpersonal forces, the process lies outside the
purview of the present discussion.

The Conscious Shift of Fields

Sometimes in a therapeutic interview one of the partners, or the
couple together, moves consciously from one field of interaction
into another. Sometimes that movement is a deliberate shift from
the present to the past. On other occasions, the transition shifts
from the present to the future, to some anticipated field of interaction. Unlike the previously examined forms of displacement, where
one dynamic field intrudes into another spontaneously, these
shifts are more intentional.

For example, a young couple are viewing their experience with a
homework task they had agreed to do during the previous week.
She is registering her disappointment with their performance,
feeling more discouraged than ever. Her depression had been the
presenting concern leading to therapy in the first place. To meet
her need for more emotional involvement with her husband, the
therapist assigned some communication exercises to be done at
specified times during the week.

She had been in individual therapy in another city for most of the previous seven years. In the first conjoint session with the marital therapist she was quite agitated by the goal of moving as quickly as possible toward termination of therapy. In that initial interview, during the history taking, she had mentioned her father's sudden death when she was twelve years old. The case material presented here takes place in the third conjoint session.

"It gets to be nine-thirty," she says, "and we either don't talk, or if we do . . . we don't really get anywhere." (She is gazing fixedly at the clock on the wall in the therapy room.) Noting that the clock lies in the forefront of her experience now, the therapist wants to explore its stimulus effect and her response.

"What would you like to say to that clock?" he inquires. Her reply to this query can disclose both its effect on her and her response. The clock, wonders the therapist, is a symbol for what?

"I'd like to tell it to stop," she replies.

"Tell it that," directs the therapist. "Talk to the clock and tell it why you want it to stop." Facilitating immediate interaction, in this instance through a fantasized dialogue between the individual and a physical object in the environment, is one of the more potent means of exploration and intervention in experiential therapy. The full scope of an interaction sequence can be traced, including the emotional impact of various themes and outcomes.

"Do I have to?" she replies, several channels in her demeanor emitting a childlike quality.

"What would happen if the clock did stop?" asks the therapist, choosing to disregard the possible displacement signified by her manner.

"I would tell it to stop, so there'd be more time," she says.

"Why do you want more time?" he asks.

"Because we always talk too late, and there never is enough time to get to the core," she responds, sighing. Her manner is one of resignation and helplessness, representing, the therapist thinks, her powerlessness to effect what she wants in her life situation, a classic condition of depression. She looks down, as though oblivious to her surroundings, and falls silent.

After some time elapses, the therapist asks, "Where are you right now?" This probe directs her to be fully in the present, to make contact right now with her experience, whatever it is.

She hesitates, and then in a slow, heavy voice, replies, "I feel slightly . . . emotionally drained. I'm talking and talking and talking and never . . . and then it gets to be too late. And the next time it's the same thing."

Hearing this, the therapist makes a preliminary inference about the clock and time and the theme of her interaction with them. Time rushes on, filled with much talk, with her husband, with therapists, but she hasn't been able to get where she wants to be.

"Where do you want to get?" he asks gently. "What do you want to talk about?"

"Well," she replies. "I. . . ."

"I want you to get there," says the therapist firmly. "I don't want you to let the clock get past nine-thirty, or let it get too late. This is the time. There's plenty of time, and there's plenty of space. What do you want to talk about?" This gives her permission to do whatever she wants with the present moment. It lets her claim it for herself.

"Um . . . ," she sighs, hesitating.

"Be there, Peg," says the therapist firmly, yet not insistently.

"Okay. . . . It's not unusual that I'm not feeling something constantly you know, whether it's feeling angry or happy, or whatever. And I've been thinking about going to the hospital to see Doug, when he was five weeks old. And I walked into the nursery. . . ." Doug, her son, had been born prematurely two years before.

"Peg," interrupts the therapist, "I'd like for you to relive it, say it in present time, as if it were happening now."

She has gone from the present interaction with the clock, her husband, and the therapist, to another time and place. The therapist's directions have enabled her to be where she wants to be, and to acknowledge that in some respects she has been there emotionally all along.

The therapist, of course, has no way of knowing where she wants to be, certainly no way of predicting this passage into the past. The experimental, exploratory nature of experiential therapy facilitates discovery of the unexpected and unpredictable. The procedures for tracing reenacted encounters with past relationships will be examined a bit later in this chapter, when we shall return with Peg to the hospital nursery.

Excursions Led by the Therapist

At times, the therapist intentionally guides the couple, or one of the partners, away from one field of interaction to another, either past or future. Excursions into the past enable the therapist to recreate fields of interaction in which one or both partners have been previously embedded. An especially important field of inquiry is the family of origin and the relationship patterns that were modeled there (Satir 1967). Parents, in their relationship, give out certain cues or models of marital interaction that are consciously and unconsciously imitated, or rejected, by their children (Bronfenbrenner 1970). How the parental couple has balanced the recurring issue of mutuality and individuality in their union significantly affects their children's mastery of this crucial task.

Each partner's relationship with each of his or her parents is another variable that can be investigated through an excursion into the past. Of particular importance here are the various relationship phases that have transpired with each parent, the times of dependency and autonomy, the times of possible overinvolvement and those of disengagement. The conditions of worth (Rogers 1959) and the injunctions (Goulding 1972) inherent in these parent-child relationships can also be examined through a focus on the past.

The replication of past fields of interaction, especially the family of origin, also can shed light on the way each partner has mastered the critical relationship tasks of being close, being separate, ending relationships and entering relationships. Such explorations can also illuminate ways in which each partner may still be attempting to master, complete, compensate for, or gain restitution for earlier relationships in his or her life (Framo 1975).

On occasion, the therapist may direct the couple or a single partner to some future field of interaction. Through the use of a guided fantasy or the simulation of some future event a set of anticipated interactions can be rehearsed and examined. This gives the therapist a means for tracing and intervening in client actions and responses in forthcoming situations.

PROCEDURES

The conceptual model previously outlined provides a set of categories for gathering and sorting information regarding couple interaction. As a given unit of interaction evolves, for instance, the reenactment of some past event, the therapist can refer to this reference structure.

The Analysis of Content

The presence or absence of concrete information bearing on some element of interaction can be noted. Where information about a category has been elicited, the therapist is justified in using those data to make inferences about patterns in the couple's relationship. Where information is missing, the therapist can explore the gaps. Process questions (Miller, Nunnally, and Wackman 1975) can be asked, such as, "What do (did, will) you see—or hear? What do (did, will) you think? What do (did, will) you feel? What do (did, will) you want? What are (did, will) you doing (do)?"

The conceptual framework acts as a check on the therapist's judgments, restraining him from drawing conclusions where data are insufficient or missing. By providing a reference structure, it helps the therapist to be careful and systematic in tracing interactions.

Returning now with Peg to the nursery, the therapist has noted her passage from present interaction to the past. The therapist's analysis is presented in the commentary following the verbatim.

Peg: I walked into the nursery and. . . .

Therapist: Peg, I want you to relive it as if it were happening now.

This directive is aimed at helping her integrate the past experience that seems to be coloring her present emotions. It will help her to bring this past event into the present. Enacting it in present terms can permit observation of the full range of her experience.

Peg: You mean feel it.

Therapist: Say it in present time:
"I'm going to the hospital."

Peg: Okay. I'm going to the hospital,
into the nursery.

Two elements of the interaction
field are introduced here: (1) the
physical environment, the nursery,
in which the drama is to be played
out and (2) Peg's action, what she is
doing, which is a walking movement. Nothing has been said about
the attributes of that physical location, its stimulus effect on her, or
her response to it. The cast of characters introduced thus far are Peg
and her infant son. The therapist
already knows that Doug was born
prematurely, but he does not have
any data regarding the stimulus
effect on Peg of that fact. He does
not yet have any information about
Peg's thoughts, her feelings, or her
intentions in making this visit. Any
themes of interaction between
mother and son are yet to be presented. Any inferences regarding
any of these missing pieces of data
would be premature and conjec-
tural. The proper attitude is one of
sustained tentativity leading to
progressive discovery.

I'm getting all scrubbed up and
everything, to go see Doug. And
I'm coming to the nurse.

She continues to describe her
own actions. A new character—
the nurse—is introduced into the
field.

And she's saying to me, "Would
you like to hold Doug?"

Peg describes (1) her sensory input, an auditory one, of (2) the
nurse's actions toward her. Three

categories already appear to have dropped from importance: the attributes of the nursery, its stimulus effect, and Peg's response. She has gone, instead, straight to the interaction among the principal characters.

And I'm feeling really nervous, because he's so small.

She describes her response, making a (1) feeling statement (nervous) associated with (2) an interpretation, an image of her son (so small).

And I'm saying, to avoid it, "Would it be all right? He's so little yet."

Peg describes her output toward the nurse, an auditory statement. But almost inadvertently she transmits an intention message (to avoid *it*—presumably holding Doug). The value of enactment in bringing covert levels of experience to the surface can be seen in this interaction. Even now, however, it is not clear why she wants to avoid this act.

And she's saying to me, "Well, I don't know if I should really let you do it, but if you don't tell anyone, I'll let you hold him for just a few minutes." And so she's going over to him and wrapping him in all kinds of stuff. (Peg begins sobbing.) She puts a hat on him . . . and everything. She's telling me to sit down over in the rocking chair. So now, I'm sitting down, thinking to myself, "I've waited for this a long. . . ." And she hands him to me, and I feel nothing. (Here, she is crying openly.) I don't feel any affection. I don't feel anything.

Peg describes her thoughts, with an implied feeling of eagerness.

She makes a statement dealing with the absence of feeling. With this statement the enactment is abruptly and dramatically reframed for the therapist, who never expected this development. His function as a facilitator, as a catalyst, to let the reenactment take its own, natural course, is exemplified in this series of events.

"I'm just thinking that by holding you . . . the situation must be improved."

She places herself in a fantasized dialogue with her son, addressing him directly.

"Because if you were dying, she wouldn't be letting me hold you."

This is the first time the subject of her son's possible death has arisen. Its emergence is spontaneous, evoked by the reenactment.

Data bearing on two interaction categories appear at once in this statement. (1) the stimulus output of the nurse, giving the infant to Peg, and (2) Peg's interpretation of that action (she would not do that if you were dying). The therapist infers on the basis of information at hand, that Peg's concern, her covert intent, is to avoid emotional involvement with Doug should he be dying.

"But I don't feel any instinct as your mother. I don't feel comfortable holding you. I don't feel sad that I can't take you home. I don't feel anything." And so I'm ready to put him back. And she takes him away.

Again, she makes a feeling statement, what she wants to feel or believes she should feel, but does not.

Therapist: Does she put him back?

Peg: She did. And I think that's the core.

She has now used this metaphor, "the core," in connection with two fields of interaction, in her conversations with her husband and in this reenacted encounter with her premature son. While the metaphor parallels both fields, Peg here places it first in the encounter with Doug, strongly suggesting that an incomplete relationship with her son then and there has some bearing on her current interaction with her husband here and now. Parallels between past and present fields of interaction strongly suggest the existence of some degree of displacement from the former to the latter, and are useful in identifying patterns of interaction between the partners.

I don't think it was grief that the pregnancy was terminated early... the loss of the pregnancy. Well... maybe I did feel all those things, but I don't feel that was the core.... Because when I'm feeling something, I have something to work on. But when I'm feeling nothing, there's nothing.

She is interpreting her own emotional state.

Therapist: I hear you saying, "Doug, I'm feeling guilty because I don't feel anything for you."

The therapist feeds her a sentence which voices the emotion implied in her former remarks. This is an interpretation by the therapist, that is, he articulates a feeling that seems to be present in her experience, but which has remained concealed or denied. Peg can participate in the therapist's statement and claim it if it fits. This intervention serves to bring out relevant but otherwise hidden information.

Peg: I always had a fear of that. After his birth the instinct was there, and I always feared its going away.

She makes another feeling statement, the fear of losing emotional attachment to her child.

Therapist: I'm sorry, I didn't follow you there. What would go away?

Peg: There was a . . . it felt as though there was a normal instinct of affection, of wanting to hold the baby and care for him. And I was afraid that by not caring for him, being with him and touching him, that the affection would be lost somewhere. And I kept trying to revive it, and it upset me so much . . . because I knew it had been lost somewhere.

Here, Peg first makes an intention statement. She wanted to feel normal maternal sensibilities toward her child.

She then repeats her feeling statement, her fear of not feeling normal affection. Then she makes another intention statement. She wanted to rekindle her maternal affection, but knew it was lost.

The dominant interaction theme thus far has to do with Peg's absence of affection toward her son— affection she wanted to feel, feared she would not feel, tried to revive, and now fears she has lost.

Therapist: Okay, I want you to be your affection.

The therapist wants to facilitate exploration of the missing emotionality. Since Peg has used the term *affection,* the therapist uses it. He directs her to assume the identity of that element of her experience and to speak for it in the first person. This directive, to become an emotion, facilitates continued immediacy in the reenactment, as opposed to a detached talking about this facet of her experience.

Peg: To the baby now?

Therapist: Be your affection and talk to the baby.

Peg: Be sure you cut in if I misunderstood.

Therapist: Where are you right now?

In Peg's preceding remark, and the paramessages accompanying it, the therapist perceived the same childlike quality that had been present before in the session. The immediate interaction, he infers, represents a subjective wish or intent, to please the therapist and the assignment of some authority position to him. The therapist wonders whether there is any significance to the spontaneous emergence of this dynamic in such close proximity to the metaphor, "affection." In short, has Peg's experience, in association with that metaphor, produced a fleeting displacement onto the therapist? And is the underlying force empowering these dynamics the lost affection?

Again, the therapist does not have to act prematurely on these inferences. There is evidence, teased out by the reenactment, to support such a preliminary hypothesis. But by waiting patiently and permitting more information to surface, the therapist can elicit more concrete data and make his judgments and interventions more suited to Peg's actual experience.

This brief episode illustrates the value of the conceptual model. The therapist can make inferences where information exists and can suspend judgments where it does not, and can refer to the model to bring out the missing pieces.

Peg: Because I'm thinking about my affection . . . lost . . . I felt that. . . . The first thing I thought of was . . . um . . . I'm afraid to become attached, because it's dead.

Therapist: Is that said to Doug?

Peg: Right.

Therapist: Could you tell him that, "I don't want to become attached to . . ."

This instruction, to say it directly, reinstates the fantasized dialogue, and thereby the experiential reenactment.

The theme is emerging of her acknowledging explicitly that she does not want to become involved with Doug.

Peg: Okay. . . . If I could just. . . . I don't want to become attached to you. I'm frightened if I'm attached to you. Because I'm afraid that I'll never be able to . . . (she begins crying).

Therapist: Tell him, Peg.

The therapist detects a resistance in her bearing, signaling that she does not want to complete her message. She appears to be at the point of an impasse, an emotional intensity which she cannot complete. This directive, therefore, is an intervention that requires her to push on through the anxiety and pain, to the finish, experiencing them in all their intensity.

Peg: To have you with me.

Therapist: Why not?

Peg: I'm afraid that while I'm gone, when I drive up to _____ tomorrow, that . . . you'll die while I'm up there.

Thus, the basic interaction theme is disclosed. Since Doug is premature and could die, Peg is afraid to become emotionally attached to him.

The outcome of this theme is yet to be clarified.

Therapist: What does it feel like to love somebody and lose them?

This query asks her to complete the interaction, that is, to lose someone with whom one is emotionally involved.

Peg: It hurts (she begins sobbing again).

Therapist: Whom are you talking about?

The therapist has inferred that she is talking about her father, but elects to probe in a neutral fashion, which still leaves the reenactment open-ended.

Peg: My father.

Therapist: Tell him that.

Peg has now gone from the nursery field of interaction to an earlier one, with her father.

Peg: I was really hurt when you left to go hunting, knowing it was against your doctor's orders . . . because of your heart. And you left me (her sobbing becomes open crying).

In this stimulus-response sequence her father leaves, against his physician's orders and when he didn't have to, to which Peg responds with feelings of hurt and abandonment.

Therapist: "You didn't have to go."

The therapist echoes an implicit

portion of her message, doubling for her and addressing the father figure directly.

Peg: No, you didn't have to go. . . . I believe that's one of the reasons it was so important for me to stay with Doug and not go up to _____. Because I felt that if I left and he died . . . that I would be deserting him the way my father deserted me.

At the conclusion of the reenactment Peg is able to put together the dynamics of the experience for herself, without the therapist's interpretation. Her father's leaving and subsequent death she interprets as desertion, a fairly common view of death on the part of a child. And part of Peg's emotionality is fixated at the time of that childhood loss and pain.

She has displaced the interaction sequence of desertion and abandonment, which originated with her father, onto her earliest encounters with her son. In the dynamics of that displacement she is both child and parent—the child back then who still fears the pain of loss and abandonment, and the parent right now, who fears to be the one who leaves and abandons another.

Therapist: When you get involved, and people die, you get hurt.

Peg: (sits up. Looks more relaxed).

Therapist: What do you want right now?

Peg: To have a beer.

At this point the therapist shifts his attention to Bob and solicits his response to his wife's reenactment (Paul 1967). We thus return to the present field of interaction.

"It seemed like I was sitting . . . letting my emotions run wild," he offers, "like, you know, really getting into it. And . . . it just seemed funny how we couldn't relate these things to each other. Maybe we did in our own ways, without . . . ," his voice fades out.

"I wasn't shocked," he continues, "when she said, 'I don't . . . I'm afraid to care about you.' . . . And I'm looking at my mind, and thinking, 'Why didn't I . . . I who would give my all, my everything, to a patient (Bob is a medical professional himself) who was going through that . . . and wouldn't even give it to my wife. And that brings a lot of guilt," he concludes.

"Could you tell that to Peg," the therapist instructs him, motioning towards her.

"I just felt like I could give that to somebody whom I was taking care of," he says to Peg, "and I couldn't give it to you. Like if a mother was there with her infant and I was taking care of the premature baby . . . I would sit down and talk to the mother about the feelings she would experience. And I'm asking myself why I didn't do that with you."

"Could you answer yourself," instructs the therapist, in effect, directing Bob to have an internal dialogue with himself.

"Maybe I thought that because I understood," he replies, speaking to Peg, "you would too."

Bob then becomes pensive and withdrawn. "I can still picture myself," he recalls, "a doctor running out of the room with a wrapped infant in his hands and me running after him, 'cause I knew it was mine."

Now, Bob has passed into another interaction field. Now, he is back at the time of Doug's birth. In subsequent narrative he recalls how helpless and frightened he felt then and how his colleagues treated him, not as an anxious and worried father, but as a colleague. He recalls their, as he views them now, callous, professional-sounding remarks to him. He felt lonely and slighted, as though they could not appreciate his inner apprehension.

Yet, he recalls, he tried to protect his wife, sensing her fear. He kept his own pain to himself, which Peg, unfortunately and understandably construes as insensitivity and disregard toward her.

Finally, the couple share their misperceptions and their missed opportunity for closeness during what had been a trying time for both.

At the sixth interview Peg announced her readiness to terminate therapy. In a follow-up personal encounter with the couple three years later, they reported continued satisfaction with their marriage.

The Marital Chronology

Past fields of interaction may be introduced into the therapeutic process through the deliberate initiative of the therapist. Knowing that past relationship states, especially those from the family of origin, can be displaced into the marriage, the therapist may make occasional direct inquiries into historical facts. In case material cited earlier when the therapist asks the female client where she learned responsibility and concern for her husband's actions, he conducts an indirect, open-ended probe of past material that might bear on her present marital state. When he then asks whether she has ever known anybody else like that, he invites her to scan her past. This puts her in touch with ways she is imitating her maternal parent and her parents' marital relationship, which contributes to dysfunction in her own marriage.

A more systematic exploration of the past can be conducted through the marital chronology or history taking. Introduced by Satir (1967) as a means of reducing threat and inducing hope in the early stages of therapy, the chronology proves a useful conceptual framework for structuring interviews and for eliciting and cross-referencing information about the past.

The scheme includes a set of probes designed to shed light on relationship models and patterns from each partner's family of origin. The state of the parental marriage, how parents handled intimacy and conflict, and a partner's interaction with each of his or her parents are some of the topics that can be explored. The investigation of ways that the client couple handles similar issues of disagreement, conflict, and intimacy often reveals parallels that suggest their replication of patterns originating in one or the other's family of origin.

For the experiential therapist the primary use of such information is not to provide insight nor to interpret findings for the couple. Instead, it is to draw inferences and to formulate patterns that can be used in the creation and direction of intervention designs. Thus, while Satir has charted the basic progression for taking a relationship history, ranging from less to more stressful issues, the therapist usually deviates from any formal outline to follow a natural flow of inquiry and response. Subjects can be pursued to the extent that seems worthwhile, and other topics can be dropped from consideration. Allowance is always made for the spontaneous generation of information, the slip of speech or the use of certain words, under the stimulus of the therapist's directed inquiry. The therapist can return later in the chronology to some topic that has been bypassed in order to track some potentially fruitful train of thought.

The chronology is an especially useful instrument in the conduct of a relationship checkup. In the following example the therapist does such a checkup with an engaged couple. In this kind of session the client couple's objective is usually, as they present it initially, preventive and educational. Their goal is the enrichment and improvement of what they perceive to be a basically viable relationship.

The verbatim material and therapist commentary will afford a comprehensive look at several features of experiential therapy. Demonstrated in this example are the use of the relationship chronology, the application of the interaction field model, and the procedures for carrying out an ongoing content analysis of data as the interview unfolds.

Presentation of the material here will be detailed for the sake of a rigorous and disciplined introduction to the model and to its related procedures of analysis. In actual practice, the therapist tries to remain flexible and spontaneous in the use of the framework.

It should be added, however, that the therapist is usually rewarded by not deviating too far from the model. Too often, on the verge of making an inference or formulating a pattern, believing himself or herself to have a good grasp of the events at hand, the therapist nevertheless patiently waits for more and firmer data. Sometimes new information abruptly and dramatically reframes the existing inference or point of view. Then, too, when the therapist is not quite sure how to assess some unit of interaction, the systematic and modulated application of the framework will often unearth the needed data.

CASE EXAMPLE

The case material to be reviewed at length here consists of a premarital interview with an engaged couple, both of whom are upperclass students at a state university. The therapist for the session, a professor and supervisor in marriage and family therapy at the same institution, is conducting a marital checkup as suggested by Jackson and Lederer (1968) and others. The interview is held in the marriage and family therapy service of the university.

An Event of Decision Making

Therapist: I'd like to find out a little about how we came to be here. (To Kathy) I believe you made the appointment for the checkup. Is that right?

The therapist is assuming that one of the partners took the lead in setting up the interview. That initiative began the interaction event which is beginning now. Right from the start, the therapist focuses on the intent behind that partner's actions.

Kathy: Yeah. When I heard that this sort of thing is available over here (the university-sponsored marriage and family therapy service), I was really interested. I thought maybe I could get to know Mark better and find some things that we might not be doing right, or that we could improve on.

Kathy speaks directly to her intent. She states her goals in preventive and enrichment terms.

Therapist: So your goal is to take a look at your relationship and perhaps to improve on it?

This question reflects back (Rogers 1959) her statement at face value. An important first step toward establishing the conditions necessary for inquiry is to demonstrate a desire to accept and understand her perspective on the checkup. The aim is to convey an attitude of implicit positive regard for her and the partner's frame of reference as the interview unfolds.

Kathy: Yeah.

Therapist: Can you remember exactly how you brought it up? Could the two of you kind of go back over that together?

This question asks Kathy to recall and describe her initial action toward Mark.

In effect, the therapist directs the couple to a modified reenactment of their interaction leading up to the decision to do the checkup. But while they are going back in time to an earlier discussion, the therapist intends to move them as quickly as possible toward addressing each other directly. His aim is to facilitate contact in the present and to inhibit a mere discussion about their earlier exchanges.

This facilitation of current encounter (Kempler 1973) provides the therapist with an opportunity to observe and trace the couple's interaction.

The question to Kathy, "What did you say?" asks her to describe her action toward Mark.

Kathy: I guess I just asked him if he would be willing to talk to you about it. I can't remember my exact

In this opening phase of the encounter Kathy interprets her own output—hesitant. She does not

words, can you (to Mark)? What I said, I guess, was kind of hesitant.

provide any description of how she sounds and looks at these times, only what her intent is. Also, she does not follow the directive to talk to Mark, except quite briefly.

Mark: She didn't know if I was going for it, I think. She thought maybe I'd be afraid to come over here or something, I don't know. But it didn't bother me.

Mark explains his partner's subjective state. No doubt, he knows how his partner looks and sounds when she is being hesitant, but he, too, goes beyond sensory data to an interpretation of her behavior. His mind reading communicates, implicitly, that he knows her intentions and thoughts without clarifying them. Mind reading can be maladaptive. The effect on Kathy can be negative, leaving her feeling exposed and angry.

Therapist: (to Mark) Kathy asked you whether you could remember what she said. How did she ask you? Could you tell her what you remember?

This question attempts once more to facilitate direct communication and redirect Mark to Kathy's earlier request for help in remembering. It asks him to describe his sensory input, what his partner said, how she appeared and sounded.

Mark: Yeah. You (to Kathy) came up to me, and it kind of seemed like you were going to ask for something . . . can I borrow some money or something . . . kind of hesitant. You looked like you were kind of hinting around. She wasn't (to therapist) really straightforward. . . .

Therapist: Could you tell Kathy (motioning toward her).

The therapist explicitly redirects him to contact Kathy.

Mark: (to Kathy) I think . . . maybe to see what my reaction was going to be. Then you asked me . . . I really don't know what it was. You said something like, "Do you want to be counseled . . . or videotaped, or something like that."

Once again, Mark interprets his fiancee's actions—hesitant, not straightforward—as well as her intent: to see his reaction. Probably without being aware of it, he has made an instantaneous mental jump from his sensory input to an interpretation of its meaning. Then, he documents his sensory input, what he heard her say.

The analysis of data already at hand in the checkup points to some preliminary inferences. The therapist infers that Kathy's stimulus output consists in making her initiatives by being hesitant and indirect. The effect on Mark, however, is to invite mind reading. He is drawn into having to read her mind. Conversely, to the extent that he reads her mind, that reenforces her hesitancy. From an interactional standpoint each partner emits stimuli which are themselves maladaptive and which have the reciprocal effect of drawing the other into maladaptive responses.

Therapist: If I'm hearing you correctly, you're saying something like, "Kathy, I don't think you were coming out with a clear request."

This intervention serves several purposes at once. It tracks Mark's account of the event and elicits more information. It also demonstrates the therapist's intent to understand his message accurately, and thus to join with him as he has with Kathy. Feeding him a sentence (Levitsky and Perls 1970), the therapist reflects his understanding of his message.

The therapist makes his own interpretation of the message implied in Mark's account and reflects it back in the first person. The client can then participate in the sentence and take responsibility for it, if it matches his experience at that point. Bringing into awareness what had been implicit enlarges, and thereby alters, Mark's frame of reference in the event.

At this moment in the interview feeding a sentence is a more appropriate intervention than reflective listening. While the latter procedure states Mark's message in the therapist's words, the former uses first person language (I don't think . . .) as a means of getting him to own his experience, in this instance to claim his interpretation of his partner's actions.

Finally, the intervention serves to mediate Mark's point of view to his fiancee, to catalyze her understanding of his frame of reference.

Mark: Yeah . . . (to both Kathy and the therapist) to feel the situation out, to see if I'd be upset or something.

Therapist: So instead of coming right out and saying what she wanted she was trying to anticipate your response or reaction.

Mark is still speaking for Kathy. The therapist accepts his statement by reflecting back his frame of reference. Such acceptance is highly important at this stage of the interview if he is to join with Mark and create a climate for inquiry.

At the same time, while the therapist has accepted Mark's experience of the moment, he has sought to expand what is implicit in it. In effect, the therapist has made an educational intervention by labeling the interaction element that is at issue here, namely Kathy's intent, and reframing how she might have handled it. The therapist says implicitly, "Kathy's intent could have been to make a clear statement of what she wanted, but instead her intent was to anticipate your (to Mark) response."

Mark: Yeah.

Therapist: (to Kathy) You're smiling. What...

The therapist notices Kathy's smile and assumes that some underlying experience is being represented in it. He acknowledges and reflects his perception of this visual output on her part and at the same time invites her to interpret its meaning. In effect, he directs her to make contact with and bring into awareness that part of her immediate experience that is being channeled through the smile.

Kathy: Yeah. You were talking about being straightforward, coming right out. I remember . . . I didn't just come out and ask, you know. I kind of felt around to see if he'd do it first. I think I should have just come right out and said something.

The therapist assumes that Kathy has been stressed to some degree by his reframing of her actions in his previous intervention. Her use of the phrase, "I should have," suggests that she is experientially accommodating the therapist's intervention. She appears to be taking responsibility for the inappropriateness of her original actions and implies a change of intent, to be more open in saying what she wants. There appears to be an alteration in both the way she views her behavior in the interaction event and in what she intends to do about it.

Therapist: Is this . . . would you say, Mark, that this has been characteristic of Kathy to . . .

This is a probe. The processing of this reenacted event is quickly unearthing the dynamics of the couple's interaction. But now the therapist wants to determine whether the patterns that are being disclosed in this one event can be generalized. Is this interaction process typical of their relationship?

Mark: Yeah (smiles at Kathy).

His response to the probe is affirmative, that this is a characteristic pattern, at least in his estimation.

Something is being conveyed via the smile. It can be conjectured, but of course not known for sure, that this visual output represents some degree of implicit anxiety that Mark is experiencing in labeling the pattern as typical.

Therapist: You would.

Mark: She doesn't . . . she'll try to get my reaction before I'll know what I'm doing. Before I can answer, she tries to feel out the situation.

Mark again interprets his partner's action. He implies that she tries to get his commitment before he knows what it is to which he is agreeing.

Kathy: You can back out then and . . .

Mark: She's keeping herself safe, I suppose, rather than committing herself and having me get into an argument with her. She just feels around it before she gets into it.

The new information in this statement is the fact that sometimes, when Kathy is initiating some action, Mark gets into an argument with her.

Mark's statement here seems paradoxical. His fiancee tries to obtain his agreement with her proposal before he is totally sure what it is, yet she also conceals or distorts her entreaty lest he become angry with her. Kathy appears to be anxious in expressing her wishes. Mark also seems to be anxious, or wary in agreeing or disagreeing with her. These data are suggestive of some kind of interaction bind in the couple's negotiation.

Therapist: Of course, that's not an uncommon problem, to come right out with what you want. That's a hard thing for me to do, particularly in some relationships, to come right out with it. It can be a stressful experience.

This statement by the therapist is a form of mimesis (Minuchin 1974), in which he identifies himself with Kathy in a common human situation. He implicitly joins with her in the stress that can be associated with expressing one's wishes in some relationships. The remark also implicitly reflects empathy with and acceptance of her anxiety.

The therapist makes additional inferences based on some recurring data. Mark has manifested a constant pattern of interpreting his partner's subjectivity, especially the intent of her actions. He continues to speak for her, moreover, even after she has announced a decision to be more open in expressing her wants. Kathy appears to be more malleable in the interview process, whereas Mark shows less ability to adapt to changes already taking place.

Therapist: Mark, would you tell Kathy what you feel when she's being indirect like this.

Since Mark has shared very little of his own experience so far in the reenacted event, the therapist deliberately probes his ability to disclose himself.

The question seeks to clarify what he feels in response to his fiancee's hesitancy and obliqueness. It seeks to elicit a very specific element in his experience at the moment and to have him speak for himself, not her.

Mark: I'm starting to notice your techniques (smiles at Kathy). I know when something's up. I've seen it so many times already that I know when she's got something on her mind, that . . . I can maybe call her at it, you know, beat her to the punch. "What are you up to now?" I used to kinda fall right into it. Now I see when she's hinting around for something. I know how she operates already; so I kinda know what she's coming up with.

Mark either does not know what is meant by the word, "feel," or he selectively ignores my question. At any rate, he once more concentrates on his partner's action, rather than saying what he feels. However, he does implicitly disclose, probably unaware that he is doing so, what his intent is at such times—"to beat her to the punch" and "call her on it." These metaphors connote that he has to be ahead of Kathy in the interaction, though how or why remains hidden from view. He also implies, again metaphorically, a manipulative situation pressing in upon him in which he finds/lets himself arrive at a place where he does not want to be—"fall right into it."

Mark uses several phrases indicating that the interaction sequence he is describing has occurred with great frequency. It can be inferred, therefore, that the pattern under examination is reflective of the couple's relationship, at least during occasions of negotiation when Kathy is taking the initiative.

Therapist: How do you handle it?

The focus is once more on Mark's experience, only this time shifting to a new element, his action. Even though the question is put in everyday speech, it asks him to describe his reciprocal action, overt or covert, in response to his fiancee's "techniques."

Mark: I just sit there and make it look as if I'm not taking her hints. I try to get her to expose her plan. I kind of make believe I'm not taking the bait, you know. She's throwing little hints, and I make believe I'm not catching them . . . I suppose to make her come out and say, "Now this is what I want."

Mark finally focuses on his experience during his fiancee's initiatives. He describes at least two elements of his response, first, his output, which is to assume an outward appearance of not understanding Kathy's entreaties, and second, his intent, which is to force her through his pretense into being more transparent with her wishes.

Mark's feigned lack of understanding appears to be a partially incongruent response on his part, as does his explanation for it. On the basis of his previous remarks, it seems that he also wants to delay agreeing or disagreeing, in order to avoid entrapment.

Therapist: I'm hearing that you won't respond or react. You hedge, as if to say, "Come on. Out with it!"

In this statement the therapist once more accepts Mark's framing of his response, to get Kathy to be clearer, and reflects it back to him. At the same time, he seeks to expand Mark's perspective by labeling the two sides of his implied ambivalence, to react (disagree) or to respond (agree).

Mark: Yeah. I make believe I don't understand what she's hinting about.

Therapist: You do what is called clarifying . . . like saying, "Kathy, I can't commit myself one way or the other until I know what you really want."

The therapist remains focused on Mark's frame of reference and uses it to make an educational intervention. *Clarification* is the process of checking out some element in the partner's message, in this instance, her intention. This intervention also implicitly reenforces Kathy's earlier announced decision to be more open in stating her wishes.

What did it make you feel when Kathy was being indirect about the checkup. I heard you say how you make contact with that?

This intervention serves both to educate and to clarify. It teaches the elements of experience by differentiating between feeling and doing. It also returns to the earlier inquiry regarding his emotions at the time of Kathy's hinting and indirectness.

Mark: (hesitates . . . frowns).

This time lag and facial expression, it can be inferred, represent Mark's effort to make contact with his feelings at the time of the event, or of similar occasions.

I felt, I suppose . . . I can't think right now . . . like I was going to get hit or attacked. So I wanted to play it cool and make sure I knew what she was asking.

Like for instance, she'll slip in a question like, "Would you like to go bowling sometime?" And I'll say, "Yeah. Sure." And she'll say, "How about tonight, with so—and—so?" And I'm kind of into ... I can't even back out.

Mark provides an eloquent script of the interaction sequence we have been exploring: (1) a general hint by Kathy followed by (2) assent on Mark's part followed by (3) manipulation towards a specific goal by her followed by (4) a feeling of entrapment and implied resentment in him.

In the first part of his statement Mark suggests the rudiments of another interaction sequence, one in which he anticipates being attacked. He implies that he sometimes feels threatened, that if he responds in the wrong way to Kathy, she will attack. The nature of that attack is not clear from the information at hand.

The further the interview goes into this subject of negotiating differences the more stress is being escalated. At this point it is too early to bring implicit conflict to the surface. There has been insufficient joining.

How the couple handles disagreement and conflict is a critical issue in the relationship and hence the checkup. Since that subject will be returned to later, the therapist decides to pull back from further inquiry on this topic for now.

Therapist: But that makes a lot of sense, I think to be sure of what you're saying "yes" or "no" to before you ... so you don't get into

The therapist addresses the more overt level of Mark's narrative and affiliates with him by further reenforcement of the importance of

something you may not really want. Don't agree to something until you're as clear as you can be about what you're agreeing to—like doing a relationship checkup. (We all laugh.)

clarification in negotiattion. Continued focus on the surface content also allows the therapist to remain joined with the couple while indirectly speaking to the implicit conflict that has been inferred. The therapist has said, in effect, "Careful clarification is the way to handle disagreement."

The therapist's final remark is designed to diminish the rising stress through humor. At the same time, the seemingly trivial comment acknowledges the seriousness of the situation, that is, the sense in which the couple's decision process leading up to the checkup appears to be a prototype of their interaction.

Thus far the relationship checkup with the couple has examined a concrete event of interaction, the decision to do the checkup itself. As the interview unfolds the therapist conducts an ongoing analysis of the couple's interaction. This analysis requires the therapist to identify specific elements in the couple's interaction and, on the basis of these observations, to make inferences concerning their relationship patterns.

This transition point in the interview is a good place to pause and summarize inferences that have been made so far. The therapist has inferred that:

1. The couple's interaction disclosed in the previously analyzed sequences is characteristic of their relationship. Both partners generalize that the event under review is a typical instance of their communication and decision making.

2. Mark does considerable interpreting regarding his fiancee's intentions and thoughts. In such mind reading he not only fails to disclose himself but also fails to let her speak for herself and clarify her own experience for him.

3. A great deal of Kathy's internal process, at least during times when she is expressing her wishes and making requests of Mark, is given over to anticipating his reaction or response. This dynamic suggests that she feels anxious, for some reason, in stating her wants and therfore acts cautiously and defensively.

4. Mark has difficulty disclosing his own feelings and wishes when Kathy is making an entreaty. He, too, feels anxious and acts with caution. His hesitant behavior implies ambivalent intentions, wanting to please, on the one hand, and wanting to avoid feeling coerced, on the other. Implicit also in Mark's hesitant behavior is some concern to avoid reprisal, that is, as he puts it, being attacked, by his partner.

5. Kathy, when she perceives Mark's hesitant and cautious behavior, tends to lead and manipulate the interaction toward her intended outcome.

6. Mark's repetitiveness, even in the face of Kathy's implied decision to be more open in asserting her wishes, reflects a degree of rigidity in his interactional style. During the reenactment new information surfaced from his partner, providing him with new inputs which could alter his expectations about her future behavior. He continues to act, however, on the basis of past images of her. He appears not to change with changing conditions.

Early Relationship Formation

Therapist: Kathy, as you look back on it, what was there about Mark that you liked initially, that you might say attracted you to him?

Inquiry into the early, formative stage of the relationship, the dating and courtship period, can provide the therapist with clues about the partners' original expectations and hopes. Mate selection being a far less conscious process than the term connotes, the early relationship contains areas of implicit difference, often slurred over, that eventually have to be confronted. Since it is an important purpose of the checkup to identify these areas of difference and potential conflict,

Kathy and Mark are directed to recall their earliest encounters.

Kathy: (in response to my question) Uh, I guess I find security in him. He's stable. When I first came up here, he was . . . like financially . . . he was really set in some of his philosophy, or something, and I was attracted to that.

Kathy's initial response to this query about Mark's attraction for her most closely approximates a feeling statement (I feel secure). Then she interprets her image of him, the traits which reflexively make her feel secure (He's stable). She expands on that interpretive statement by adding that he was "set in some of his philosophy, or something." Missing from her remarks is any sensory documentation of these interpretations, although she alludes to some aspect of his finances.

And he doesn't bug me at all. He's pretty understanding of me. He doesn't give me any hassles, you know . . . like if I wanted to go out, he's pretty understanding . . . doesn't tie me down too much.

Kathy's remarks here virtually describe a stimulus-response sequence that has been enacted with some significance in the relationship. She alludes to an intention on her part, "to go out," and then provides a sensory description of his reciprocal action (doesn't hassle me). The sequence outcome leaves Kathy free to be separate. She interprets his response as "understanding." She concludes with yet another perceptual statement about his action (doesn't tie me down).

Therapist: Could you say more about what you meant when you said . . . how did you put it . . . that Mark's pretty stable?

This is a clarifying question to get Kathy to provide the sensory data that were deleted from her original interpretive statements.

Kathy: Yeah, stable.

Therapist: What do you mean by that, his manner, or what?

The word "stable" which she attributes to Mark has several connotations—firm, steadfast, enduring, unchanging. The word "set" carries a range of connotations—fixed, resolved, or perhaps rigidly prescribed. The therapist clarifies her meaning by asking her to document the sensory inputs of his actions that have gone into the formation of her image.

Kathy: How he runs his money, that's one. He always knows where all his money's going to.

Kathy makes her earlier allusion more explicit by documenting Mark's care of his financial affairs.

Therapist: So you see him as pretty organized?

This question attempts to expand her image by reflecting in the use of the word "organized" a further meaning implicit in her interpretation.

Kathy: Yeah. And when he first came up to school, he was pretty sure about getting to classes on time . . . making sure he didn't miss class and stuff like that. He was pretty determined to do well in school . . .

Kathy really begins to specify, that is, document some of Mark's actions that she has observed and which form the basis of her image of him. She also infers his intention implicit in those actions (determined to do well).

which was just the opposite of me. I was just here, not going to classes, and he kinda took over and helped me get going.

Kathy interprets her self-image as the opposite of Mark and describes her behaviors that go into the composition of that image (not going to class). The opposite of "set" and "determined" would be such traits as "apathetic" and "inert."

Kathy then describes another stimulus-response theme: some action from Mark toward her, the outcome of which was to "get her going." She does not document his actions, how he "took over."

Therapist: I hear you saying, 'I was less organized, less with it.'

This sentence reflects her message.

Kathy: Um hum.

Therapist: 'And Mark was good for me.'

Kathy: Um hum.

Therapist: In what way? Did he provide you with a model? Or did he actually do some things. Do you see the difference in what I'm asking?

This is a clarifying question, to distinguish between Mark as a stimulus who could indirectly influence her, and a more direct agent who took specific actions toward her.

Kathy: He did some modeling, . . . you know, like in going to classes. I looked atthat and thought maybe I should go to class.But at the time I didn't care whether I went to classes or not. And with his money . . . he always made sure where his money was going. And then I started watching my money.

Kathy makes very clear sensory and intention statements (I saw his going to class and his handling of money, and I wanted to imitate those actions).

And then he did kinda help me . . . like he'd sometimes call me in the morning at eight to make sure I'm up for my class. So I guess he did both; he modeled and actually took some action to help.

Kathy documents very clear sensory impact of Mark's action.

Therapist: (to Mark) What was your purpose in calling her—I like the concreteness of that example?

The therapist probes Mark's intention in making this kind of clear and visible output. An implicit image of Kathy is probably connected with

Mark: I suppose I was brought up that way . . . by my family. If someone wasn't, kind of . . . help each other, you know . . . just to make sure they didn't forget or something.

this action. The therapist explores her stimulus effect on him, leading to his taking such action.

Mark spontaneously and abruptly shifts to his family of origin. He volunteers that he, and apparently others in that environment, were the recipients of actions on the part of some family member (or members) to remind them, to keep them from forgetting.

Therapist: Who would?

The therapist is tracking the stimulus-response sequence in Mark's family milieu to ascertain who is emitting this reminding behavior.

Mark: My mother, I suppose, mostly. That's probably where I got it from.

So Mark, who was the recipient of his mother's reminders, of her actions toward him, is imitating his parent's behavior in his own action toward Kathy. This is not an inference on the part of the therapist, but a self-interpretation by Mark.

She's always reminding me of dental appointments . . . everything. She'd call us up at school to make sure we went to the dentist right after school, in case we forgot. . . .

A very clear documentation of the mother's actions.

So I supppose it was, like I was developing a relationship with Kathy. And her attitude was . . . she was here because there was nothing else to do. School wasn't her main purpose . . . and I suppose, since I wanted the relationship to continue . . . if I didn't help her along by getting her to class, she might not be up here that long.

Mark provides information concerning his image of Kathy (apathetic and disinterested) and further data of the intentions connected with his actions (to keep her in school—and thereby in their developing relationship).

Since the interview takes a new direction at this point, this is a good place to pause and develop inferences drawn in the foregoing interaction unit. In the early stages of Kathy's and Mark's relationship, it can be inferred that:

1. There is a strong need in Kathy to experience security in the presence of a stable and involved significant other.

2. There is likewise a strong tendency in Kathy to be autonomous and unrestrained. In fact, she expects to be permitted to pursue that impulse and to have it accepted by another.

3. There is in Kathy a strong predisposition to be underresponsible and indifferent in response to the college environment, to be apathetic and inert.

The strength of these needs and tendencies is indicated by the fact that Kathy identifies them as general attributes of herself at the time. They are not merely occasional or mild characteristics.

4. Emanating from Mark, both as exemplary model and as an active agent, are nurturing actions and intentions. He aids and rescues her from her passivity. A corollary inference, subsidiary to the others made here, is that Kathy encourages or reenforces Mark's involvement and directing of her school activities through her continued forgetfulness.

5. Finally, Mark, in assuming responsibility for Kathy's affairs, reenforces her continued apathy and passivity, while Kathy in her carefree behavior reenforces his continued rescuing behavior. An interaction pattern is thus formed in which his effect on her is increased dependence and her effect on him is continued overinvolvement. The actions of each partner become cues for reciprocal responses from the other. Our data up to this point provide no indication of the outcome of this sequence.

In the above portion of the checkup the therapist conducted an ongoing analysis of the couple's reported interaction during the formative period of their relationship. Information was tracked and sorted in accordance with preciously specified interaction categories, and clarifying questions were asked to surface missing bits of information. Inferences about the relationship were made, based on this analysis.

The outline of an interactional pattern was formed in the therapist's mind. Mark was, or is, responsible not only for organizing his own affairs at college, but in an overresponsible manner, for Kathy, too, who thus remains underresponsible.

Even while he is tracking the couple's description of their early relationship, the therapist is raising several potentially relevant questions in his own mind. Is the overly nurturant behavior Mark is emitting confined to his interaction with Kathy, or is it a pattern learned in another field of interaction and being repeated with her? Is Kathy's behavior, which lacks self-direction and invites Mark to take over, confined to this relationship, or does it represent a replication of interaction models learned in another milieu?

In replying to my inquiries about his intent in calling and reminding Kathy about classes, Mark spontaneously volunteers that he was brought up that way. His rather abrupt introduction of personal history into the interview was surprising. He clearly draws his own parallels between relationship models in his family of origin and his present interaction with Kathy.

Mark's Family of Origin

Mark's mention of his upbringing opens a potentially fruitful avenue for exploration. In following the unexpected lead that he has provided, the therapist is able to move into historical material in a natural, unforced manner. Having set out with a plan to investigate the couple's earliest contacts and perceptions, he turns aside from that course to pursue the line of inquiry opened by Mark's response. He can begin to elicit and cross-reference information about such variables as Mark's interaction with his mother and its parallels in his relationship with Kathy. Later, if it seems advisable, he can redirect the interview to the topic they are now leaving.

In making this shift in focus, the interview data becomes qualitatively different. Until now, interaction analysis has been directed toward communication exchanges between Kathy and Mark. Each has been able to amplify and give immediate corrective feedback to the other's narrative, which is a major advantage of the conjoint approach of seeing them together. Now, the data arise entirely from Mark's self-reporting, from his account of his relationship with the maternal figure. His narrative will provide access to the mother-son relationship, as viewed from his frame of reference.

In order to establish an empirical base for drawing inferences about that relationship, the therapist will once more follow systematic procedures of interaction analysis. The following unit of interaction will be broken down into its constituent elements: (1) the actions, the stimulus inputs, that Mark sees and hears from his mother; (2) the effects her actions have on him, as indicated in his interpretation, his feelings, and his intentions; and (3) the reciprocal action, the stimulus outputs, he makes as evidenced by what he says and does overtly or covertly. The therapist will be trying to identify themes and outcomes of various stimulus-response sequences, in short, the feedback loop that defines interaction between the two.

If other elements come into the field of interaction, they too, will be tracked. These can be: (1) the attributes which Mark assigns to the field in which he and his mother interact, including the attributes of any extended cast of characters; (2) the stimuli which that field places on either Mark or his mother; and (3) their separate or joint responses to these stimuli.

This unit of interaction proceeds thus:

Mark: She'd (his mother) call us up at school to make sure we went to the dentist right after school in case we forgot.

Mark initially makes a sensory statement, documenting his mother's action toward him (an auditory stimulus, calling). He then infers her intent, to remind him. There is a parallel between his reading his mother's intent and his tendency, manifested earlier in the interview, to interpret his fiancee's motives.

It is impossible to know from Mark's account what his mother's purpose was in her reminding behavior. But the therapist would like to elicit more information about this apparently recurring theme of interaction, especially its effect on Mark.

Taken at face value, the result of the sequence, if repeated over time, would be to reenforce in Mark a position of dependency and a self-image of forgetfulness. His mother would be reenforced in his mind as a nurturing figure from whom he could expect management of his time and behavior. This outcome, incidentally, parallels Kathy's position with Mark (forgetting classes).

Therapist: How did you—or how do you—feel about your mother's being responsible for you?

The use of both verb tenses reflects the fact that the therapist does not as yet know the outcome of the interaction process, whether this apparent overinvolved relationship phase is confined to an earlier developmental stage in his life, or whether it continues to define the relationship. The query about his feelings is designed to clarify the effect of the sequence on him.

Mark: I suppose I never thought about it until I got up there.

Therapist: You just took that way for granted

Mark: But it was a secure feeling.

He replies to the probe. His feeling parallels Kathy's reported response to his original action toward her (security).

I never had to worry about anything, like dentist appointments, or being here or being there. She was always there . . . she didn't work at all. So she was always there when I wanted her. We always had a meal

Mark projects a very positive image of his family milieu and his mother's actions in it. Dependable, reliable, and structured are all attributes implicit in his interpretation. He documents her actions in

on the table at set times. You could always be sure that when you came in five minutes before supper, it'd be ready.

support of this image, always available, meals on time, reminders.

Therapist: I'm hearing that you found that a pretty firm structure.

A statement reflecting his positive image of his family environment. That image parallels Kathy's initial picture of him.

Mark: Yeah.

Therapist: And you really came to count on it.

Even though the therapist can discern a possible overinvolved relationship pattern in his mother's actions, he is here deliberately demonstrating his understanding, acceptance, and respect for the positive frame of reference he ascribes to his mother and the environment she provided(s). The therapist does judge the family model he is presenting, but takes it as the given, the interaction field, in which Mark had to adapt. That setting was, for him, reality itself.

Mark: I just figured everybody's family was like that—with the mother there all the time. Now I can see . . . talking to Kathy . . . people weren't like that.

Mark implies that he now realizes that other family environments are different from his own, and that he learned this through his relationship with Kathy. His remark offers a natural lead to explore yet another significant variable in the checkup, Kathy's family of origin.

At this juncture, however, the therapist chooses to stay with Mark's narrative. The therapist has already made inferences based on the previous exchanges, and wants the opportunity to verify them with Mark.

Mark: Until I came up here I was never on my own for any length of time. And the day I came ... when I saw my parents leave, drive away after they dropped me off, I kinda got a real empty feeling. Like, you're 250 miles away now, and you've got to do it on you own or die.

This new element of thought emerges around the theme of separation, and Mark lays out a major interactional event in which it was first manifested. He has arrived at college (the environment), sees (his sensory input) his parents (the other two persons in the cast of characters during the event) drive away (their action), and the effect on him of their leaving is a feeling of emptiness.

In effect, his childhood interactional field, so stable and reliable, was differentiating. Abruptly, he felt deprived of that environment in which he had been grounded, deprived of its outputs toward him, and which he came to expect. "Empty" is a rich metaphor for the lack of support and care that previously nourished him. Now he faces a new environment (the college) with a new set of conditions. It presses on him (its stimulus) by its very absence of previous support patterns, and a new set of responses is required on his part, one of self-reliance. The theme of this new situation is crisis, a make-or-break transition, in which he can develop appropriate actions or fall into maladaptedness.

The task inherent in this watershed developmental stage is movement from an apparently overinvolved relationship phase to one of greater autonomy and individuation.

Therapist: I'm hearing, "When I got up here, I had to provide my own structure."

The therapist reflects his message by feeding him a sentence.

Mark: It's like someone throwing you in the pool and saying swim.

Another rich metaphor in simile.

Therapist: (Laughs). Yeah, water won't support you unless you make some motion in it.

This is feedback by amplifying his metaphor. The metaphor encompasses several foci in Mark's new interactional field at once: the new fluid environment, constrasted with a firm and secure one; the initial splashing and insecurity; and self-propelled movement forward. The life cycle itself throws people into unknown states, transitions, and challenges.

Mark: There's nobody there to hold you up anymore; so you've got to make it on your own.

The real void in the new environment becomes personified. Mother is not there to support him.

Therapist: But you know, Mark, if she . . . if she was coming on so overresponsible like this, she would have to be sending you the message, "I see you, as needing to be cared for." And the effect of that message on you would be, "I need someone to structure things for me."

This intervention feeds back to Mark the overinvolved interaction sequence and outcome the therapist has been inferring. The intervention is expressed in a "yes . . . but" format (Napier & Whitaker 1978). That is, having first followed and demonstrated acceptance of his frame of reference concerning the parent-child relationship (it provided support), the therapist now challenges that very perception. He wants to enlarge Mark's framework to include the overinvolved relationship phase implied within it (it reenforced your dependency).

Mark: Yeah.

Therapist: So when that's taken away . . . "I've got to do it myself."

The therapist emphasizes the feeling of anxiety and the promise of autonomy.

Mark: Adjust pretty quick . . . Like in the morning . . . I never had to set an alarm. She'd be up there to wake me up, for school and. . . . When the alarm . . . the first time I heard an alarm up here for class, it was a rude awakening. You don't have someone waking you and keeping after you, you know. So I took it on myself to get to class. I had to get to class, set my own schedule, budget my own time. Because I was on my own. I didn't have anyone to fall back on.

Mark accommodates the reframing and, in effect, articulates his transition from dependency to autonomy in the concrete terms of an alarm clock.

Mark introduces important new information concerning his mother's actions (keeping after you), implying a frequent and persistent pushing. And once more he provides data on his emotional reaction to his newly impoverished environment (the alarm, a rude awakening). Afterwards, he began to take new actions to organize his life in the new setting (set alarm, fix schedule).

Therapist: So it was both good and bad to grow up in that environment, to have that kind of security.

The therapist is trying to say that patterns learned in a particular family are both good and bad. They adapt people to one field of interaction and thereby, at the same time, possibly impoverish their capacity to respond in some other time and place, in other relationships.

Mark: But I got too dependent on it.

The reframing is congruent with Mark's self-understanding. It brings to awareness and relabels what lay dormant in his experience.

Mark: Right. Like right now, I can stand on my own two feet. But when I go home my mother doesn't realize that I've come to be able to stand on my own. She still wants to hold me up all the time. I don't need it anymore.

Mark uses a metaphor, (my own two feet), to make an interpreting statement. The metaphor suggests self-support and independence. Then, once more, he mind reads, interpreting her subjectivity (she doesn't see that I'm self-sufficient) and what she wants (to hold me up). He implies that he is moving towards a more autonomous phase while she continues to view him out of the earlier overinvolved interaction.

Deleted from his statement is any sensory information, no description of her recent behavior leading to this present image.

Therapist: How have you handled that?

Whatever the facts about the mother, Mark relates to her as he views her. Thus, this question, clothed in everyday speech, seeks to clarify his response, his action toward her continuing responsibility for him.

Mark: Well, it's hard. Because I'm not home that much to show her that I'm responsible now. I think she still wants to take the mother role and help me along . . . you know, push me and be behind me all the time . . . and make my decisions for me when I want to make my own decisions now. Sometimes we get into conflicts, you know . . . like I want to be able to do things,

Again, he says what he thinks she wants.

This statement documents the mother's action, implying that she suggests, advises, and solves problems for Mark. The effect on him of such hovering guidance, the taking over of so much initiative in his behalf, can be a continued dependence.

'cause when I'm here at school I do them all the time. But when I go home she wants to, all of a sudden, take over for me. I don't like that.

He also clearly does not like this continued pushing, but suggests that the interaction pattern is hard to break.

Therapist: You want to say, "Hey, look—I'm grown up."

The therapist feeds back Mark's self-image of autonomy and self-initiative.

Mark: Yeah.

Mark said this with a manner that reflected that this was as far as he wanted to go on the subject of the conflict.

Therapist: (After reflecting a moment) How is your mom with the rest of your family?

With a fairly clear pattern in mind of the mother's continuing overinvolved relationship with her son, the therapist now wants to develop the implications of her behavior for the rest of the family. Since this one subsystem, the mother-son, is interconnected with other subsystems—and since he has some sense of mom's behavior in this parent-child dyad—the therapist wants to see how her functioning is manifested with others in the nuclear and perhaps in the extended family. For that family of origin provided Mark with his model, his interactional cues, for intimate relationships.

Mark: My mother was kinda like the central figure in our family. Everybody relied on her. She took care of most of the financial matters, like shopping, and paying the bills. 'Cause she didn't work, and she was home all day. Whenever anything came up, she was there.

This is a very compelling interpretation of the mother. She is the central figure on whom others depend.

Therapist: Is she the same with your father?

The marital relationship is a critical model for Mark, and broaching the subject can be an emotionally charged area for him. Yet he has given the therapist a natural lead, to examine how the mother's central role in the family affected her relationship with her husband.

Mark: Was she that way with my father?

Therapist: Yes.

Mark: (Pauses). I would say so . . . yes.

Mark looks reflective, as if pondering his models through the stimulation of the question.

The child learns by observing and imitating others. Marital behavior is, therefore, contagious. What the child sees, hears, and experiences in his parent's relationship becomes a potent model for his own learning (Bronfenbrenner 1970). How the parents show intimacy, how they handle disagreement, and how they provide for both individuality and mutuality in their relationship provide stimulus cues for the child's imitation (Satir 1967). Thus, with Mark the therapist is trying to get a picture of his model of marriage.

And I suppose my dad's even kinda used her as a crutch, to lean back on . . . because she was there. I suppose just one less responsibility he's gotta accept.

Mark ascribes to his father a tendency, a response towards the mother's central position. The interaction theme is one of leaning, being supported. He provides no sensory data documenting that image.

Therapist: Would you say he's in a kind of dependent relationship with her?

This response both reflects and seeks to clarify the interaction theme implied in his previous metaphor, the crutch.

Mark: I would say so. I think he's a lot more dependent on her than she is on him.

For the sake of time, the therapist accepts his interpretation without asking for documentation.

Therapist: Do you have some idea where your mother learned this kind of superresponsible behavior?

This is a fairly broad rubric under which to investigate Mark's extended family and possibly some intergenerational dynamics. Patterns of interaction are often transmitted down through the generations (Bowen 1978).

Mark: I can see it in my grandparents, in my grandfather more than my grandmother. I think my grandmother depends heavily on my grandfather. He used to tell me about how hard he worked during the depression and how he had to watch his money. I think if he died first, she'd go to pieces.

The therapist notes parallels between the mother's involvements in family finances, her father's concern about money, and Mark's preoccupation with that theme.

Therapist: Like somebody's got to be dependent on somebody else.

This statement seeks to feed back and confirm a pattern of overinvolved and dependent relationships in Mark's family of origin.

Kathy: His parents live really close to their own parents. They're only two houses away—it's her parents they're close to. I can see how his mother's taken over controlling his grandfather, kinda.

Kathy provides a map of the physical environment in which Mark's parents live. Geographical proximity in and of itself indicates nothing about relationship boundaries in Mark's extended family. His mother can live two doors away from her parents and have very clear and appropriate relationship boundaries with them. Conversely, she can live physically close and have very rigid and disengaged or enmeshed relationships with her parents.

Therapist: So you know them?

Kathy, however, sees enmeshed patterns in her future mother-in-law's actions towards Mark's grandfather. She suggests that she has seen (her sensory data) some behaviors indicating a controlling pattern in the mother's interaction.

Kathy contributes to this exploration of Mark's family model. It is possible that her participation reflects a cross-encounter (Paul 1968) process taking place as she listens. Such involvement affords her an opportunity to draw parallels and analogies between Mark's model for marriage and her own developing relationship with him. As she tunes in to the consequences of enmeshment in relationships she can amplify that learning and transfer it to her own behavior with Mark.

It is noteworthy that Kathy, after hearing Mark's description of his mother's behavior toward him and toward his father, interprets the parent's actions as controlling. This is a more powerful action than the verbs used by Mark, namely, reminding, waking, pushing, and taking over.

Kathy: Yeah, I know them. Like on

Kathy presents sensory data in

the telephone once, when they were fighting, she made your grandfather (looks at Mark) come over to eat dinner when your grandmother was in the hospital or something. She really gets mad if your grandmother is controlling your grandfather.

support of her interpretation of the mother as controlling (on the phone once, she made him).

Therapist: Sounds as if she's super-responsible in her family. You know, I bet there's a sense in which that's uncomfortable. It's a familiar role, because she's been at it a-while. But I bet she'd like to relax and get out of it a bit.

Although there's far more material that could be traversed in Mark's family of origin, the therapist has a rudimentary sense of his model. Included in the configuration are some further questions about the dynamics already excavated, for example, the intrapersonal effects for Mark's father of a sustained dependent state, the implications for Mark of the father's modeling, the impact on the mother of pronounced overresponsibility. Each of the these considerations points to additional interactional themes and outcomes, including impasses.

The therapist chooses one of these implications and reframes it for Mark and Kathy (it may be uncomfortable for her always to be overresponsible). This intervention potentially facilitates empathic understanding of Mark's mother.

Mark: You know, I think she's kinda into it and doesn't know how to get herself out.

This is a poignant description of an impelling and repetitive interaction sequence.

Therapist: She's got a lot of momentum . . . that's the way many patterns are.

This brings to a close a line of inquiry into Mark's family of origin and the model of marital interaction that it exemplified for him. From this investigation a number of inferences can be derived:

1. That Mark in his nurturing actions toward Kathy was imitating and identifying with behaviors modeled for him by his mother. The mother's reminders, pushing, and taking over provided her son with cues for his own acts of imitation.

2. That the effect on Mark of his mother's overresponsible nurturing was to shape a state of dependency in him. Behaviors like reminding, advising, and suggesting transmit a covert message that, in her eyes, he was incapable of providing these functions for himself.

This infantalization process, as Napier (1978) calls it, is often motivated by the wish to be helpful. The parent guides and directs the child through activities that can be done independently, thus inhibiting the development of autonomy and self-reliance. The assumption of so much initiative in planning and thinking for the child, what Mark refers to as taking over, is the hallmark of an overinvolved or enmeshed relationship phase. To repeat, it frequently, if not usually, is well-intentioned.

3. That Mark regarded his own model as typical of families in general. To have been immersed in his family, he assumed, was to have experienced the reality of family life. Presupposing this, it was inevitable that he would generalize some of the patterns he learned there to other relationships. It seemed natural for him to assume responsibility for his fiancee, just as his mother had previously done for him. At least part of what Mark brings to his relationship with Kathy, then, is the expectation that old patterns, learned and adaptive in one set of interactions, would also fit new ones as well.

This assumption, in the new relationship with Kathy, fits up to a point. But it can also bind the emerging relationship. Specifically, the overresponsible nurturance which Mark received, took for granted, and now imitates with Kathy, and which she apparently needed to a degree, can become increasingly maladaptive. Such overinvolved interaction can, in time, arrest the growth of each partner, as well as the development of the relationship.

4. That Mark views his family model in part with appreciation. It provided him with stability and security during his formative

years. More specifically, he regards his mother's care in positive terms, as reassuring, dependable, and fixed.

5. That Mark presently views himself as achieving greater independence and self-reliance. Such individuation was forced by the demands and challenges of a new field of interaction, the college, where the structure on which he previously depended was missing. This new state did not evolve without anxiety, without the shock, insecurity, and instability that accompany a new developmental stage and relationship phase.

6. That Mark also recognizes the limitations of his family model. The very structure that was so dependable instilled dependency, thus making the task of differentiating from it all the more difficult.

7. That the task of individuation remains problematic. Mark suggests that his emerging self-image, autonomous and self-reliant, is not matched by his mother's perception. This lingering bind is most evident when he goes home, where his mother persists in actions to "hold him up." Presumably, this means that she remains in an overinvolved relationship state toward him. The data reported by Mark suggest that the enmeshed phase is maintained by the mother. She, he implies, wants to rebalance the relationship to its former state.

8. That the data available concerning Mark's family of origin suggest a generally overinvolved model. This inference is indicated by his reporting of at least four enmeshed dyads: Mark and his mother, his mother and father, his mother and her father, and his maternal grandparents. Kathy provides corroborating observations in support of this view.

Development of the Relationship

As yet, the outcome of the overinvolved pattern in the couple's early relationship has not been ascertained. Now the checkup turns to an investigation of that subject.

Therapist: Where does that original pattern stand with you now (said to Kathy), of his helping you get organized?

Kathy: It's changed.

Mark: Yeah.

Kathy: Last year it changed.

Therapist: It's changed?

This is surprising. Just when a fairly clear conception of the relationship state seems to have emerged, all of a sudden the interview takes a new twist.

But the abrupt turn illustrates the value of strict adherence to the model. Realizing that he does not have data on the outcome of the couple's early interaction, the therapist intentionally probes for it. And suddenly, his perspective is jolted by new and unexpected information. Like cascading water, one wave flowing over another, a whole new perspective begins to emerge.

Mark: It's kind of, almost, reversed itself. Like I used to be . . . got to class and . . . she didn't care. And now she's really into all her classes.

Kathy: Yeah.

Mark: She's really . . . she'll read every chapter of every book of every class. Her grades are like a hundred percent better, and I may be a little bit progressed over where I was.

Therapist: I hear you saying, "I'm as organized as I ever was, but Kathy has. . . . "

Mark: Much more with it.

Therapist: How do you feel about the change (to Mark)?

This query is a probe based on previous inferences. If Mark has been acting overresponsibly towards Kathy, and she has become more self-reliant, the therapist wants to explore where that leaves him. If the relationship balance has shifted, is Mark stressed by the change, or is he comfortable with it?

Mark: I like it. I'm glad. Because when we first met, she . . . moneywise, she'd lose money, and it didn't bother her. We've already talked about how in my family we're all money managers. Now, her checking account . . . she knows where every penny's going—more than I do mine.

Mark feels pleased with the change and is sending Kathy very positive messages about her present behavior.

Therapist: It's better having her responsible for herself, instead of your having to be responsible for her.

This feedback delineates the more differentiated, less enmeshed relationship.

How is it with you, Kathy?

Kathy: I like it a lot better.

Mark: I feel more at ease now. I don't have to worry like when we get married . . . I don't have to worry where the money's going.

Therapist: I can see how the earlier pattern was fraught with a lot of pitfalls. You know, in time (to Kathy) you could have come to resent his pushing you, crowding you to account for every check . . .

This statement expands the couple's present perspective, to show the consequences that could have eventuated had the pattern persisted. Using the metaphor of the checking account the therapist points to a continuum of action on Mark's part in which he could have moved from reminding, to pushing, and from there to controlling. Kathy's reciprocal response to those actions could have been an emotional continuum ranging progressively from compliance, to resentment, to defiance.

Kathy: I could see that coming. I used to throw away money foolishly, and he'd get mad at me. And I'd say, "Well, it's my money!"

Mark: Yeah, and I'd say, "Well, someday it might be mine."

The reframing of the enmeshed pattern has catalyzed to the surface emotions that have already been present in the relationship, Mark controlling, Kathy defiant.

This cursory mention of arguments over finances affords the therapist with a lead-in to one of the most discriminating variables in the checkup repertoire, the couple's handling of conflict. That subject brings to the foreground the whole issue of differences in the relationship. The extent to which the partners can tolerate and preserve separate thoughts, wishes, and emotions reflects their capacity to balance individuality and mutuality in their interaction.

At this juncture, however, the therapist chooses not to follow this path. The surfacing of implicit conflict is potentially stressful for the couple and for the checkup, and he does not yet feel sufficiently joined with them to broach this topic directly. Then, too, the checkup really has not examined Kathy's relationship model from her family of origin. Without such data, and without a deeper understanding of their present patterns of interaction, inquiry into conflict resolution, or impasses, might not be as fruitful as it otherwise could be. The therapist will return to this subject later in the interview.

Previously in the interview, exploring the couple's earliest interaction, the therapist had wondered about the origins of Kathy's initial position in the relationship. Had her original apathetic and dependent state been derived entirely through interaction with Mark? Or had it arisen in another interaction field and been displaced onto her fiance? An investigation of Kathy's childhood milieu might shed light on these antecedent considerations.

Kathy's Family of Origin

Therapist: Kathy, in your upbringing was there anyone who played the kind of role that Mark did initially, that is, being responsible for you and trying to organize you?

This question reiterates the previously identified interaction pattern and asks Kathy to scan her history for persons who once embodied a nurturing overinvolvement for her.

Kathy: I don't think I had anybody being responsible for me. I was on my own pretty much. I think I kind of wanted somebody to take an interest . . . er . . . I don't know whether it is to take an interest . . . or what.

As Kathy scans her childhood relationships there is an absence of such nurture towards her. But she had wanted (an intention statement) to put someone in that place (the actions of taking an interest). Thus, she immediately characterizes her model as lacking.

Her self-image in the family of origin is clearly an autonomous one (on my own pretty much).

Therapist: Let me take a crack at it, and I'm going here by what seems to be implicit in what you said, "There was no one who took that much interest in helping me set limits, or letting me know what he or she wanted or expected."

Kathy seems to be struggling to formulate what she wanted in her family of origin. The therapist tries to help her put something in place in that field. He conjectures that it has something to do with stability and structure, since these functions are the ones that Mark provided. He let her know what he expected. Perhaps she can associate with the words, "limits" and "expectations," and use them as metaphors enabling her to be more concrete and specific.

Kathy: Um hum.

Kathy has a reflective look.

Therapist: Was Mark like a reaction against what you had known, you know, someone who would really get interested in you and tell you what he wanted or expected?

The therapist is trying to put together a pattern which Kathy herself has implied but which she appears to be trying to understand more fully. If Mark provided for her what was missing in her family of origin, then he was a reaction to that earlier deprivation.

Kathy: Yeah (almost muted).

Therapist: You're saying, "yes"?

Kathy: I think nobody ever cared whether I was economical or not . . . and because nobody cared or nobody gave me any push at all, I just didn't do it.

Again, her family of origin is characterized by an absence of certain actions, a lack of caring and pushing. The therapist notes the parallels in her use of the verb, "push." Mark pushed her; nobody in the family did. Since nobody expected limits, she did not set them for herself.

Therapist: Are you talking about your mother or father, or both?

Kathy: Father.

Therapist: So Mark was making up for some gaps that you had with your father.

Kathy: I think so. He didn't . . . I might not have known it then. . . . I see some differences that I hadn't seen before. But I always pictured him as not giving me . . . not too many expectations on me, you know. Like he'd say: "I want you to

She appears to be reframing her image of the father, that is, changing her interpretation of his actions from one view to another. His behaviors, which she once regarded as permissive and encouraging of her autonomy and self-reliance,

make up your own mind." Or, "I don't know how to help you with that." Or, "You've got to decide that for yourself."

And it wasn't that he . . . I don't think that he . . . I don't think it was in a good way. I wanted some kind of . . . advice . . . some example to fall back on, which he didn't even give me . . . no example.

Therapist: Um hum.

Kathy: I would still have liked to make up my own mind, but I didn't have anything, you know.

Therapist: You wish your father would have said what he wanted or thought, if nothing more than to be a sounding board.

Kathy: Yeah.

Therapist: You would have still made up your own mind . . .

Kathy: Um hum.

Therapist: But at least you would have had somebody else's thoughts on the matter.

Kathy: No models . . . I don't know . . . I just felt like I wanted to do it all then. I got really determined to do

she now sees as disengaged, as not providing the support and involvement she needed.

This remark reflects back an aspect of the parental function she missed in the family or origin, someone to listen and to help her clarify her thoughts, feelings, and wishes on matters. The data strongly point towards disengaged relationship boundaries in the family.

She would have maintained her autonomous state.

well and to show my dad that I could.

Therapist: I'm not following you.

A shift has taken place in Kathy's experience at this point. She sounds angry. Just when she has finished talking about the disengagement she felt with her father, she suddenly exudes, through her tone, frustration and resentment. Her response to those feelings is a kind of gritty impulsive determination, as though saying, "I'll show him. If he won't help me, I'll do it myself!"

Kathy: Maybe a rule in our family was not to be responsible, or something . . . I'm not sure.

Kathy has gone way ahead of the therapist in her stream of thought.

Therapist: I'm sorry. I'm still not with you.

Kathy: I don't know . . . when I was in the seventh grade until my senior year, the only person was my dad and me, who lived together.

Therapist: You haven't mentioned your mother.

The therapist had been wondering where her mother was, and here was a natural place to inquire.

Kathy: No. She died when I was twelve. In my senior year my dad remarried. So the only person I can relate to is my dad.

Therapist: And the sense I've been picking up from you about him is that you saw him as unavailable, not quite there for you. Is that accurate?

This response reflects a composite image of her father, to verify it.

Kathy: He's hard to get in touch with. It's mainly his job, I think. He owns a business, and he spends lots of time there. And about the only time I'd see him was early in the morning, when he'd take me to school, or late at night, when he'd come home. But that's about the only time, when school was going on, that's the only time I'd see him. He worked pretty late down there.

Kathy sounds almost apologetic. Perhaps she is somewhat protective of her father here, as though explaining his disengagement through the job is more tolerable than of his interpersonal inaccessibility.

So the rigid boundary between them was physical and temporal, as well as interpersonal. The pattern of an extremely disengaged family field is taking definite shape.

Mark: I think that's where I was more exposed to money management than she was. Her father wasn't there most of the time. I don't think she got a lot of background in it. Like I said earlier, I was exposed to financial matters through my parents, especially my mother . . . since she didn't work, and she takes care of most of the financial matters. So I guess that's where she didn't get as much logical backing, like in money matters.

Therapist: (to Kathy) But you're shedding more light for me now. You're saying you were really on your own.

Mark may be missing the interpersonal dimension in the subject being traced here, and so the therapist chooses to block him with selective inattention. It seems he has heard his fiancee's sense of deprivation, but he interprets it at a content level instead of an empathic resonance with her emotions. His response right now in the interview, ironically, parallels the one she is attributing to the father. Mark's emotional interaction is rather rigid.

Kathy: Um hum.

Therapist: Did you have to grow up fast?

The therapist draws an inference that Kathy's family model would require her to develop autonomy and independence quite early. This probe tests that inference.

Kathy: Yeah. I got real close to my friends . . . and most of the time a personal relationship with a guy a lot. I didn't play the field that much.

Kathy may have, as she makes this statement, a subjective, unmet need for closeness, which she found in a sustained relationship with one person at a time.

Therapist: Um hum.

Kathy: 'Cause it was secure like that.

Her use of "secure" here parallels her initial feelings in the relationship with Mark. Accumulating data seem to support the inference that Kathy carried an unresolved need for closeness and security out of her family milieu.

Therapist: Have you told your father of your plans to be married?

Getting close to another man implies a realignment of relationship boundaries with the father. The transition of marriage implies a separation from the father, and the therapist wants to learn his response to that step as Kathy has sensed and interpreted it. He knows that Kathy carries into this new stage a lingering sense of deprivation, but wants to probe where the individuation implied in marriage leaves the parent. His response will reciprocally color how she handles this transition. A pronounced disengagement on his part could leave her feeling even more emotionally cut off, with a lack of support and belonging.

Kathy: Yeah, he knows. We haven't announced it yet.

Therapist: Have you gotten a sense of his feeling about it?

Kathy: I don't know. It's hard to get any sense of anything from him. He likes Mark a lot.

Therapist: Um hum.

Kathy: But he doesn't say . . . like he's glad or anything.

Therapist: You really don't know. There, once again, you don't know where he is.

Here is concrete evidence of her father's inaccessibility. Kathy has no sense of how he feels or what he thinks about her future marriage.

So when Mark came on real strong at first, when you first started going together . . . letting you know what he thought you should do that was a sharp contrast to what you'd known.

In effect, this reflects back to Kathy and tests a possible pattern. In their matching process Mark provided for Kathy the kind of external structure she had missed in her relationship with her father.

Kathy: It really was.

Therapist: Do you know your step-mother?

This question opens the door to additional elements in Kathy's family of origin. It can potentially shed light on more of the relationship patterns modeled there.

Kathy: Yeah. You know, just a couple of minutes ago I kinda got an insight . . . I was thinking . . . I don't

This is Kathy's image of her step-mother, with no sensory documentation for that interpretation. She

know if this means anything or not, but my stepmother is . . . is really kinda flighty-like, irrational. Maybe . . . I just . . . my dad wasn't putting that role on me anymore.

Therapist: Like somebody in your family has to be flighty . . . Is this what you meant a little while back when you said that a rule in your family was, "Don't be responsible?"

Kathy: Maybe. I'm not sure. I just thought about that. I can't say that it's right or wrong.

Kathy: My stepmother doesn't have any bearing on her children. She doesn't have any control over them at all. She doesn't handle money at all.

Therapist: That sounds familiar.

refers obliquely to a theme in the family interaction field in which the father imposes a flighty, irrational image on someone else.

The therapist is going back to cross-reference information here, to explore whether this statement is connected in any way with her former remark about a family rule. This is the beginning of a probe as to whether this rule is actually an injunction, an implied expectation, laid down by the father.

This statement appears to reflect the emergence into the foreground of some new element of experience. Its rudimentary state suggests experience in formation.

Once more, Kathy expresses images of her stepmother, this time referring to her parenting and her handling of money. Exact documentation to support her interpretations (no bearing, no control) is missing.

This is a deliberate attempt to lift up a parallel. Kathy has implied an interaction theme in her family of origin in which either she or her stepmother played a flighty, irresponsible role. This theme of the irresponsible female has recurred throughout the checkup; in interactions between Kathy and Mark, between Kathy and her father, and between the father and stepmother. The frequency with which the theme appears suggests a major sequence that has been repeated significantly in Kathy's life history.

Kathy: (Smiling) Yeah, I was thinking about that, too. She's just always running around, every place, always on the go . . . never settles down at all.

Kathy documents the flighty image of her stepmother, providing concrete perception of an impulsive, capricious behavior.

Therapist: That sounds like where you were. Is there any sense in which. . . .

This is a probe. It raises questions concerning further parallels. A list of adjectives has already been used to describe Kathy early in the relationship: "just here," "not caring," "irresponsible," "illogical," "carefree." The therapist wonders whether two others should be added, "flighty" and "impulsive." That is, could these traits also be descriptive of her in the early days of the relationship with Mark? The therapist is working towards a comprehensive picture of her earlier most characteristic responses in fields of interaction.

Kathy: Yeah.

Mark: I can see that.

This is evidence of Mark's cross-encounter with his partner's narrative. As with Kathy earlier, such resonance enables him to tune in to his fiancee's family interaction models and to draw analogies for his own current relationship with her.

Therapist: You can see this?

This query invites Mark to elaborate and amplify his perceptions and learning.

Mark: Yes, between her and her stepmother now . . . and the way Kathy used to be. Like she has no set plan of what she's going to do today. And Kathy used to be like that, too. She'd get up in the morning, and whatever happened, happened.

Mark draws the parallel. His insight demonstrates the process of amplification, in which he expands on a point and in that act internalizes its implications for himself.

This is a added interpretation by Mark of Kathy's former behavior. The depiction is one of a passive self on whom forces act rather than a self-directed agent who shapes events.

Therapist: Yeah.

Mark: If she just wanted to take off and go for a 100 mile trip, she'd do it. And if she decided to stay in bed all day, she'd do that, too. She didn't really set any plan. And her stepmother's like that now.

Mark provides two documentations to support Kathy's former impetuous image. Implicit in one of them is information which, by inference, could amplify a pattern previously recognized in the checkup. In that interaction Mark called to get Kathy up in case she passively decided to stay in bed all day, instead of going to class. He was the active agent to offset her passivity.

Therapist: Let me ask this question. Was the time when you started becoming less flighty, more responsible, anywhere concurrent with your father's remarriage? In terms of time, I mean?

The therapist is investigating the hypothesis of a contiguity of events (Bowen 1978). A major family event like marriage can produce realignments in long-standing, repeated relationship sequences. Often, the origins of these shifts are so tacit, so complex that they cannot be traced. The family simply experiences the effects, the obvious changes that have taken place.

Kathy: It was after that time that I started changing.

Therapist: How soon after?

Kathy: About a year.

Mark: I can see how her stepmother, maybe . . . took over that role in their family. Like there was first Kathy and her dad, and now her stepmother's in that role. And Kathy's getting out of it. I don't know. Maybe she doesn't feel she has to fill that role anymore . . . doesn't have to do all those things.

Therapist: Could be. But at least you don't have to play that script.

It seems that there is far more depth in Kathy's story than the checkup has excavated so far. But it has confirmed the realization that her behavior has changed. She no longer has to fulfill a rigid, repetitive role in a field of interaction.

Kathy: I don't have to be dumb. Yeah.

Therapist: Does that mean illogical?

Kathy: Um hum.

This is a good place to pause and draw together the inferences drawn during these most recent exchanges concerning Kathy's family, which are:

1. That the preponderant body of data points to a very disengaged model in Kathy's family of origin. Her mother died when she

was twelve, which was presumably a major experience of loss. The remaining parent, her father, with whom she spent her adolescent years, was physically and temporally unavailable and psychologically inaccessible. This deprivation, another loss for her, left her with strong unresolved needs for care and closeness in relationships with significant others.

2. That Kathy, within her family milieu, developed strong traits of autonomy and independence. Since she had grown up with this freedom, this permissiveness, she expected it from any new relationship, and therefore, she valued Mark's tolerance for her separateness.

3. That associated with Kathy's autonomous tendencies are feelings of resentment and frustration. Wanting closeness, but encountering inaccessibility, she developed secondary feelings of resentment, perhaps rejection, though the data are inconclusive here.

4. That a theme running throughout Kathy's history is impulsive, carefree, flighty behavior. Both she and Mark report such conduct by her during the early stage of their relationship. Both also see parallel traits in the stepmother.

Inferences about the father's function in this interaction sequence cannot be made from the data at hand. Very little information was given regarding the father's behavior in relation to the daughter's and wife's carefree ways. In fact, precisely this disengagement on the part of the father, Kathy suggests, led to her having no external structure for learning self-discipline. There were no models, no one expressing expectations and opinions, which she could use as a reference point.

5. That Mark filled the interpersonal void, her lack of closeness and stability through his nurturance. She perceived his hovering, pushing, support and concern as supplying the external structure she had missed. In short, Mark enriched her disengaged interaction model.

Handling Differences

Therapist: Some time back you mentioned that you used to have some

The therapist feels sufficently joined with the couple now to esca-

conflicts over money. Are there any areas now where you have some differences?

Kathy: Something that we don't get along with?

Therapist: Let me tell you my intent in asking that question. I'm really broaching the subject of how you handle disagreements.

late the stress inherent in this topic.

How the couple copes with conflict is one of the most critical variables in the checkup. For in such times partners have to cope with the task of balancing individuality and mutuality. The partner who has not mastered the task of interpersonal closeness can become anxious at the prospect of entering into agreements and obligations. Agreement can be experienced as intrusive and confining. The partner who has not mastered the task of individuation can become anxious at the prospect of differences and separateness. Disagreement can be experienced as disregard or rejection.

Conflict, then, can bring into operation all the intrinsic differences that were present and glossed over during earlier stages of the relationship. It can challenge all the assumptions and expectations that each partner projected on the other in happier times.

Kathy: I can explain how we handle disagreements. I can't think, off hand, of any . . . of any certain one. I think at first we'll just blow up . . . or get in a fight.

Therapist: (Gesturing towards

Since Kathy and Mark are once

Mark) Could you talk to Mark. Tell him how you see the two of you handling disagreements.

more converging on their interaction, the therapist directs them to address each other directly. This will promote immediate encounter

Kathy: And then I'll just shut up and get really closed up inside myself and think about it for awhile. Then I think I come back, and we sit and talk about it. I think I come to you and say, "I want to have a talk. I think we should have a talk." And then we usually sit down and talk about it. Usually, it turns out for the good.

Kathy's response to a fight is, at first, covert and internal. She turns inside herself.

Then she initiates rapprochement by suggesting a talk (an action output). The outcome of such interaction, she reports, is beneficial.

Therapist: Initially you're angry and turn inside youself. How could you describe that? Could you tell Mark what's going on?

After reflecting back to Kathy the behavior she attributes to herself early in the conflict, the therapist asks her to make contact with her internal experience at that time and to transmit it to her partner.

Kathy: (Hesitates)

A latency period or time lag can be the reflection of (1) Kathy's contacting and sorting out her experience, her feelings, thoughts, and intentions, and (2) the anxiety connected with expressing that interior experience directly to Mark.

I use it as a weapon, I think. I get real quiet and won't talk about it.

"Weapon" is a metaphor for, as Kathy implies, an instrument of interpersonal attack. She is quiet and silent, but passively exuding aggression toward Mark. Though nonverbal, her demeanor expressed through other representational channels is attack.

Talking directly to Mark here in the interview takes courage, for it requires her to take considerable interpersonal risk. Intense anxiety can be aroused. She is taking responsibility for her anger instead of passively acting it out through silence.

Therapist: Your intention in withdrawing and getting quiet is what? Tell Mark.

Her preceding remark implied an intention in using passive aggression toward Mark. The question seeks to clarify this intent, to have her contact it and own it.

Kathy: Like I'm mad or something. If he . . .

This confirms the above inference, that the silence contains anger.

Therapist: To Mark (motioning toward him).

Kathy: If you make me mad, I just shut up to make you mad more.

This statement implies that her hostile silence is a reaction to some output from Mark. Some action of his, she implies, provokes this reaction in her. The interaction sequence runs thus, "Since you do something that makes me angry, I'll be silent to make you angry, too." She has not specified what Mark's action is that makes her angry.

Therapist: "That's my way of punishing you." Is that what you're saying nonverbally?

This sentence contains the therapist's interpretation of what she said. She has to claim the message by actively identifying with it and paricipating in it.

Kathy: That's what I'm saying.

Therapist: (to Mark) Do you know when shes like this?

The therapist moves now to Mark's side of the sequence, beginning here with his sensory input.

Mark: She kinda like . . . . Her reactions . . .

Therapist: To Kathy (waving in her direction).

Mark: I get the idea your reactions are to . . . kinda work on me, make me feel sorry for you, I think. And I'll say, "You're mad," and then you'll say, "Oh, forget it!" That makes me mad.

Mark does not provide sensory data indicating how he recognizes Kathy's state. Instead, he interprets her intention (to make me feel sorry for you). This is essentially the same pattern he manifested earlier in the checkup.

Then we'll be in a heated argument (to therapist), and nobody wants to give in. Then she'll say, "Well, forget it," and it puts you off balance, you know. And you soften up, I suppose, and she'll end up getting her way, or something.

In an argument, Mark assumes, someone has to "give in," which implies to yield. Implicit in yielding, furthermore, is the giving up on one's separateness, one's own feelings and wishes, in the conflict. Moreover, Kathy's manner has the effect of swaying his emotions (you soften up), imposing on him, so that he yields to her wishes. Implicit in Mark's remarks is an element of interpersonal fusion (Bowen 1978), a susceptibility to strong emotions in the other. He is sentitive to his partner's wishes, even to the extent of yielding his own.

Therapist: Does it work on you?

This asks the composite effect on Mark of the partner's output.

Mark: Most of the time.

With great frequency, then, Mark surrenders his autonomy in the face of Kathy's passive pushing.

Therapist: Tell her what you feel at that time.

This is designed to clarify the feeling associated with the act of yielding.

Mark: Frustrated . . . I suppose, that I'd let you have your way. I think I let you have your way too often.

This is perhaps the inevitable emotional outcome of his thwarting and nullifying himself.

Therapist: Are you saying that . . . you think that what she's doing is trying to have her way.

This reflects his interpretation of his partner's intentions. Whether accurate or not, he acts on the basis of what he thinks she is doing.

Mark: Kind of . . . yeah, she'll do it so I'll give in or something.

We have surfaced a great deal of implicit conflict in Mark—he's turned from directly contacting Kathy to talking with the therapist.

Therapist: I want to check out something. Do you feel coerced?

This question seeks to clarify his emotionality during this particular interaction sequence. Once more, Mark is having difficulty contacting and/or expressing feeling. Here, the therapist labels and reflects back an emotion which seems implicit in his experience of the moment.

Mark: Kinda. Yeah.

Therapist: Indirectly coerced.

This statement delineates the interaction sequence: Kathy indirectly acts on Mark through silence, and he feels the effect as coercion.

Mark: I guess I give in, I suppose, just to quit arguing . . . to let it drop or something. It's not really that important to me.

He describes his response to the sequence, an outcome in which once again he nullifies himself. Implicit in this action is the state of discounting himself, as though his own experience is of no consequence.

Kathy: And I'll know that you're

Kathy states her interpretation of

doing that. And I feel that I didn't win it, and you didn't win it. Neither of us won it.

his giving in, his resignation, that the exchange is abortive. She doesn't describe Mark's stimulus output when he gives in, that is, how he appears and sounds at the time. She frames the unsuccessful negotiation in terms of winning and losing. She sounds frustrated.

Therapist: You win, but you lose.

Kathy: Um hum.

Therapist: You win, but you don't like the outcome.

This reflection speaks to the outcome of the conflictual interaction. Two levels are addressed at once, the overt level in which Kathy wins the argument, and the covert level in which there has been an unsatisfactory interpersonal outcome.

Articulating the covert level is directed to the interaction bind present in the couple's relationship during times of conflict. Neither partner has been able to be fully himself or herself. They have been unable to be separate, to disagree, and then move from there towards mutual accommodation of differences.

Therapist: You sound as if you're not pleased with that outcome.

This reflects the emotionality connected with the incomplete outcomes, displeasure and disappointment.

Mark: I'm not pleased. I wish I could get my point across, to prove I was right. But I'll just let it go. 'Cause I know I was right, and she'll know I

Mark is dissatisfied, too. But he is referring to the overt level of conflict, which he frames as a matter of being right and wrong.

was right. But she won't admit it or something.

Therapist: Um hum.

Mark: And she'll just. . . .

Therapist: (motioning toward Kathy). Could you say it to her.

Mark: You know, I think it's kinda understood at times that I'm right or something. Sometimes . . . later, you'll agree that I was right. But at the time, when we're disagreeing on something . . . and I know I'm not going to get you to change your views, I'll just say, "Oh, you're right."

Mark interprets his partner as sometimes agreeing with him, and offers sensory input in support of that judgment (her saying later that he was right). But during the argument she is intransigent.

Kathy: (to the therapist) I think we've got it that I'm supposed to be illogical. I think he's placed that on me.

This new and rather sudden turn is surprising. Kathy's phrase, "we've got it," sounds like a repetitive interaction sequence. She implies that a certain pattern has been repeated enough in their interaction to become somewhat fixed. The sequence, she suggests, begins with Mark's imposing an illogical image on her.

Her statement points to parallels to her relationship with her father, with whom she also played an "illogical" role. "He's placed that on me" is a phrase which has been applied to both her father and her fiance. The presence of such parallels gives rise to the hypothesis of displacement. The fact that this script existed in Kathy's experience prior to her relationship with her fiance suggests that she could be projecting. Some antecedent intrapersonal need could be contributing to the creation and maintenance of the pattern.

Therapist: (directs her to talk to Mark).

Kathy: You say things like, "You're not making any sense," or "You're not being logical about it." You know what I'm talking about?

Kathy very specifically documents Mark's actions, leading her to conclude that he sees her as illogical.

And so, sometimes I just get really illogical just to freak you out. I mean, I know I'm being illogical, but I'm just saying it . . . just 'cause, you know? (looks at therapist).

She describes her own behavior. She sounds angry right now, as though reexperiencing the resentment she feels during times of conflict.

Therapist: "So if that's the image you've laid on me, I'll give it to you in spades!"

The therapist intervenes as a double with her, mimicking her emotional intensity, and expressing in metaphor the exaggerated reaction she makes to his name-calling (illogical).

Kathy: I'll deny being illogical, but I'll know I'm doing it. But I'll do it to make him mad.

Again, Kathy describes her behavior and the intent beneath it, to make him mad.

Therapist: Um hum.

Kathy: Or make him feel illogical, too : . . (pause) But I wish we could just (the emotional intensity has subsided) . . . when we get into those arguments over who's right . . . sometimes I can say, "OK, you're right." But other times, I don't feel

After one final experience of anger and vindictiveness, Kathy becomes reflective and pensive. She seems a little sad and remorseful, as though regretting the unsuccessful negotioation.

like I want to give in. Sometimes I think I'm right, too.

I then realize that the name calling on Mark's part and the exaggerated, self-denigrating reaction on Kathy's both follow on the heels of the interaction bind. During conflict, when they are blocked in expressing separateness and differentness, that impasse explodes into verbal and emotional aggression.

Mark: I don't think I impose it on her, that she has to be irrational. I just think that at times she isn't, actually, looking at it rationally. But sometimes I feel inside that I'm right . . . and that she isn't, she's not looking at it objectively—the problem or situation.

This statement by Mark appears internally inconsistent. He says he doesn't see his fiancee in an irrational role, but then goes on to say that at times she's illogical. He is trying to distinguish between Kathy's being occasionally illogical or unobjective, and irrationality as a general trait of her personality. Perhaps it is Kathy who cannot make this distinction. Any time he treats her as being illogical she experiences that as a symbolic reenactment of the old and painful script. This fusion does indeed disrupt her objectivity, and she is thrust back into unfinished emotional binds from the past.

Kathy: I guess we see that we both can't be right.

Therapist: But there can be autonomy for each of you. You can have your thoughts, your feelings, your wants, Kathy. And Mark, you can express yours. Then you can work out some way to make provision for both of you. We can talk about this some more in a few minutes.

This educational intervention lifts up the values of individuality and mutuality, in contrast to the idea of winning and losing.

Therapist: (to Kathy) This is just a probe. Real early in our interview you spoke of being kinda indirect when you're expressing your wants. Have you been saying during the last few minutes, "I sometimes express my hurt indirectly, too."

Early in the interview it was established that Kathy has difficulty expressing her wishes openly and that her hesitancy is due in part to her partner's guardedness in responding to her requests.

The inferrence now is that part of Kathy's bind in the relationship comes in having to be so cautious and restrained. She, too, becomes fused, having to be sensitive to and take responsibily for his emotionality. Then, being hesitant and meeting with Mark's indecisiveness and delays, she becomes frustrated, disappointed, and angry. Then, she indirectly punishes him for his inaccessibility. This inability to approach Mark's feelings and wishes has direct parallels with her situation with her father.

Kathy: I think so. Sometimes I do.

In the previous portion of the checkup the couple's interaction during times of conflict has been examined. The predominant pattern which may be derived from the data is an interaction bind. Specifically, it can be inferred that:

1. Kathy, in making initiatives or proposals in the relationship, is tentative and hesitant. It is not clear from the interview data how she looks or sounds when making indirect hints or intimations. But both she and Mark recognize the behavior as a characteristic stimulus ouput on her part.

Her intent in conveying her wishes covertly and indirectly is not entirely clear from the data. But such actions have been conditioned in part through interaction, initially with her father and, more recently, with Mark. Each of these important persons in her life has been circumspect in responding to entreaties and suggestions. Her father was inaccessible and remote in sharing his thoughts, feelings and wishes, Mark is hesitant and guarded in expressing his. Sensing that her entreaties produce the effect of binding Mark, rendering him hesitant and wary, she becomes tentative and oblique, "feeling him out." Thus, she has to be responsible not only for her own initiatives, but also for their effect on her partner. She is fused.

Having to be so covert and indirect, however, binds Kathy. She cannot be clear and transparent in expressing her own intentions, her wants and wishes. The emotionality associated with such distorted assertion of her wants is frustration and resentment.

2. Mark, as the recipient of his partner's initiatives, is hesitant and guarded in his response. Once more, how Kathy looks and sounds when she is being indirect and tentative cannot be determined from the data available. It is clear, however, that Mark knows when his fiancee is emitting such behavior.

Mark's delay in responding also reflects fusion. On the one hand, he wants to please his partner; but on the other, he wants to be autonomous. If he doesn't accommodate to her entreaties, he feels guilty and fears her punishment, which takes the form of passive aggression. If he defers to her wishes, "gives in," as he puts it, he nullifies his own individuality and then feels resentful.

His hesitancy has been shaped through a history of interaction. His fiancee's reaction, when he does not accommodate to her initiatives or does not state his agreement or disagreement, has been a passive aggressive silence. He now expects to be "hit" or "attacked," as he puts it, by this indirect "weapon," as she labels her reaction. Whether out of guilt, the wish to please, or the fear of retribution, he usually yields to her wishes.

3. Confronted with her fiance's hesitancy and guardedness, Kathy becomes angry and frustrated. Her behavior at that point is to become silent, although her intent is to punish Mark.

Withdrawing into herself in the face of Mark's closeness parallels her behavior when her father was inaccessible. Faced with the father's disengagement, she felt alone and deprived, and responded with a gritty autonomous resolve.

4. Mark interprets his partner's silence as disappointment at not getting her way, and as a means of coercing him into compliance. He apparently sometimes empathizes with her disappointment and

defers to her entreaties. His intent in this response is to please and, feeling fused, to rescue her from disappointment. At other times he appears to yield to Kathy's silence out of fear of emotional punishment. His intent in this action appears to be to appease.

Thwarting his own feelings and wishes in order to appease, Mark feels resentful. He appears to disown his ambivalence and, instead, blames his fiancee and holds her responsible for his resultant frustration.

5. When Kathy observes her partner giving in, she is dissatisfied. While she has ostensibly gotten what she wanted, that outcome produces emotionally abortive interaction. Our data do not reveal how Mark looks and sounds when he accommodates to his fiancee's initiatives. But it can be assumed that through some auditory or visual outputs he represents his internal defeat and resentment. Sensing his resignation, she, too, is disappointed.

6. On occasion the interaction bind erupts into a more explosive outcome. Mark tends to state his views through reasoning. Sometimes, during moments of disagreement, he labels his partner as unreasonable. Although the data are inconclusive here, the probability exists that (1) his view of Kathy on some of these occasions is contaminated by earlier images of her as illogical, flighty, and carefree, and he transmits this dated image to her or (2) her reaction to even the slightest hint of this imputation is mixed with past associations to that image. In her reaction she magnifies her unreasonableness with glib argumentation, exaggerating the image ascribed to her. Thus, when the interaction impasse escalates out of control, the partners resort to behaviors destructive to the self and to the other.

The Sudden Reframing

With the interview hour drawing to a close, the therapist wants to move toward the couple's evaluation of their experience in the checkup. He also wants to give them some feedback regarding findings and recommendations. This interaction unit goes thus:

Therapist: I'd like to know what benefit the checkup has been for you.

Mark: I think I got a lot out of this, 'cause I got to talk about things that normally wouldn't come up in my daily routine . . . you know, material I never really talk about.

This statement by Mark is confirmation of a finding that has been made throughout the interview, namely, that he is not accustomed to focusing on emotional and relationship matters.

Therapist: So it helps to bounce it off a sounding board.

Mark: Yeah.

Therapist: Kinda filter things through someone else's lenses and let them give you some feedback.

Kathy: These are all things I think about . . . that go through my head lots of times. I'm really interested in stuff like talking with people and getting close to people. So it's comfortable for me, enjoyable, you know.

Therapist: Um hum (to Kathy). Let me check something out with you. I get a sense that you hoped the interview would help Mark. Was there anything of that?

This question arises out of the opposites implied in each partner's previous remarks, Kathy interested in relationship concerns, Mark not so inclined.

The therapist inferred that Kathy's intent in the checkup was to enrich her fiance's skills in interpersonal interaction. He speculated further that an impetus for the checkup, for her, was the bind already coming into the relationship during times of negotiation and disagreement.

Kathy: I keep wanting to pull him up, you know.

Kathy sees herself dominant in relationship skills, and her intent is to nurture her fiance's development in this area of personal growth.

Therapist: In what way?

Kathy: To help him get his feelings out more.

She seems to be very aware of the locus of Mark's internal and interpersonal dilemma.

Therapist: To become more comfortable is. . . .

Kathy: It's so hard. Because I've learned so much in school, in my family relations classes, but I can never go back and explain everything I've learned to him. I can't give him the same approach I've learned.

Here, once again, Kathy expresses a nurturant intent, to bestow or set forth for her partner the relationship abilities she claims for herself.

Therapist: Um hum.

Kathy: I wish he could be with me to hear the same things I do.

I infer that a major, if not the prime, objective of the checkup for Kathy was just that, to have Mark undergo a guided process of encountering and reflecting upon relationship experience.

In these few concluding remarks the entire checkup is unexpectedly reframed. Drawing the interview to a close we uncover a principal objective that has been present, though unannounced, all along. Kathy's originally stated purpose, to learn more about her fiance and to discover some things they might do better, becomes more sharply focused. In this reframed perspective it can be inferred that:

1. Kathy had hoped to provide an experience in which her partner could become more comfortable in expressing emotionality and in which they could undergo some resolution of the interaction bind that was creeping into the relationship.

2. Kathy experiences concern over her fiance's inability to express his feelings, and especially over his immobility during times of disagreement. Since he is sometimes emotionally bound, unable to act on his feelings and wants, she, too, is placed in a bind. Anxiously, she has to be cautious and restrained in asserting her wishes, lest she intrude on him. Then, paralyzed by mixed emotions, he gives in, which is unsatisfactory; or the conflict escalates out of control, which is painful.

Therefore, Kathy feels responsible to nurture her fiance in the development of greater spontaneity. Though her intent was perhaps covert and not clearly formulated in her own mind, the checkup, she hoped, could demonstrate the importance of and facilitate more openness in her partner.

Kathy's intent and action thus appears to parallel an attitude attributed to Mark's mother. She, too, nurtured by planning, leading, suggesting, and generally speaking, guiding. Like his mother, Kathy has to be wary of her partner's mounting touchiness over such overinvolved leading. In many respects, she had to be covert and indirect in initiating the checkup, as we learned in the opening minutes of the interview. How the interview came to be done, then, was a paradigm of the couple's relationship. Kathy hinted. Mark hesitated. But then he went along. Being unable to break that all too frequent sequence has brought the relationship to an impasse.

CRITIQUE

In this section some of the more obvious comparisons and contrasts between experiential and other systems of marital therapy will be examined, with particular reference to perspectives and approaches to the gathering and sorting of clinical information. As much as possible, the review will seek to avoid purist classifications among systems and, instead, will focus on constructs in and of their own merit, in whatever theory they are grounded. This approach, in this writer's view, will contribute to ongoing theory construction in the field.

The foundation on which the experiential approach is based is the concept of therapy as environment. In this model, expounded in the work of Goulding (1972, 1979), therapeutic design entails the creation of an experiential enactment or simulation which replicates the client's life situation as much as possible. Using a mixture of methods, gestalt exercises, sculpting, psychodrama, communication directives, and systems, the therapist aims to make visible, auditory, and mobile the basic feelings, attitudes, and behaviors in a client's life script. Intrapersonal and interpersonal dynamics are projected into the therapeutic environment where they can be traced directly.

As a dramatic enactment the environment functions as a living, changing projection experiment. An individual's frame of reference can be revealed and carefully traced. His or her perception of the physical environment, to employ the interaction field model, can be followed, together with the responses that are made to it. Interaction sequences, themes, and outcomes among the cast of characters can be carefully monitored. And concealed, denied, and distorted experience can be evoked and brought to bear immediately in the enactment.

For Goulding, operating basically from the theoretical framework of transactional analysis, such hidden experience consists of injunctions or conditions of worth that the client encounters in the family of origin and which have resulted in deep-seated decisions affecting his basic stance in life. The re-created environment enables the therapist to trace the ego states (child, parent, adult), the key words (should, ought, must, *et cetera*), and the interaction themes that represent that script and the self-destructive, and interpersonally dysfunctional, consequences that go with it. The client is confronted with his or her life patterns with present immediacy.

Goulding's appreciation of the importance of past and unconscious material both in assessment and intervention is shared by the experiential marital therapist. But whereas Goulding interprets such material under the rubric of transactional analysis, the experiential therapy presented here is grounded more in psychodynamic (Boszormenyi-Nagy 1965, Paul 1967), modeling (Satir 1967) and Bowen (1978) theories. It should be noted that Boszormenyi-Nagy notes considerable similarity between the concept of

the script in transactional analysis and that of the repetitive interaction sequence in his own psychodynamic approach. Attention to
such factors as slips of speech, to key words, to subject-object
assignments, to symbolic interactions, and to parallels between
past and present patterns are all based on a recognition of psychodynamic factors. Such bits of information are clues to the displacement of past fields of interaction into present ones.

The experiential therapist is concerned, therefore, to unearth
past patterns of interaction, especially those models from the
family of origin, as they may be imitated and replicated in the
marital relationship. Relationship patterns learned with various
members of the childhood family are considered, especially where
they may be projected into the relationship with the partner. Also
worthy of investigation is evidence of unfinished relationship
tasks, resulting in an undifferentiated selfhood that becomes fused
with the martial partner (Bowen 1978). Such lack of individuation
often renders a partner vulnerable in interactions filled with intense emotionality, with anxiety about closeness or separateness.
These emotional impasses produce binds that can restrict interaction or produce outright conflict. Psychodynamic evidence of
losses and disappointments from the past, where they result in an
emotional fixation, are likewise kept in view. Such loss, when
denied and unresolved, can result in unconscious attempts to
restore the emotionally unrelinquished person through interactions with the marital partner (Paul 1967).

Thus, experiential therapy shares with the psychodynamic approach a recognition of the role of displacement in marital process.
And, like the psychodynamic approach, the experiential therapist
attends to such factors as slips of speech, subject-object assignments, parallels, and repetitive interaction sequences in pursuit of
clinical data, through the so-called elusive function of listening
with the third ear.

But in the creation of the therapeutic environments as a method
of exploring and teasing out information, the experiential therapist
differs rather markedly from the psychodynamicist. In the dramatized enactment of a field of interaction the experientialist initiates
a direct and immediate observation of interaction patterns, emotions, intentions, incomplete relationship phases, displacements,

and other relevant information. Moreover, operating throughout the course of an evolving enactment with an attitude of sustained tentativeness, the therapist remains fully empirical, prepared for the surprising developments, the new disclosures, and the reframing (Watzlawick, Weakland, and Fisch 1974) of events which are so crucial in genuine therapeutic change.

A notable exception in the psychodynamic approach is worth noting here. Paul (1975), operating out of this perspective, creates a unique and effective therapeutic environment through the use of videotape playback interventions. In self-encounter a marital partner is confronted by his or her own previously recorded interaction. In the language of experiential therapy, the partner is provided through audio-visual materials with an exact replica, a mirror image, of his or her own action outputs in the relationship. One is given the opportunity to see and hear himself or herself, to sense the observable self that the partner experiences. It is revealing and sobering to hear one's auditory messages, such as tones, speech rates, and pitch, or to see one's visual outputs, such as facial expressions, body posture, and movements. One is confronted head-on by one's own acts that contribute to the creation and maintenance of dysfunctional interaction.

It is apparent by now, that for the experiential therapist symbolic and metaphorical language is highly important. In turning to this topic, we broach one of the frontier areas of marital therapy. Therapists can be distinguished increasingly by their appreciation for or discounting of these orders of data.

Haley (1976), in his distinction between digital and analogical language, has focused this theoretical issue. In digital communication a bit of information refers to one specific referent and to no other. When communication contains not just one, but multiple levels of reference, it is analogical. When the behavioral therapist, for example, establishes quantified base lines on specifically observed behaviors or charts measurable changes in the shaping of new ones, he or she is applying a digital approach to information gathering. Other levels of data, such as internal emotions or intentions lying behind the observed acts, or their possible conditioning in the family of origin, are beyond the purview of the behavioral orientation. It should be noted, however, that the element of interpretation or cognition of events is increasingly becoming incorporated into the behavioral approach (O'Leary and Turkewitz 1978). This distinction between observable acts or sensations and their interpretation is, as previously noted, very much a part of the interaction field model in the experiential framework.

Similarly, when some systems therapists selectively focus on certain behaviors and interpersonal processes at the expense of others (Sluzki 1978), that approach is deliberately digital. In this perspective, the therapist filters in those orders of data which are relevant to a cybernetic feedback model of marital interaction. He or she focuses on observable effects of interaction, instead of on intentions or other levels of intrapersonal experience. The impact of one action or another, the organization of interaction sequences, and the mechanisms that maintain homeostasis in the system are the relevant bits of information, both for problem definition and therapeutic intervention. Inferences beyond these observable effects to underlying motivations, or to other elements or levels of experience, is regarded as irrelevant. Since the interruption of the dysfunctional feedback loop is the object of systems therapy, the concrete alteration of that sequence alone is sufficient.

Other systems therapies are not so digital in approach. In the couple communications training program of Miller, Nunnally, and Wackman (1975) intrapersonal dynamics are taken fully into account in an instance of interpersonal interaction. Immediate feelings, intentions, and cognitions are considered as critical in a given communication event as the more overt behaviors and perceptions with which they are connected. The model of the awareness wheel developed in their perspective has been synthesized into experiential therapy as a framework for tracing intrapersonal process in a particular unit of interaction. In their training program the awareness wheel framework is used for the structured shaping and enrichment of couple communication skills.

The systems therapy of Bowen (1978) is likewise less digital in information gathering than that of the so-called systems purists. Fundamental to this perspective is information bearing on the degree of a partner's individuation. Differentiation of self has to do with being neither diffusely caught in nor emotionally cut off from one's family of origin and being able to function in a wide array of intense human relationships without becoming emotionally fused, that is, rationally incapacitated by them. Failing such individuation, a person cannot work out appropriate separateness and mutuality with the marriage partner. This finding is also observed by Satir (1967), and is central in the theory of experiential marital therapy.

Highly original in Bowen therapy is the responsibility placed on the client to surface information relevant to his or her individuation process. Information gathering is conducted by the client himself or herself, with the therapist's coaching. Through such procedures as person-to-person conversations with family members, the client researches his or her own family and, through those encounters, undergoes the emotional intensities and clarifications that facilitate differentiation from the family ego mass (Bowen 1978).

Contrasting with these approaches, an analogical perspective on marital process is multidimensional. Intrapersonal elements of experience in all their complexity are taken fully into account, along with their interconnections with interpersonal patterns of interaction. The past in its overlap with the present is also fully considered. An analogical perspective on marital process embraces levels of conscious awareness and action in the relationship, as well as levels of covert, deleted, concealed, or denied experience. It recognizes that human experience can be manifested on many levels at once and that messages transmitted via one channel can both match and be incongruent with messages sent at another. The analogical view holds a profound appreciation for what can be called the dimension of depth in marital process and attends to the multitude of ways that this depth can be manifested.

An analogue is based on the intrinsic similarities or correspondences between two or more dimensions of marital process. As such, analogues participate in at least two levels of marital reality at once. One facet of an analogue, at one level of marital process, essentially resembles one or more other levels of interaction. An analogue, then, can represent or stand for something which it is not itself, yet in whose power and meaning it participates (Tillich 1959). It functions in a two-edged manner, opening up two levels of reality at once. In its capacity to mediate between levels of intrapersonal and interpersonal experience, an analogue can point beyond itself in its more apparent significance and disclose meanings which otherwise would remain hidden and obscure. An analogue transcends itself, and provides access to material which the couple and the therapist need to reach, which might not be revealed in any other manner. The analogue is fundamental to the epistemology of experiential marital therapy and is employed in information gathering, problem definition, intervention and outcome evaluation.

To illustrate, when Peg, in her reenactment of her visit to the hospital nursery, is told by the therapist to talk to the clock, a metaphorical analogy is being used. In the forefront of her awareness, drawing her fixed stare, the clock nevertheless is not the heart of Peg's concern. It is an analogue for something else, for some other level, or levels, of reality in which it participates and toward which it points. Nevertheless, as a symbol, this object participates in and stands for dimensions of Peg's experience that at the time lie hidden from sight, unknown to her, to her husband, and to the therapist. In directing Peg's imaginary dialogue with the clock, the therapist elects to use the analogue, in its mediating function, to gain access to this otherwise veiled level, or levels, of her experience.

Conversely, the clock in its more apparent level is an analogue, the overt representation, of hidden levels of concern and anxiety which Peg is currently experiencing in her marital relationship. Nine-thirty comes and goes, she reports, and she and her husband might talk and might not. Either way, she says in a resigned tone, they do not get to "the core." The clock symbol has now opened up a new metaphor, the core. So, in responding to Peg's preoccupation with the clock, the therapist meets her at that level of her experience and tracks that symbol to its association with another one. And this second metaphor, in turn, opens up further levels in the deep structure of her experience. Evoked from this structure are her unresolved grief over her father's death and the projection of anticipated future pain in the possible death of her premature son.

The experiential therapist makes constant use of analogues in gathering information on marital interaction. Presenting symptoms are often analogues of relationship impasses, as Haley (1976) has shown. The creation of an experiential enactment and the data evoked during it are based on the analogous correspondences between the simulation and the interaction field which it represents. Within that enactment objects and persons often stand in for, that is, analogously represent real people, concerns, and meanings in the clients's life situation. Metaphors and symbols are often directly employed as vehicles for exploring and revealing facets of experience that would otherwise remain hidden. The client may be told to "become a symbol," for example, to personify some dream image on the premise that such an experiment can disclose the deeper levels of the dreamer's experience represented in that analogue (Simkin 1972).

Actually, most therapies use some form of analogical thinking. Structural therapy, basically a systems approach and a good case in point, makes considerable use of correspondences in its information gathering and mapping functions (Minuchin 1974). Seating arrangements among family members often represent relationship structures. Probes, sometimes taking the form of manipulation of physical space, often yield valuable information regarding the family's flexibility or resistance to change. Communication sequences become analogues useful in locating the family spokesman, the power struggles, and the coalitions that exist in the family. Family performance of an in-session task, such as having a lunch together in the company of the therapist, correspond with patterns of enmeshment, disengagement, and triangulation that are presumed operative at home. The way a homework directive is carried out during the week reflects the family's adaptability to change. Thus, when the therapist tells a disengaged mother to teach her daughter, the identified patient, how to use matches, that task stands for, corresponds to, a more clarified and functional boundary between the two. The homework task becomes an analogue for opening up the relationship. In each of these instances the observed functioning of the family becomes an analogue for its basic structure, and the therapist uses a task related to the former to map and restructure the latter.

Experiential and structural approaches are alike, then, in viewing therapy as environment, with certain activities, like tasks, standing for other levels. Each therapy uses analogues at one level to explore, trace, map, and intervene in marital and family process at another. They also share similar views on the role of the therapist as director, actively catalyzing this therapeutic environment towards discovery and change.

The two therapies differ radically, however, in the extent to which they use analogical thinking. The experientialist joins the structuralist in viewing certain overt activities, like communications sequences or tasks, as analogues for such dynamics as triangles or coalitions in family process. But he or she then wants to explore those same triangles or coalitions as analogues for what Bowen (1978) calls the family projection process. How, the experientialist wants to know, has the marital conflict worked its way into the child's life, in what detours or breaches of parent-child boundaries? And what can be learned, via this projection process, about the marriage itself, about the lack of differentiation between the partners, about the intergenerational transmission process that may have filtered down into this child's symptomatology?

The efforts of therapists to give consideration to these multiple levels of interaction are sometimes viewed as suspect, lacking sufficient empirical evidence, by those of more digital persuasion. Attention to factors such as metaphor and displacement are regarded as too subjective, and therefore too problematic. Therapeutic functions like listening with the third ear seem all too ethereal and mysterious, perhaps saying more about the therapist than the client couple. For the experiential therapist this position can be altogether reframed, and this redefinition raises considerations that lie at the very heart of therapeutic epistemology.

The experiential approach, it can be argued, is based on a radical empiricism that pursues data throughout all dimensions of marital interaction. Many levels of reality, intrapersonal and interpersonal, past and present, are viewed on a unified continuum (von Bertalanffy 1968). The experientialist refuses to prejudge or to select any level as more real or more relevant than another. Persons have histories. They dream. They express themselves in metaphors and rituals, often saying more than they know and knowing more than they can say. They communicate with great skill and with great clumsiness. They exert overt, visible effects on each other through their behaviors. They assign and comply with covert subjective states that are tacit and hidden from view. And no one of these orders of data is more or less real and germane than another.

Empiricism can only be preserved by an attitude of sustained tentativeness. The intent to pursue knowledge wherever it leads is the essence of objectivity. The predetermination of which findings are most real and valid for therapy, in contrast, is the essence of subjectivity. The digital approach, paradoxically, most radically demonstrates the complementarity principle in epistemology in which the inquirer imposes his own subjective prejudgment on reality. The therapist's presupposition of novelty and the unexpected in a dimension of depth which can and often does exceed his or her grasp is the essence of experiential knowing.

The experientialist knows that in the quest for some elusive objectivity, he or she cannot be delivered from responsibility for the personal judgments that are made throughout the course of therapy (Polanyi 1958). Recognizing all too well the operation of his or her personhood in therapeutic interpretation and action, the experientialist seeks to build controlled and systematic procedures for data collection. Therapeutic epistemology is best served, not by delimiting and prejudging marital process *a priori*, in some digital manner, but by constructing clinical methods of inquiry that can enable the therapist to organize his or her subjectivity vis a vis the dimension of depth. For the experiential therapist, therefore, the tracing of interaction is a matter of ongoing content analysis (Stone et al. 1966). Knowing that he or she must make continuous judgments in an interaction field of great depth, the experientialist derives a set of procedures for systematically making these inferences. Specifying in advance a set of categories, the elements of the interaction field, the therapist traces the presence or absence of data related to each one. Inferences are made where data exist, and they are suspended where they do not. Where information bearing on some category has not been surfaced, the therapist can elicit it through a variety of experiential procedures.

Therapy becomes a process of cascading waves of exploration and discovery within the dimension of depth. The relation between therapist and couple therefore, becomes an ongoing interaction loop. Interaction occurs, is perceived and interpreted by the therapist, who then makes some intervention that, in turn, catalyzes some new effect in the clients. The subject-object complementarity that exists between the therapist, as the knower, and the couple, as the known, cannot be avoided in a detachment made in the name of an ethereal objectivity. The experiential therapist seeks to take responsibility both for the dimension of depth in marital process and for his or her own methods in the pursuit of it.

Chapter 2

Patterns

Another therapeutic task closely related to the gathering and sorting of information but with functions all its own is patterning. If the task of information gathering is to yield specific inferences regarding a couple's interaction, that of patterning is the organization of these findings into meaningful and therapeutically useful configurations.

In patterning (Fagan 1970) the therapist works towards an understanding of all the events and levels, both intrapersonal and interpersonal, that go into the makeup of the couple's interaction. Made up as it is of an intricate and complex structure of interconnected elements, the pattern of the couple's interaction is extraordinarily difficult to comprehend. Yet the therapist, in the experiential approach, works to conceptualize as cogently as possible the network of interaction, the combination of events, levels, and components that form a unified whole. Within this unified conception of many dimensions the therapist also seeks to specify the points of connection between elements and levels.

Once the interaction in its many dimensions is conceptualized, a number of differential considerations and options become available to the therapist. Those points within the pattern where the greatest strain or impasse exist can be identified. Parts of the pattern that appear to be less consequential than others can deliberately be dropped from attention. The therapist can decide to pursue those elements of the couple's process that seem to offer the optimum opportunity for change. Recognizing that marital interaction dimensions are interconnected, the therapist can act on those which can bring about the alteration of other structures. Where the therapist realizes that certain disruptions will have to be made in the course of therapy, the risks to be taken and the value choices to be made can be explicated.

In experiential couple therapy this function of patterning is never complete and finished. This function, like others, is characterized by its own set of discrete tasks that are given relatively greater emphasis at certain points in therapy than at others. Just as the operations of information gathering are never-ending, with new data constantly pouring forth in unexpected discoveries, so it is with patterning. The therapist continually updates and revises his or her conceptions of marital process. Points of stress and objectives of change are constantly reworked in the light of new findings and discoveries. The patterning process evolves, enriched by the unearthing of new and more salient information. And these new constructions of the couple's interaction, in turn, lead to new and ever-changing intervention designs, which is the next function of therapeutic activity.

In the present chapter we shall examine the patterning process in detail, using Kathy's and Mark's relationship as our case material. We shall follow the workings of the therapist's mind in forming an understanding of the couple's interaction, in identifying areas of need, in specifying objectives for improvement, and in delineating points of risk and potential in therapeutic intervention. Following this discussion, in the critique at the end of the chapter, we shall compare and contrast patterning functions as they relate to assessment and goal setting in other systems of marital therapy.

PHASES AND STAGES*

The checkup of a couple like Kathy and Mark has particular value for the examination of interaction patterns in an intimate relationship. Theirs is a relationship in formation and can be viewed from the standpoint of that stage in the cycle of marriage. Past the dating and courtship period, engaged, and moving towards the formal ceremony, their relationship provides a fairly close and detailed

---

*For this subtitle I acknowledge my debt to Willie Nelson, country singer and fellow Texan.

look at the earliest origins of marriage. Unlike those couples, deeply pained, hurt, disappointed, or angry, who so often make up the bulk of the therapy population, Kathy and Mark are in a developmental transition. Already they are starting to experience the demands inherent in any intimate relationship, to change and adapt along with emerging conditions. They are beginning to recognize some inherent differences that were either not obvious or, more likely, selectively ignored in their earliest encounters. And they are experiencing the diffiuclty of disagreeing and being separate persons. This stress, sometimes producing outright conflict, contains the seedbed for disrupting their relationship. The ingredients are there, as they are in a close relationship, for greater intimacy and mutuality or for greater conflict and alienation.

Fortunately for them, through Kathy's initiative, these pangs of growth are being acknowledged and brought into the open. Such warning signs could be, and often are, unheeded, discounted, or suppressed, but they probably will not go away. In fact, failure to cope with the symptoms will tend only to exacerbate them, turning a relatively normal, developmental process into a malingering, long-term pattern of maladaptation. If this normal life crisis is not mastered, it can spill over into later stages and phases.

To this early stage of relationship formation each partner brings his or her own unique personality. The personality of each partner reflects a distinctive approach to close relationships, a pattern molded primarily within the milieu of the family of origin. To the growing child, as child development studies have shown (Bronfenbrenner 1970), the family of origin with its particular cast of characters is embued with great power and status. The parents, siblings, and others of the family comprise the major sources of support and control, both physical and emotional, in life. This field of interaction, in the mind of the developing child, constitutes reality itself. Family life as he or she experiences it is, for all practical purposes, the model for close relationships in general. What he or she sees and hears in the interactions of others provide cues for imitation and identification. The example of the parental relationship is especially crucial in this regard. Interactions with persons in that childhood setting likewise serve to mold basic assumptions and expectations about human interaction.

A partner's patterns of relating, then, are built up through incalculable occasions of interaction in that family environment. In often unnoticed and seemingly inconsequential events of daily life both explicit and implicit patterns evolve, defining how, when, and with whom family members relate. Some of these rules, as Minuchin (1974) calls them, are observed in the actions of others. Some are experienced directly and immediately in firsthand encounters. Coping with these multi-faceted demands, conditions, and changes over time, a person forms basic assumptions about close human relationships.

In the course of his or her unique history within a particular family environment a person passes through many stages of development. Each stage, in turn, is characterized by distinct yet changing relationship phases, as Boszormenyi-Nagy (1965) calls them. One must learn how to be close without becoming emotionally fused with others, how to be autonomous without being disengaged, how to individuate from the family of origin without becoming emotionally cutoff (Bowen 1978), and how to dissolve old relationships and form new ones without projecting the old into the new. This latter capacity is called for especially at times of death, divorce, and other forms of separation. The life cycle confronts everyone with the task of mastering these different phases of interpersonal relating.

The fully individuated person who has completely mastered these many phases, however, stands as an ideal on a continuum of interpersonal competency (Bowen 1971). Such a person would be able to participate in a wide spectrum of relationship phases, all the while remaining objective and comfortable with the level of emotionality appropriate to each. This individual could give care and nurture to others, where fitting, without becoming overinvolved and overresponsible for them. He or she could also receive the care and support of others without becoming unduly enmeshed or dependent on them. Such a person would be capable of self-initiated action and self-reliance without becoming estranged and disengaged from others, and would be able to allow others the same autonomy and individuality. This fully functioning person could maintain his or her own boundaries of selfhood while respecting the integrity of others. He or she would not transgress the boundaries of others, nor would this person fall short of responsible involvement with them. A repertoire of interpersonal competency would have been built up over the life cycle of such a person, enabling him or her to maintain the delicate balance between individuality and mutuality in close human interaction.

Most persons bring to marriage gradations of incompleteness with respect to these development tasks in human interaction. One partner, coming from a history of overinvolved (Boszormenyi-Nagy 1965) or enmeshed (Minuchin 1974) family relationships, may not know how to be appropriately separate and autonomous. Coming from a family environment marked by disengaged (Minuchin 1974) or alienated relationships, another partner may not know how to be comfortably and suitably close and supportive. Growing up in a family where strong conditions of worth were present, another mate may have learned to deny, distort, or conceal elements of his or her selfhood. Deposits of lingering resentment and disappointment (Goulding 1972) are often laid down in the personality of such a person. In the quest for individuality another partner may be locked into an extreme sense of isolation from his or her family of origin, with the emotional cutoff that accompanies this position (Bowen 1978). Another partner's life may have been filled with times of deprivation or exploitation in the family of origin, laying down an enduring sense of imbalance (Boszormenyi-Nagy and Spark 1973) in relationships. This person carries into marriage a chronic sense of relationship deprivation, on the one hand, or of being intruded upon, on the other. For yet another partner, times of relationship dissolution, such as death and divorce, may remain emotionally unresolved, with enduring emotional fixations around such feelings as grief and sadness (Paul 1967). For another partner, estranged from certain members of the original family, feelings of forgiveness and acts of rejoining remain blocked.

Marriage, then, presents mates with new and most critical life tasks. Ways must be found for responding appropriately to the partner in the present, for continuing the resolution of unfinished relationship tasks from the past, and for mastering the never-ceasing challenges and vicissitudes that inexorably arise in the course of marriage (Overturf 1976). Success comes in meeting this task in ways that are balanced, mutual, and reciprocal for both partners. In patterning, the therapist seeks to understand the interaction process through which a given couple is meeting these tasks.

In relationship formation several dynamics occur at once. There is, on the one hand, a tendency on the part of each partner to repeat and to continue interaction models observed and experienced in the family of origin (Napier 1978). Partners overtly and covertly seek to replicate relationship patterns experienced in that field of interaction, for at least they are familiar. On the other hand, each partner hopes to enrich (Napier 1978) his or her original developmental milieu, to have what was not present and available in that childhood environment. This unconscious longing to vary one's earlier history lays the basis for an intuited, implicit hope for completing unresolved relationship tasks. Partners then seek in their mates the kind of interaction that will enable them to correct, to master, or to gain restitution for unfinished business from the past (Framo 1975).

The matching process in relationship formation is uncannily accurate and complementary. Coming into the relationship with their individual expectancy sets, partly conscious and partly unconscious, partners intuitively find in the partner certain objective traits and characteristics that meet their respective subjective needs (Boszormenyi-Nagy 1965). The mate whose history was grounded in a disengaged family model strives for a sense of involvement with the other, for overt and covert levels of closeness and support. The mate whose history has been lived out in an enmeshed field of relationships seeks overt and covert levels of personal freedom and autonomy, thus establishing the basis for a clearer differentiation of self (Bowen 1971, Napier 1978). The mate emotionally cut off from his or her family of origin covertly seeks in the partner one who is still deeply involved in an extended family with the belonging that state affords. The partner whose antecedent experience has been replete with an inordinate amount of exploitation or deprivation may seek out that mate with whom his or her undiminished disappointments or resentments can be repeated and redressed (Goulding 1972). The unexpressed hope is that the partner can help to complete, or at least complement, one's own unresolved relationship tasks and impasses (Satir 1967).

In its earliest origins, then, the intimate relationship is comprised of complex and interlocking system of intrapersonal and interpersonal forces. Individual expectancy sets and needs have to be met through interactional patterns that are mutually satisfying and balanced. Partners can relate to each other adaptively, by recognizing and preserving their separate identities. But they can also relate with varying degrees of maladaptive interaction, in which past patterns are displaced onto the present, where they are out of context and inappropriate. The emerging relationship then becomes characterized by the symbolic reenactment and reconstruction of earlier unresolved and uncompleted interactions. The new partner is then covertly maneuvered into being an overinvolved, disengaged, critical, deceased parent, or other important personage from the timeless past (Framo 1975, Paul 1967).

PARALLELS AND DISPLACEMENTS

In the previous chapter a verbatim transcript and therapist commentary was presented of the relationship checkup with Kathy and Mark. Each portion of that record discloses a distinct unit of interaction, one focusing on the couple's decision process leading up to the checkup, another having to do with their handling of disagreement and conflict, and the other two focusing on each partner's relationship with the parent of the opposite sex. In tracing the field of interaction in each of these units the therapist conducted an ongoing content analysis of data. Empirically supportable inferences concerning the couple's interaction were derived from these analyses. Also unearthed were certain relationship models afforded each partner by his or her family of origin.

It does not demand a close scrutiny of these findings to discern several rather obvious and striking parallels, as Paul (1967) refers to them, between the different fields of interaction. The existence of these similarities is strongly suggestive of some degree of continuity or overlap between each partner's interaction with the partner in the present and with the parent in the past. The present section of this chapter examines this hypothesis as a first step in understanding the couple's interaction pattern.

The most prominent parallel in Mark's pattern of interpersonal relating lies in his difficulty in being separate or individuated. Over the years he has become symbiotically dependent on his mother's nurturing.

At one stage in his development, during the early childhood years, such an overinvolved relationship phase was necessary and adaptive. And even later, as he recalls it now, her guidance in the form of reminders and suggestions provided him with a stable and dependable family environment and model. In such a milieu, through his mother's modeling, Mark learned how to receive care and support and, as we shall see later, how to provide these resources for others. Such involvement, the giving and receiving of care, are important relationships skills amply provided to Mark in his family of origin.

It is the inability of this nurturant relationship phase to change over time, to adapt to the child's unfolding development, that induces an inappropriate pattern of interaction. A maladaptive infantilization process (Napier 1978) sets in. Under the guise of continuing help and guidance, a parent, or both parents, condition the child into a state of prolonged, maladaptive dependency. Activities that could be done independently continue to be directed by the parent, stripping the child of opportunities to develop self-directed planning and thinking. Movements towards autonomy and self-reliance are thus thwarted.

As family therapy has discovered, such continuing overinvolvement on the part of a parent can mask a family projection process (Bowen 1978). This lingering overinvolvement on the part of Mark's mother, an enmeshment now extending into his young adult years, could be functioning to shield or detour her from an implicit, perhaps explicit, marital conflict. Any attempt to apply this concept to Mark's situation, however, would be entirely speculative, since no compelling evidence to that effect exists in the verbatim record.

Stimulated by the challenges of his new college environment, by the rewards of autonomous action, Mark is developing greater independence. He sees himself now as capable of increased self-initiative and self-reliance. Hence, his relationship with his mother should be changing, as he views it.

But when he goes home, prepared to act upon that newfound autonomy, he finds the old interaction pattern resistant to change. His mother persists in expressing her opinions and making her suggestions. Mark is then confronted, through the mother, with a relationship phase that has been in place over a long period of time. Acting out of customary and habitual responses to her son, she tends to maintain the status quo, the prior homeostasis.

In his visits home, then, Mark is beginning to feel gradations of discontent and annoyance. He feels his newly won autonomy imperiled, if not violated. Feeling his boundaries intruded upon by his mother's continuing enmeshment, Mark is becoming frustrated and, we may conjecture, resentful.

Mark is now faced with a real dilemma. If he deviates from the original overinvolved relationship, thinking his own thoughts and taking responsibility for his own actions, he risks stressing his parent and thereby his relationship with her. That stress could presumably erupt into the withdrawal of her affection and support, leaving him feeling rejected and isolated. It might also come forth in a variety of overt and covert guilt-inducing actions by her, maneuvers designed to restore the relationship to its former basis. To oppose the one who once provided such care and support would in itself be enough to induce the guilt of disloyalty and ingratitude.

But to acquiesce to his mother's continued overinvolvment confronts Mark with another set of emotions. To deny his own thoughts, feelings, and wishes is to frustrate his own selfhood, his emerging individuation. To "give in," as he frames this bind, is to counteract his growth as a differentiated person. Thus, the strained visits home evoke a range of mixed emotions: feelings of guilt and disloyalty for wanting to change the existent relationship pattern, feelings of resentment for her continued intrusion, feelings of frustration and anger with himself if he squelches his own emerging independence.

It is difficult to know from the facts at hand how much of Mark's dilemma is real and how much is fantasy, a figment of his own imagination. The probability is great, however, that his framing of the impasse approximates the true situation, since that perception has been built up over time in countless events of interaction. For Mark, on the threshold of a major shift in relationship alignment, the transition seems problematic. Positioned on one side of a changing relationship boundary yet to be clarified, the emotions that are to be felt, the actions to be taken, and the images to be reframed in that process are yet to be experienced. The shifting relationship boundary is alterating Mark's emotions and frame of reference towards the mother. Feelings and actions once framed one way are now being felt and viewed from an entirely different perspective. Accompanying this transitional phase is an emotional state of intense and highly disquieting anxiety.

With Kathy, Mark experiences the same bind, and therein lies the first parallelism in the data. His partner approaches him with a seemingly harmless probe about a relationship checkup. Mark senses, however, that her query clothes something that his partner really expects or wants. Although the interview verbatim provides no data on the way Kathy looks and sounds when making these indirect intimations, it can be assumed that Mark has learned to recognize the relevant verbal and non verbal cues.

It is not clear why Kathy is so circumspect, so covert and indirect in asserting her intentions. The data suggest that such behavior has been shaped in part through prior interaction with her partner and before that, in her relationship with her father. Mark has in the past been guarded and hesitant in responding to her entreaties. From prior encounters she knows that the expression of her wishes renders him cautious and wary. This often repeated interaction sequence has, evidently, reinforced her progressively into indirect and oblique behaviors.

Kathy's probe sets off in Mark both an internal and interpersonal ambivalence. On the one hand, he wants to accommodate to her wishes; but on the other, he wants to be true to his own feelings, thoughts, and intentions. He feels obligated to please her and guilty if he does not. Yet to "give in", as he puts it, is to run roughshod over his own wishes, to nullify himself. To do this is to feel frustrated and resentful.

Moreover, Mark knows from prior encounters that failure to comply with his partner's wishes is to invite her retaliation in the silent treatment. In a not so subtle pout she expresses both her disappointment and her anger. In a passive, yet aggressive manner she acts in a way designed to induce guilt. Mark then feels "attacked," to use his words, punished for not going along with her manipulations.

Faced with this ambivalence, this impasse, Mark hesitates. By remaining closed and tentative, he avoids outright agreement with the self-denial that goes with this alternative, or disagreement, with the open conflict that can ensue with this one.

Usually, as Mark reports it, he "gives in", but feels resentful, and then a state of open conflict erupts. During this hostile episode from him there may be instances of name-calling and denigration.

The parallels are pronounced between these two relationship patterns in Mark's life, the one with his mother, the other with his fiancee. In each, first of all, the female partner acts out of an overinvolved relationship phase. Mother nutures through reminders and suggestions, Kathy through taking initiatives towards greater closeness and togetherness. Moreover, Kathy is now assuming responsibility for her partner's growth in relationship skills.

Coming as he does from a family where relationships were enmeshed, at least certainly with the mother, it is inevitable that Mark would seek partly to repeat this familiar pattern. Relationship patterns and the adaptations they represent are not easily relinquished. It is not surprising that Mark would seek, in the new relationship, patterns that he had known in the family of origin. Though sometimes painful and unsatisfactory, old patterns are at least familiar.

In each of the two relationships Mark is striving for a new sense of individuation. With his mother he is beginning to feel capable of more independent thought and action, less in need of her direction and guidance. With his fiancee he is becoming more aware of his own thoughts and wishes over against hers. With each, then, Mark is struggling towards an emerging relationship phase, one where he is more free and autonomous. He is plainly becoming deeply concerned to achieve a clearer and more autonomous boundary for himself in each relationship.

And in each relationship Mark is acutely aware of being in transition. He is not yet confident and sure of himself in his newly emerging state. In fact, as he puts it, "it's hard" to be over against his mother at times when she persists in directing and guiding his affairs. With Kathy, too, there is still hesitancy and guardedness, fearing that what he wants or thinks on a given matter will not meet with her approval, will disappoint her, or will make her angry.

And in each relationship he is beginning to feel intruded upon. When the two women continue to press him, the mother with her suggestions, Kathy with her hints, he feels coerced. He resents their trespassing on his autonomy, his mother still trying to lead even while he wants to be more self-sufficient, his fiancee attacking him indirectly when he wants to be free to have his own views. Fearing the continuing overinvolvement from his mother, Mark is beginning to feel trapped in his relationship pattern with her. Fearing Kathy's coercion, he feels restrained in any movement towards differentiation.

Parallels are to be found in Kathy's story, too. If her partner's history is marked by too much interpersonal involvement, hers is characterized by too little. If in Mark's family the model of relationships is enmeshment, in Kathy's it is disengagement.

Kathy's disengaged family model was no doubt shaped heavily by the death of her mother. This event is mentioned in the checkup almost matter-of-factly. Thus, there is virtually no indication in the interview of the impact on Kathy, or on the family system, of this loss. The therapist did not explore this event further. Such times, as has been found (Paul 1967), exert powerful effects on family members. Major realignments of relationships boundaries can take place. Unresolved losses, where relationships remain in an undissolved phase, can create emotional fixation points that continue to press on the family system, and on future relationships, in diffuse and unclear boundaries. An unresolved relationship phase can then spill maladaptively over into future patterns of interaction. Any or all of these results could conceivably have occurred in Kathy's family. Suffice it to say that, at minimum, her mother's death established a family model of deprivation and loss in Kathy's history.

That model was exacerbated by her relationship with her father. He was unavailable to her, first of all, in the sheer fact of his long, late working hours. In the checkup, Kathy initially masks another, more devastating form of disengagement by presenting it as a matter of physical time and space. But later she describes her parent as inaccessible and remote. She felt shut out and deprived of appropriate involvement with him. There was, as she reports, a pervasive lack of a clear and transparent parent-child boundary in which she could develop. When she needed him to be there, available with his expectations, his feelings, his thoughts, or his values, he was not. He was, instead, distant and seemingly uninvolved.

Kathy's response to this family milieu was, as could be expected, the development of a great deal of independence and self-reliance. She had to learn to take care of herself. She cherishes and takes pride in that autonomy even now, and does not want to feel restrained or "hassled", as she puts it.

Fused with Kathy's development of autonomy, however, are some other, more painful elements. Wanting to move from a disengaged relationship phase with her father to one more involved and supportive, but meeting with his continued distance and inaccessibility, Kathy developed feelings of frustration and resentment. The closeness and nurturance she had every right to expect in growing up were missing in her life.

Left to her own devices, Kathy developed tendencies of carefree and flighty behavior. Devoid of an external family structure in which to learn discipline and self-control, she reports a history of impulsive, disorganized ways of living. Both she and her fiancee report that this personality pattern was operative in the earliest days of their relationship. Both also see parallels between the carefree, flighty actions of the stepmother, as she is now, and Kathy, as she once was.

The fact that the two women, stepmother and daughter, play out such corresponding roles in relation to Kathy's father is strongly indicative of a repetitive interaction sequence, or script, in which he is exerting considerable subjective influence. Why this is so, or the exact nature of this script, however, cannot be determined from the checkup record. Suffice it to note that, for whatever reason and under whatever impetus, Kathy is moving away from this script both in her attitudes and her actions. And she likes herself better for it.

With Mark, Kathy confronts the same distance and closedness. Once more, she faces the arduous task of getting close to another person significant in her life without running the risk of alienating him and ending up isolated or rejected. Specifically, she constantly confronts the bind of trying to discover his feelings and wishes on some topic or issue, while at the same time trying to accomplish her own intentions in the interaction. When he keeps his inner experience obscure or hidden, her energy goes into drawing him out, while delicately not intruding too far. So she has to anticipate his responses and reactions, knowing how difficult it is for him to communicate in a clear and open matter. Pushed too far, she knows, he can become anxious and stressed, and can withdraw. Worse still, he can give in, and then feel resentful and sometimes be verbally abusive.

Then, feeling squelched and suppressed by this insufferable bind, or being deprived of what she wants, Kathy reacts. She goes into a sullen pout which clothes her disappointment, on the one hand, and her anger, on the other. This not-so-passive aggression plays into Mark's set by inducing guilt and resignation, and he feels "attacked" which, of course, he is. If he then accommodates to her initiatives, gives in, she feels guilty, manipulative, and unsatisfied. There is no joy in getting what she wants. Her satisfaction is empty.

If Mark, feeling himself trapped, attacked, and intruded upon, then lashes out in name-calling, Kathy, too, becomes extreme. "To freak him out," she says, she becomes irresponsible and somewhat self-destructive. Such behavior, it can be inferred, masks her underlying feelings of disappointment, hurt, and rejection. She then acts out an old and all-too familiar image of being carefee and irresponsible.

In Kathy's interaction patterns with these two important persons in her life, her father and her fiance, there are marked parallels. Each relationship is characterized by a quality of disengagement, though the boundary appears more rigid with the father than with Mark. The former apparently was pervasively distant and aloof, while Mark, himself the product of an enmeshed family, is capable of considerable involvement and support. But he makes distancing and withdrawal moves when he begins to feel unsure of his own autonomy and threatened by his fiancee's approaches for greater intimacy. The capacity for interpersonal involvement, however, is present in Mark, a feature which Kathy no doubt intuited.

In each relationship, then, Kathy is seeking a new relationship phase, one of greater emotional involvement and support. She has for all practical purposes given up this quest for nurturance and accessibility with her father. But with Mark the pursuit goes on. During the formative period of the relationship she invited and reinforced his care and overinvolvement. She sought and received support through his efforts to bring order and structure in her life. Even now she continues to take initiatives towards intimacy and closeness in the relationship.

And in each relationship she finds her search for closeness thwarted or denied. She once framed this deprivation with her father as a positive quality, as his being permissive and thus encouraging of her independence. Now this view has been reframed. Now she is more in contact with the feelings of disappointment and resentment she harbors over his disengagement.

With Mark her frustration has more to do with the seemingly insurmountable impasse that occurs in their interaction. Once able to be caring and nurturing, he seems now to withdraw when she tries to get close to him. Instead, there is an anxiousness and guardedness in him which can, if pushed too far, result in defensiveness and anger. Thus, she lives on the thin edge of apprehension that her initiatives for closeness may drive off the very closeness she is seeking.

The presence of such extensive parallelism between past and present relationship patterns affords inescapable evidence of displacement. Patterns originating in one field of interaction, the family of origin of each partner, have intruded themselves into the couple's contemporary interaction.

This is not to say that these earlier patterns were inherently maladaptive. If anything, they were probably quite creative, grounding each partner in the family field in which he or she belonged. Kathy's autonomous responses were perhaps the best an adolescent girl could make in a disengaged and deprived setting. Mark's dependent responses were probably inexorable, the almost inevitable consequence of a highly enmeshed family of origin.

In the partner, especially during the formative relationship stage, each mate seeks both what he had and did not have in the family of origin. Certain patterns learned in the family environment are simply repeated. Such responses are generalized expectancy sets and assumptions that seem self-evident and right, and thus worthy of replication. Mark, for example, having been the recipient of the nurturance which his mother modeled for him, drew upon her actions as cues in his early support of his fiancee. He imitated and replicated her behavior, the calling and reminding, as if it were the intrinsically fitting and proper thing to do.

But past patterns can be repeated for other, more covert reasons. A partner may seek in the relationship with the mate what he or she did not have in the family of origin. With exquisite accuracy, as Warkentin and Whitaker (1967) poetically express it, mates covertly and intuitively select each other in order to complement, enrich, vary, master, redress, or complete relationships from the past.

This complementary principle can be seen operating in the personality opposites which Mark and Kathy represent. He is seeking autonomy, and she has majored in this orientation. She is seeking closeness, and this has been his history. She found in her fiance one whose whole development has included order and stability. She was conscious of the fact that his organized way of life she sorely lacked, so that his actions could complement what was missing in her own personality. Kathy, it should be noted, is more aware of the ways Mark initially complemented her personality (more dependable) than he is of hers (more autonomous).

Mates also covertly hope to enrich their antecedent experience. For Kathy, Mark represented the possibility of a closeness and mutuality that could offset and compensate for the deprivations and omissions of her childhood family. With him, she hoped, she could vary her history and receive the nurture that she had missed and for which she still longed.

Though it was never fully explicated during the checkup, it can be surmised that Mark, too, with Kathy, hoped to vary his historical experience. Even though he sometimes denigrated her spontaneity and impulsiveness, these traits in her personality enriched his more restrained, dependent, and well-ordered approach to life.

By far the weightiest displacements occur in the projection of incomplete relationship phases from the past onto the present, where it is inappropriate and therefore maladaptive. Such displacement can be found extensively in Kathy's and Mark's interaction. When the past is transferred into the present, transgressing it, the past is no longer just past. It is present and operative in the deep structures of interaction.

Both Kathy and Mark have brought into their relationship unfinished business from the past. Mark brings a strong, unresolved need centered around the theme of enmeshment and individuation. Kathy, in turn, brings an unmet need clustered around the theme of distance and closeness. Each is predisposed, therefore, to project these unresolved sets into the relationship with the other.

When Kathy approaches her fiance with a suggestion, a hint, or a request, Mark perceives that initiative as a symbolic enactment of his mother's expectations and hovering overinvolvement. Evoked in him at that point are hosts of emotions connected with an unfinished impasse, the wish to please, guilt if he does not, and resentment if he surrenders his autonomy. His bind is heightened by the fact that, not having learned how to cope with these intense emotions, he is helpless and immobilized. The present impasse becomes, for him, a symbolic reenactment of the antecedent one. A fusion of past and present, parent and partner, occurs. In this fusion it is no longer clear to him with whom he is interacting. He assigns to his mate certain expectations and assumptions that have arisen in an earlier field of interaction. He also displaces into the situation the anticipation that certain themes and outcomes will be repeated. His range of options for realistic and purely present-centered response is severely restricted.

But, as Boszormenyi-Nagy (1965) observes, there is in displacement not only a subjective assignment by one partner, but also a compliance with the assignment by the other. Kathy is not just viewed by Mark as hovering, intrusive, and attacking, but in her actions she exudes these characteristics. She hints, probes, and manipulates, and not getting what she wants, passively attacks or punishes. His memories of the past lead him to expect overinvolvement and intrusiveness, and that is exactly how Kathy acts. But for him the interaction becomes too close, too involved. His fiancee's behavior confirms his expectancy set, and stirs into motion his subjective replication of a past impasse.

The subjective need projected by Kathy is the pursuit of intimacy and the fear of distance. Disengagement she has known all too well, and closeness, security, and togetherness are her unmet relationship needs. Involvement, stability, and nurture are, for her, symbolic metaphors of closeness and interpersonal engagement. Yet withdrawal, distance, or rejection, she fears, can occur at any time, especially if she pushes too hard or manipulates too much. Like her partner, she too, is wounded by the past. Having failed to resolve this interactional impasse in the past, she is rendered anxious and unsure of herself in the present. She, too, is faced with a restricted range of action, as if the script is bound inevitably to repeat itself.

Mark is a suitable object for his fiancee's assignments. Tentative, guarded, and hesitating, he invites her pursuit, and eventually her intrusion. Yet he also can get involved, can nurture, and can feel obligated to respond to her initiatives. He can also feel defensive and resentful and, if pushed too far, can erupt into name-calling and disparagement. His objective traits of personality match her subjective expectancy set, making him a fitting participant in her script.

When the moving force behind displacement is a mate's covert wish to alter, complete, or vary relationship concerns originating in the past, it is maladaptive for at least three fundamental reasons. First, the partner finds himself or herself the recipient of projections that are vague and confusing. In the course of interaction one partner is assigned certain roles, is expected to carry out certain actions, or is presumed to have certain attitudes, all of which seem unrealistic and extraneous to the matter at hand. When Mark says, "It's not that I *want* her to be unreasonable. . . ," he is probably attempting to counteract an assignment Kathy placed on him which arises out of repeated, unresolved interaction with her father. When Kathy takes initiatives towards closeness and mutuality, she has no way of knowing that for her fiance these actions are symbolically intrusive, reminiscent of his mother and threatening to his emerging autonomy. The net effect of these displacements is to strip the partner of separate and original action in an interaction event. Mark cannot express his disagreement without being perceived by Kathy as critical and rejecting. Kathy cannot pursue closeness without being perceived by Mark as intrusive and smothering.

To the extent that the assignments are covert, usually beyond the awareness of the person making them, they cannot be clarified. Since they remain unconscious, they are not likely to be satisfied. Kathy ultimately cannot stand in for Mark's mother while he attempts covertly to complete an unresolved relationship transition with the parent. Nor can Mark ultimately stand in for Kathy's father in his fiancee's covert quest to fill an antecedent void in her life.

Displacement, secondly, also inhibits the maker's own further individuation (Boszormenyi-Nagy 1965). The symbolic reenactments that are generated in displacement serve only to deflect or postpone the painful process of resolving the original impasse. When Kathy, in the early days of their relationship, covertly invited Mark's nurture, she was probably delaying the painful realization that her father had not been and may never be capable of closeness. Full contact with that fact can evoke long-dormant and intense feelings of hurt and loss: All her maneuvers to counteract her history through projected assignments onto Mark cannot alter that past.

Moreover, so long as Kathy continued to play out her carefree, flighty script with its chronic frustrations and smoldering resentments, she merely postponed the time when she could opt out of that scenario. Apparently, the father's remarriage expedited her passage through this particular impasse, though the checkup data do not reveal how.

Likewise, so long as Mark continues to experience his interaction with his fiancee as a precarious balance between overinvolvement and individuation, he delays his task of finding a suitable balance between individuality and mutuality in relationships. For him, now, the boundary between closeness and distance is diffuse and tenuous. Since that confusion arose in his relationship with his mother, it is there that the impasse is founded. And it is there, in the final analysis, and not symbolically with his partner, that the unfinished task of differentiation will have to be completed.

Displacement also retards individuation by hindering the realignment of relationship boundaries in which the impasse originated. Mark's images and perceptions of his mother, and Kathy's of her father, are based on the child's viewpoint. Each has no doubt been so caught up in his or her own concerns and anxieties in the parent-child encounters that the parent's situation has been overlooked or discounted. But as Goulding (1972) and Bowen (1978) have noted, coming to an awareness and understanding of the parent's framework and history is a further relationship phase on the road to individuation. Such empathic regard for and acceptance of the elder's framework creates the basis for a rejoining and clarification of the relationship with him or her.

Frequently, the impasse of unresolved relationships is transmitted from one generation to the next in families. There is some evidence suggesting this to be the case in Mark's history. His mother, he reported, has lived her entire married life next door to her parents. Such physical proximity in and of itself may mean nothing with respect to her interpersonal closeness or distance in relation to her parents. She can conceivably live beside her family of origin and maintain very clear and functional boundaries between herself and them. Mark, however, views his mother's closeness as reflecting her continuing overinvolvement with her parents. He documents those perceptions with observations of her behaviors towards them, constant checking, advising, reminding, and caring for them. There is strong evidence, therefore, supporting the judgment that Mark's enmeshed family model reaches into his extended network of relationships.

If the mother has not completed the task of individuation herself, then the emergence of this push in her son's life could reactivate her own developmental impasse. In his impending differentiation, as Paul (1970) has found, she can reexperience all the disquieting anxiety associated with her own unfinished family business. Her son's becoming more differentiated can threaten to bring back all the mixed emotions, invisible loyalties, guilt, sadness, and submerged resentments, that she has avoided and repressed up to that point. Confronted anew with her own incomplete individuation, embodied for her in her son's passage towards autonomy, she can attempt covertly to ward off her ambiguities. Unaware that she is doing so, she can tacitly enjoin Mark to postpone or defer individuation, prescribing her own impasse.

As part of his own individuation process and as a way of rejoining his mother on a new basis, Mark needs to hear her story. In this new relationship phase Mark can recognize the members of his family of origin, especially his parents, as real human beings with their own unfinished tasks, ambiguities, joys, and miseries. Such a family voyage (Guerin 1973) would enable Mark to experience his parents' struggles, to trace the origins of the conflicts they have transmitted. Implied in this new relationship phase are elements of understanding and emotions of acceptance and forgiveness. Displacement hinders the actualization of such intergenerational empathy, and thus restricts the growth of an important relationship phase. The therapy of intense, person-to-person encounter between individuals and members of their family of origin (Bowen 1978) facilitates the accomplishment of this relationship task.

Displacement, then, inhibits personal growth. It restrains the completion of the original interpersonal binds out of which it arises. And finally, it arrests and puts in jeopardy the couple's relationship. When partners' interaction becomes repetitive and fixed, homeostatic, the likelihood is great that a recurring replication and reenactment of unresolved relationship impasses is occurring. Boundaries between past and present, between parent and partner, between symbols and reality have become fused and slurred.

AN INTRUSION-REJECTION PATTERN

Kathy's and Mark's relationship is bordering, perhaps even in the early throes of, such rigidity. They appear to be still struggling, and the checkup itself could be regarded as an effort to break out of the impasse and to achieve greater openness and flexibility.

The pattern that characterizes their interaction is what Napier (1978) calls the rejection-intrusion dynamic. In this pattern one partner seeks closeness and mutuality, while the other desires separateness and independence. The roots of the dyanamic usually lie in each partner's relationships in the family of origin, in models very much like the ones found in Kathy's and Mark's backgrounds. One mate, like Kathy, comes from an essentially disengaged family and has experienced considerable abandonment, deprivation, and loss. The other partner, like Mark, has known a basically enmeshed family style, and therefore has experienced overinvolvement, engulfment, and intrusion.

The deprived partner, like Kathy, strives for closeness, togetherness, and mutuality. The engulfed mate, like Mark, pursues personal freedom, autonomy, and individuation. When the closeness-seeking partner, Kathy, makes initiatives towards mutuality, the distance-seeking mate, Mark, becomes anxious, and may handle the perceived intrusiveness by withdrawing. Such withdrawal, in turn, only seems to increase Kathy's anxiety, and the abandonment, deprivation, and rejection she has so much expected and feared is perceived anew. Anxious, she clasps even harder, leading only to the imprisoned mate's further retreat. Thus, Kathy, eager for closeness but anxious about rejection, experiences herself chronically tied to a mate who is constantly retreating from intimacy. And Mark, eager for autonomy and fearing intrusion, chronically experiences himself tied to one who perpetually seeks to be closer.

As Napier (1978) observes, these apparent differences can conceal some fundamental, covert similarities between the partners. In his transition toward differentiation Mark carries lingering needs for approval and nurturance. Part of his anxiety, then, lies in the fear of rejection and loss of approval. Covertly and obliquely, Mark can vicariously satisfy this continuing need for closeness in the intimacy-seeking initiatives of his fiancee. At the same time, he can shield himself from these threatening dependency feelings by distancing them, externalizing them, and warding them off in the person of his mate. Paradoxically, his very withdrawal only intensifies her pursuit of intimacy and thus guarantees that the issue of closeness remains in his life.

In a similar vein, Kathy, who remains so angry and frustrated when Mark is closed and withdrawn, is to some degree still anxious about closeness. When in her upbringing has she really known genuine closeness and thus had an opportunity to become comfortable with it? At one level, then, her fiance's overt fear and withdrawal from intimacy enable her to avoid a closeness that could be threatening and anxiety-provoking. Also, too much mutuality could encroach on the autonomy and freedom she has known and valued. Thus, her intrusions paradoxically guarantee the maintenance of the distance she requires.

Despite their protestations to the contrary, therefore, the couple maintains an intuitively balanced level of distance (Napier 1978). Mark can covertly preserve the closeness he needs while overtly embracing autonomy, while Kathy can covertly vouchsafe the distance she needs while openly espousing closeness. Paradoxically, in the present state of the relationship, either partner would be threatened and vulnerable at getting what he or she claims to want. Anxiety levels would escalate to a high pitch.

STRATEGY AND TACTICS

In the patterning process, thus far, the therapist has conceptualized the general structure of the couple's interaction. Points of connection among various elements, together with their influence on one another, have been identified. The therapist is now thus prepared to specify the points in the mates' process where stress exists, where intervention can be addressed to improve the relationship, and the order in which these interceding actions most appropriately can be made. A broad strategy can be formulated, along with intervening tactics to reach desired results.

In the history of Kathy's and Mark's relationship, she appears to have undergone the most change. From earlier carefree and flighty attitudes and actions she has developed a more organized and responsible way of living. In her communication with her fiance she has been able to identify the skill that she most needs to improve, namely, the clear and transparent expression of her wants, or intentions. During the checkup itself she displayed the intent to work on this skill in future communication. She can see dysfunctional consequences of her hinting and indirectness. Likewise, she can see the origins of some of her relationship needs in her deprived relationship with her father. She has reframed that relationship. She was also able to draw parallels between her former self and her stepmother.

Implied intent to work on certain communication skills and insight into relationship and family of origin patterns do not by themselves constitute change. But they do reflect Kathy's flexibility and capacity for change. She manifests an extensional orientation to the relationship, one in which she is willing and eager to expand her understanding and to enlarge her skills. This finding indicates that intervention to shape and stabilize her skill in expressing intentions would be an important first step in therapy. This tactic, as Bowen (1978) recommends, would serve to maintain the apparently more flexible partner at an unfluctuating level while other more tenuous points in the interaction are addressed.

Modeling and Experiential Shaping

Were the therapist to continue working with this couple, then, a number of interventions could be useful for implementing this objective with Kathy. Instances of reflective listening, for one, would afford her an opportunity to move through her anxiety, her defensive caution and indirectness, and to express her wants. Empathizing with her at such times, and attending to all channels of her communication, verbal and nonverbal, the therapist can articulate the intention that is implicit, but not fully transparent, in her messages. Such an intervention might be, for example, "Kathy, much of you seems to be saying that you'd like to come right out with what you want without having to be apprehensive about it."

Feeding a sentence is a similar, yet qualitatively different, procedure for facilitating this objective. The therapist, having listened to and observed Kathy, can give voice to her implied intention. There is an interpretive element in such an intervention, but one that can be grounded in and related back to her experience, to her auditory and visual cues of communication. An intervention such as, "I would like to come right out with what I want without being so cautious," gives her an opportunity to respond to the therapist's offering and either claim or reject it.

Doubling adds a further experiential dimension to the procedure of feeding a sentence. The therapist can actually move beside Kathy, and this physical proximity brings the sentence closer to the client and facilitates her testing it and owning or disclaiming it.

Moreover, the very act of the therapist's physically moving closer to her place in the therapeutic system metaphorically differentiates the sentence as hers. Such manipulation of space can potentially demarcate and strengthen her boundary, her uniqueness. This same action by the therapist serves a corollary effect of signaling Mark that the statement is his partner's, in her separateness, and thus indirectly restrains his tendency to speak for her.

When the intervention, saying it directly, is added to the above procedures, an interpersonal aspect is introduced. The doubled sentence described above is spoken directly to Mark. Such a message becomes, for example, "Mark, I want to come right out and let you know exactly what I want and to stop all my hinting around." The therapist, with a nonverbal movement may motion to Kathy to look directly at her fiance while this sentence is being spoken. Such visual contact, seemingly trivial, epitomizes the rehearsal of new behaviors that cut through the heightened anxiety levels. Complying with this directive, she has to go beyond, pass through, her reticence and anxiety. In it, the emotions aroused by direct and immediate contact cannot be avoided. If Kathy, after participating in the message, owns it as reflecting her wishes, the further step can be taken of having her repeat it. This procedure of saying it again, with its implied emphasis on taking responsibility (Levitsky and Perls 1970) for the message, once more differentiates her as a separate person whose wants are worthwhile.

If the foregoing exchanges have been videotaped, an additional intervention entails the playback of these recordings. Kathy can observe herself sending more open and transparent messages, which can be self-reenforcing. Any existing stress which might be disclosed in the videotapes she can experience first hand. She can observe any auditory and visual anxiety cues as they are sensed by her partner. If even earlier recordings are available, she can contrast her original pattern of hinting and obliqueness with her new and more transparent style of expression, thus seeing and hearing the differences in her observable behavior.

Rehearsal (Levitsky and Perls 1970) is yet another procedure that builds on the above skills and extends them. This intervention can provide Kathy with an opportunity to express herself at length on some personal or relationship issue. In rehearsal, the therapist creates a situation which permits her to practice interaction with Mark on some concern. Since this procedure simulates an anticipated actual event, it is somewhat less stressful than the more direct encounters described above.

If this rehearsal has been videotaped, playback once more can provide Kathy with an opportunity to observe herself in action. She is thus given feedback on the way she looks and sounds when speaking her wishes. Distorted communication can be contrasted with a more congruent style. Kathy can encounter herself as her fiance experiences her, thus confronting her own contribution to a dysfunctional or functional communication pattern. Soliciting Mark's responses (Paul 1968) during or following such playback adds his observations and input to this learning process.

Even as the therapist makes these interventions with Kathy, steps are concurrently being taken to interrupt and redirect portions of Mark's maladaptive communication. Since he frequently interprets and articulates his partner's subjective states, especially her intentions, he transgresses her boundaries as a separate and unique person. Checking this mind-reading tendency, therefore, is an important therapeutic goal.

When the therapist actively listens and attends to Kathy's communication and shows empathy, acceptance, and a desire to understand her frame of reference, he or she is modeling new behavior for Mark. When the therapist asks questions to clarify her exact point of view on some matter, such checking out provides the client with observable cues for imitation. The modeling of these very specific communication skills demonstrates to Mark a more adaptive way of interacting. Through the emulation and shaping of such skills Mark can more functionally recognize his fiancee's individuality and behave so as to preserve her boundaries.

In a similar vein, the therapist's interaction with Kathy is based in part on sensory awareness, on listening to her tone of voice or attending to her facial expressions. When these sensory impressions are reflected back to her by the therapist, yet another communication skill is modeled for Mark. Since, as we have seen, Mark often interprets his fiancee's experience without documenting (Miller, Nunnally and Wackman 1975) or specifying any sensory inputs leading to his thoughts, the addition of these skills can enrich his communication repertoire.

When the therapist says to Kathy, as he did at one point in the checkup, "You made an expression at that point," he demonstrates the process of listening and attending to different representational systems. Documenting and feeding back his own sensory awareness, the therapist provides Mark with behavioral cues for imitating this competency.

The therapist can more actively intervene in this mind-reading tendency of Mark's by blocking it (Minuchin 1974, Sluzki 1978). Such blocking can take place indirectly through the therapist's selective inattention of Mark's references to his partner's subjective state. By continuing to concentrate on Kathy's messages and by actively soliciting her further self-disclosure, the therapist discourages and gives negative feedback to Mark's mind reading. Even more direct blocking can be accomplished by the therapist's physically holding up one hand to block Mark while drawing Kathy out with a motion of the hand. These gestures in physical space metaphorically delineate each partner's boundary.

The therapist can also help Mark decelerate his mind-reading behaviors by actively helping him to replace them with more functional communication. The client can be helped to acquire such skills as active listening or clarifying messages. Instead of passively modeling these competencies, as we saw earlier, the therapist actively facilitates Mark's practice and shaping of them.

Doubling, for instance, is a mediating intervention that can facilitate Mark's acquisition of the new skills. In this procedure the therapist, rather than reflecting back Kathy's statements as therapist, moves over beside Mark and functions alongside him. The therapist still continues to reflect, to clarify, or to use some other communication skill, but he or she does so by speaking for Mark, as though these behaviors were his. Mark then participates in and claims this doubling as his own, gradually emulating the skills and progressively internalizing them as part of his natural repertoire. Success with the new competencies, together with his fiancee's greater satisfaction at being understood, can become Mark's inducement for continued practice and improvement.

In addition to arresting this mind-reading tendency and replacing it with more adaptive skills, a major therapeutic objective with Mark converges on his making contact with and learning how to express his own emotionality. A severe emotional constriction in him contributes importantly to the couple's interaction bind. Feeling dependent, intruded upon, guilty, angry, and fearful, and projecting these intense emotions into his interaction with his fiancee, Mark places the relationship at an impasse. Rationality and emotionality become fused in projections and displacement. Boundaries between past and present, between parent and partner, between reality and symbolic reenactment become diffuse.

A major therapeutic objective with Mark, consequently, lies in the provision of a relationship that can enable him progressively to become less anxious and defensive. The creation of conditions of genuine regard, empathy, and acceptance, manifested through careful listening and understanding (Rogers 1959) can facilitate his becoming less guarded and threatened.

This is not to say that Mark is fundamentally fragile or vulnerable, for in many respects he is quite self-assertive and capable of handling himself in the couple's interaction. But through interventions that communicate empathy and acceptance of his feelings, Mark himself can begin to evoke and express his emotions more fully. He can discover that he experiences a wide range of feelings that are understood and accepted by the therapist, and more importantly, by his fiancee. He can learn to feel close without risking intrusion, autonomous without risking punishment, separate without risking guilt or rejection. He can learn how to move in and out of these different and changing relationship phases without avoiding them, on the one hand, or getting stuck in them, on the other.

The therapist's interventions to join with and to understand Mark can model such behaviors for Kathy. Such processes as empathic understanding and reflection of her fiance's feelings can provide Kathy with cues which she can then emulate. She can audibly and visibly observe behaviors through which she can make it easier for him to be more open and less threatened. For Kathy, these new actions enable her to create new conditions of interaction, conditions in which she can be sensitive to Mark's feelings without feeling deprived herself, accepting without risking his withdrawal, clarifying his messages without incurring his resentment.

As with Mark, the therapist can double with Kathy in the practice and progressive shaping of these skills. Even though the therapist is still providing the reflective listening, by his moving beside her and doubling with her, an intermediate stage of learning is provided on her way to more complete imitation and replication of the skills. Sitting beside Kathy, the therapist might say, looking at Mark, "So you feel manipulated when I just hint around about going bowling, or something. And you feel angry." Such rehearsal can decelerate her previous communication behaviors, which leave her feeling anxious and threatened, with ones which provide regard for and tolerance of her fiance's separate and unique experience.

Even while Mark is rehearsing a more congruent expression of his feelings and wishes, Kathy may still be stressed. Once again, the playback of videotaped recordings can provide her with an opportunity to hear and see her reactions. Such self-encounter can afford her a concrete demonstration of her nonverbal behaviors that activate and reenforce her partner's anxiety and defensiveness.

The foregoing intervention design is based on a number of patterning considerations. It is a strategy, first of all, aimed at the more overt levels of the couple's interaction. Kathy's hinting and Mark's hesitancy are behaviors readily observable to the partners themselves. Furthermore, during the checkup they identified these stress points as problem areas. To the extent that they themselves have isolated these maladaptive behaviors, the impetus to modify them is internally generated. The therapist can then work with the momentum of the couple's concerns. Problem definition is intrinsic to them, not externally imposed by the therapist.

This strategy also has the advantage of matching the couple's initial purpose in doing a checkup. Kathy framed the interview as an exercise in learning what they might be doing wrong and how they could improve it. Therefore, the preceding design represents what would probably be perceived by the couple as a response to their presenting concern, as framed in their language. It is a strategy formulated by using the momentum they bring to the session (Watzlawick, Weakland, and Fisch 1974).

The tactics employed are basically modeling and the experiential rehearsal of new communication skills. The therapist sometimes passively provides communication cues that the mates can see, hear, and then imitate. Cues are introduced into the couple's communication pattern precisely at those points where old behaviors are to be extinguished and new ones accelerated. Partners also indirectly learn the sequence of effective communication, for example, that clarification is an appropriate next step in response to an unclear message.

The Structured Communications Training Group

Another design that could suitably be used to enrich this couple's communication process is the structured training group (Miller, Nunnally, and Wackman 1975). In this approach communication skills are shaped generically within a group of four to six couples. Meeting for a predetermined length of time over a defined number of sessions, the group is trained in a variety of distinct yet interconnected skills, methods that offer practice and performance.

In session one, for instance, the design is focused on self-awareness and the transmission of personal information. In a mini-lecture the concept of the awareness wheel is presented, illustrated by brief, pointed examples and modeling by the trainer. This presentation constitutes a review of material already read by group members prior to coming to the session. Group members are provided with concepts that can enable them to discriminate, sort out, recombine, and express the various elements of their internal experience in a given unit of communication. Without a great deal of discussion, participants move immediately into the practice of the skills "in slow motion," sending, for example, a sensory or a feeling message. Concepts are thus internalized through practice and rehearsal. Other group members are assigned explicit tasks of observation during these structured exercises. By feeding back where and how they see and hear certain skills being performed, positive reinforcement is given, helping to shape the competencies, as well as widening the scope of each participant's learning. This rehearsal of discrete skills is followed by other exercises designed to facilitate the learners' abilities to combine elements of self-expression and to cope with greater complexities in performance.

Partners are then directed to use the awareness competencies in sending messages to each other, beginning with lighter, less weighty material but moving to more risky issues if and as they are ready.

Couples thus retain control over their own stress levels during the session. Provision is made for the couple to decide together how they will handle a given task or assignment in the program. Likewise, the design affords each couple opportunities to fit the general program to their own idiomatic needs. Kathy and Mark, for example, working both individually and together, could determine that she would concentrate particularly on the expression of intentions during the program and he on the expression of feeling. In homework assignments the partners chart their performance on the agreed-upon skills, thus adding further to the shaping of new communication patterns.

Self-awareness elements are followed in a second session with training in listening skills, in the ability to clarify messages, feed them back, and arrive at shared meanings. In this session training is given in empathy and reflective listening, since very often couple communication entails one partner's helping the other to clarify his or her experience. Skill in empathizing with, articulating, and reflecting the mate's experience is an important intimacy-building capacity. In this session, like in all others, emphasis is placed on the structured exercises and rehearsals so crucial to an experiential approach to learning.

In subsequent training sessions couples work on combining and sequencing communication elements. They examine and simulate different styles of couple interaction, those where issues are avoided, those where one partner attempts to coerce or change the other, those that are more tentative and guarded, and those based on effective communication. Couples give one another feedback on their style, or blend of styles. Their skills built up, couples in later sessions apply what they have learned in coping with weightier issues in their relationship. These exercises enable partners to work on the task of balancing individuality and mutuality. Using communication competencies, they rehearse how to disagree, that is, how to understand and value the partner's point of view while maintaining one's own. In negotiation training, couples rehearse the use of communication skills in identifying individual or joint needs, setting mutually acceptable goals, and in reaching agreements and decisions that are satisfactory for both (Bockus 1975).

From time to time in group sessions the therapist may apply the modeling and doubling procedures discussed earlier. He or she can announce the rule early on of being available for consultation to a couple during an exercise. If a pair reaches a stress point or impasse, the therapist can intervene immediately and facilitate continued movement. If the therapist can quickly grasp the couple's concern or bind and can intervene with a doubling procedure, he or she can expedite their exercise and keep it moving. Such consultation can also be made available to a couple privately as an adjunct to the group process. If some matter cannnot be dealt with adequately in the group, the therapist can model and double with the partners in the set of skills and rehearsals where they are blocked.

The effectiveness of these designs is supported by extensive outcome studies. As Jacobson (1978) has shown in a study of outcome research in marital therapy, behavioral communication training and relationship enrichment approaches have demonstrated results. Brief, time-limited, and structured, the modalities discussed earlier offer great promise in a situation like Kathy's and Mark's, where enrichment and improvement are the articulated relationship goals.

In the patterning process with Kathy's and Mark's relationship the therapist has identified other stress points as well. The couple's overt interaction is connected with other, more covert levels that lie beneath the surface. Mark is already experiencing stress in relation to his mother, and that bind is being projected into his interaction with Kathy. The changing but still incomplete relationship transition with the parent is being displaced symbolically, creating numerous parallels and binding his interaction with his fiancee. Likewise, Kathy, who has grown in the relationship, is nevertheless stressed by the impasse that sometimes occurs with her partner. She then is confronted by the symbolic reenactment of old relationship wounds.

At this point, then, the therapist has to evaluate the risks and rewards of certain intervention strategies, the trade-offs that are always a part of the patterning function. To address Mark's relationship with his mother at this time would appear to present more risk than promise. Even though Mark introduced the subject spontaneously, never in the checkup does he frame the mother-son relationship as a full-blown problem. It is emerging and problematic. Not really a part of the couple's presenting concern, as they frame it, the therapist's convergence on the issue now would probably not match the couple's felt need. Focus on covert process at this time would probably disturb intrapersonal elements that do not need more agitation. Moreover, these underlying forces may be resolved in time, given a chance to follow their own developmental course. The therapist, therefore, thinks small (Haley 1973), converging on concerns defined by the couple and thus having their support, their willingness to invest time, energy, and money.

The strategy of focusing on communication enrichment contains a further advantage. Since the more overt levels of the couple's interaction are connected and continuous with the more covert, action on the former can potentially impact on the latter. When Mark learns how to express his emotions with his fiancee, to be differentiated with this person in his life, that ability can potentially transfer over to his relationship with the mother. With her, too, he can potentially become more spontaneous. Change induced at one level of interaction, in his relationship with his fiancee, can potentially spill over into other levels, into the impasse of the mother-son dyad. If the intra- and interpersonal forces that created the couple's relationship bind stand on an interlocking continuum with one another, then in principle, that very continuity can be utilized in reversing and freeing their interaction.

But the therapist's foregoing analysis and consequent strategy may not be borne out. The forces generating Mark's impasse with his mother, and now with his fiancee, are long-standing and deep. They are grounded in primary levels of interaction, in an overinvolved relationship phase that spans a lifetime. Breaking out of it can call into motion powerful forces of constraint, both in himself, as we have seen, and perhaps in his mother. The odds favor homeostasis as much as change.

The factor most in Mark's favor is the contextual appropriateness of his growth towards individuality. This is the time in his life when differentiation is demanded. In fact, failure to master this task will place severe restraints on his future development. It is already encroaching on his ability to cope with a new task in the cycle of life, the formation of an intimate relationship in marriage. And should he and his mate fall short in that task, the likely consequences would be the projection of any resulting conflict, explicit or implicit, onto their children. A triadic process seen so often in family therapy would stand a high probability of being set in motion.

To hedge the therapeutic strategy against these more negative possibilities, therefore, the therapist needs to leave open the door for future contact. He or she can converge on communications training for now, but make provision for continuing access. Following Erickson's (1973) excellent example, the therapist can express interest in being kept informed, for research and professional purposes, in the ways the couple accomplishes their objectives, *not* if they run into trouble, which virtually prescribes failure. The consultation process can be kept open during this time when Mark, individually, and the couple together, are passing through this developmental and interpersonal stage.

Accordingly, the couple was referred to a couple communication training group that the therapist expected to conduct within the university marriage and family therapy service. For all the foregoing considerations, that course appeared to be the most fitting strategy for the current state of the couple's interaction pattern and to its improvement.

CRITIQUE

Nothing distinguishes the various approaches to marital therapy more than their orientation to the question of intervention goals. In some therapies the final objectives of intervention converge on what has been called here overt levels of interaction. Goals, in such systems, are present-oriented, are addressed to specific problems introduced initally, are stated in the couple's own vernacular, and often are observable and measurable. In other therapies the objectives of intervention are formulated in relation to more covert reaches of interaction. The completion of unresolved matters from the family of origin, the clarification and breaking up of displacements and projections, and the reduction of disquieting anxiety levels and emotional fusions are some of the stated goals in these latter perspectives. Not surprisingly, these differences correspond to the ways different therapies approach the task of information gathering, that is, what they regard as relevant data within their particular perspective. In recent interpretations of the field some of these more evident concordances and splits among the various marital therapies have been classified (Gurman 1978). Such analyses have served to clarify positions and the presuppositions lying behind them.

It is the thesis of this critique that in the concept of patterning it is possible to transcend some of these apparent differences and to construct a more integrative perspective. Such theoretical construction can open up new alternatives of thought and action for the therapist, and thus for the client couple.

In the fine distinction he draws between cybernetic and open systems in living organisms, von Bertalanffy (1968) provides insights useful in understanding patterns in marital interaction. Von Bertalanffy is an innovator of the general systems theory whose tenets appear prominently in contemporary marital theory and therapy. According to this theory, living systems possess both primary and secondary regulatory processes. Primary regulations, those which are most fundamental and primitive, are of the nature of dynamic interaction. They are based on the fact that living organisms, including social relationships like marriage, are open systems. They maintain themselves in a steady state by the continuous exchange and increase of information.

Superimposed on this dynamic interplay of primary processes are those regulations that can be called secondary. They are characterized by fixed arrangements of the feedback type. A cybernetic system, though accomplishing its control through an exchange of information between its component parts, is nevertheless closed. Information within such a system does not increase.

The principle of progressive mechanization, then, as von Bertalanffy calls it, states the relationship between these two orders of control in the organization of systems. At first, systems are governed by the dynamic interaction of their components. Later on, fixed arrangements and conditions of constraint, or control, set in. These latter patterns of organization make the system more efficient, but also gradually diminish its adaptability and equipotentiality. That is, since new information cannot enter into these processes, the system cannot find new or alternative pathways to the realization of its needs and goals.

A number of implications for marital therapy exist in von Bertalanffy's discrimination. Perhaps most importantly, it tends to emphasize the fact that the surface structure of marital process, as Bandler and Grinder (1975) call the manifest and observable framework of language and thought, is only the upper level of interaction. Symptoms, the rigid and reified relationship patterns which are the targets of intervention among the systems purists or behaviorists, are the final stages of interaction that has run down, become progressively mechanized, lost its energy, and become severely diminished in its ability to cope. The claim of these therapies to be doing systems therapy is in fact, an assertion of prerogative in only certain orders of systems, those at the cybernetic or homeostatic level of interaction. The reduction of the general systems model in marital therapy to this special order of systems (Steinglass 1978) is, to this writer, an unfortunate development in the evolution of the field. Of course, the goal of intervention in this cybernetic approach is to interrupt the rigid feedback process in a couple's relationship, and by arresting these reified patterns, to set more dynamic energies in motion. But by focusing only on the way observable sequences of interaction are organized and modified, the systems purist disregards other orders of systems that may account for the etiology and progressive mechanization that evolves into symptomatology.

The concept of patterning embraces not only surface structure of marital interaction, but the deeper structure as well. To the experiential therapist, symptoms are surface or final stage systems, when other more primary processes of interaction have broken down. A rigid, reified interaction sequence represents the gradual unfolding of entropy, the dissipation, blocking, and diminishing of energy in the relationship.

Applying von Bertalanffy's model of primary and secondary

process, the course of symptom development can be followed. Taking Kathy's and Mark's impasse as a case in point, it can be argued that their relationship symptoms originated initially in the breakdown of primary processes of interaction in each partner's family of origin. Thus, in Mark's case the nurturant relationship phase, mother toward son, was at one time in that field of interaction appropriate and adaptive. If in time that phase shifted to a more maladaptive, overinvolved one, that state could be corrected by the action of other forces in the field, for example, Mark's father. Failing that, the interplay of other dynamic forces could still intervene, correcting the system and enabling it to realize its potential. A force of this type is currently operative in Mark's inherent tendency towards individuation, a developmental drive emanating out of his particular stage in the life cycle. The family system has built into itself its own morphogenesis, in this case, in Mark's emerging differentiation of self.

When that developmental task is left uncompleted, however, entropy begins to set in. Inherent in Mark's developmental impasse is an emotional and interactional fixation point. Energy that could be released by the completion of the task is blocked and, in many respects, is now being dissipated in intense anxiety and emotional ambivalence. Homeostatic constraints maintaining the status quo have usurped the usual dynamic interplay of system energies.

The impasse becomes progressively constraining; it is then displaced into Mark's relationship with his fiancee. The task unfinished in the family of origin is projected into the new relationship, creating a fusion of intellect and emotion. The past ceases to be past and is present. The partner ceases simply to be partner and is contaminated by a host of feelings, assumptions, and expectations that originated in another interaction field, in another time and place. Adaptation to present relationship conditions is impeded and imperiled by his displacement of past patterns onto the present.

The observable sequence of interactions in Mark's and Kathy's communication, then, represents a surface level that rests on a very deep structure of antecedent events. The guardedness and restraint that so rigidly and repeatedly appears in Mark's interaction with his fiancee is but the final stage in a progressive system of control and constraint. His and his mate's overt feedback loop reflects a mechanism for maintaining a mutually intuited boundary of closeness and distance. In it, almost mechanically, Mark wards off intrusion while guaranteeing closeness, while Kathy pursues closeness without risking rejection. It is a fixed arrangement that is devoid, in its present form, of openness and flexibility.

Thus, the surface structure rests upon and is an analogue for the deeper structure. Observable symptoms and the framework in which they are cast are continuous with, participate in, and represent the deeper dynamic of the relationship. Conversely, deeper and antecedent levels of interaction progressively build up to a point of rigid fixity and are manifested as overt symptoms. The symptom, then, reflects and potentially can disclose the dynamic field in which it is grounded. A symptom, as Haley (1976) observes, is not a "bit" of information denoting one discrete and circumscribed problem. It is an analogue that fits or resonates with a complex and multi-faceted situation.

A couple's interaction pattern, therefore, is comprised of both overt or surface levels and covert or deep structures as well. These levels, moreover, are interconnected and continuous with one another. A therapeutic objective targeted at one level can have impact on another, either through indirect influence or through transfer. The therapist can, through the use of metaphor, paradoxical reframing, or the manipulation of observable symptoms, indirectly address other more covert levels of dyadic or intrapersonal process. The enrichment or modification of overt communication structures can transfer to deeper levels of intrapersonal and interpersonal process. Thus, the rehearsal by Mark of more open and differentiated experession of emotionality at the overt communication level with his fiancee, can potentially result in a less anxious, more individuated pattern with his mother.

Conversely, the completion of unresolved relationship phases from the family of origin can disrupt the fusions and displacements existing in the deep structure and release emotional energy for the effective reshaping of communication patterns and behavioral exchanges at the more overt level. Recognition of this multidimensional and interconnected structure of marital process enables the therapist to be differential in setting intervention goals. In fact, the often advocated but sometimes unheeded injunction, "different strokes for different folks," becomes a matter not of lip service but of necessity.

In the light of this comprehensive view of the couple's interaction pattern, the therapist can take into consideration a number of issues in defining the objectives of therapy. One of the first and most important variables to be taken into account is the adaptational and developmental stage of the marital partners. Erickson (Haley 1973), a master of this viewpoint, regards the life cycle as the broad frame of reference for determining strategies of intervention. Against this backdrop, his larger goal is to get the life cycle going again. Also, by thinking adaptionally and developmentally, Erickson is able to avoid the labeling and the pathological bias that can accompany therapeutic overinvolvement, or intervention overkill.

Studies of developmental stages and transitional turning points (Caplan 1967) have shown them to be fraught with considerable stress and disequilibrium. Life changes associated with biological development, such as pregnancy, childbirth, or old age, those linked with social transitions, such as engagement and marriage, becoming parents, or changing jobs, and those connected with times of loss, such as the death of a family member, create novel situations for both individual partners and for the marital relationship. For a relatively short period of time the individual, or the couple together, is faced with unfamiliar tasks not easily and quickly solved by the usual coping processes. It is not uncommon for a period of confusion and frustration to set in. Grappling with the new adaptational situation, one or both partners can become tense and emotionally distraught, perhaps even anxious and depressed. Fears of mental breakdown can even ensue.

Such manifestations, Caplan's findings show, are signs of normal adaptation and change. Effective coping during these moments requires perserverance in facing problems and trying to solve them despite stressful confusion and frustration. Feelings of anxiety and distress are openly expressed. Mates, friends, and primary providers of professional services, usually physicians and clergymen, are consulted to gain understanding about what is happening and to receive guidance and support.

Thus, during such times of transition the therapist can function with adaptational and developmental attitudes and methods. Once, when a newly married couple consulted him for an emerging sexual difficulty, Erickson (Haley 1973) suggests to them that their problem is not uncommon and that in time it probably would resolve itself. In so doing, he frames their situation as a normal transitional task that nevertheless will require their attention, joint cooperation, and experimentation. This latter suggestion, in effect, prescribes the playfulness, the mutual discovery and learning, that is so crucial in sexual therapy and which is an appropriate adaptational task for a new couple. The therapist, as a representative of the wider culture, also implicitly gives the couple permission to experiment. Operating from this adaptational position, the therapist avoids a pathology bias and a labeling of symptoms that could become iatrogenic, that is, therapeutically inducing a loss of self-esteem. By expressing continued interest in hearing how the solution goes for the couple, the therapist leaves open the door for future contact, should the problem, in fact, persist.

An adaptational outlook guided the therapist's thinking in determining an intervention strategy with Kathy and Mark. The therapeutic tactic of conducting a relationship checkup was informed by a recognition of the couple's developmental stage, which was relationship formation. The expressed goal of examining and improving their interaction was consistent with their particular stage in the life cycle. Furthermore, following the checkup, the therapist's recommendations were informed by adaptational thinking. Improvement would be accomplished by the circumscribed goal of enriching the couple's communication repertoire. Mark's changing relationship with his mother might, in time, resolve itself through normal developmental interaction and therefore could remain undisturbed for the time being.

Where the therapist observes the operation of displacement in the couple's interaction pattern, adaptational thinking provides a corrective to a pathological attitude towards it. Displacement is maladaptive, but it is understandable. Coping patterns learned in the family of origin are long in their formation and durable once formed. Given all the forces in a family field of interaction, with its system of demands and constraints, relationship patterns are, from one point of view, quite creative. They represent the family member's efforts to come to terms with that environment, however painful and dysfunctional that coping may sometimes be. Adaptation to one's family, like that pertaining to all organisms, binds one to a particular time and place, to a specific field of relationships. The coping mechanisms learned there are not easily relinquished. They are carried forward into new relationships, where efforts are made to replicate them, to complete them, to master them, or to enrich them. From this perspective, displacement does not reflect pathological but learned behavior that is being repeated in a new relationship, where it is no longer necessary or appropriate.

Viewed adaptationally, Mark's well-formed dependency is essentially an inexorable consequence of his family milieu. Characterized though it is by enmeshed relationship patterns, it nevertheless represented for him an unquestioned reality. For him to replicate these overinvolved actions towards his partner in their early dating was, from one point of view, inevitable and natural, although from another vantage point it was maladaptive. For the therapist to accept Mark's dependency as a learned pattern instead of as pathological behavior may, as Menninger (1963) has noted, make considerable difference in the way the client responds to and progresses in therapy.

A second set of considerations for the therapist's reflections centers on the location of therapy objectives. Intervention goals addressed to the surface structure of the couple's interaction generally bear the quality of enrichment. Such enrichment takes many forms. A relatively closed and reified interaction loop is interrupted and, at specific points of dysfunction, new behaviors are injected through the therapist's directives. For example, when Mark makes an unsubstantiated reference to Kathy's subjective state, he is asked what he senses that is leading to his inferences (Sluzki 1978). Thus, mind reading or projection is differentiated from sensory documentation. Mark's interpersonal repertoire is thus enriched by the addition of greater sensory awareness or of greater skill clarifying or checking out his partner's subjective states.

Enrichment can also take the form of extinguishing certain dysfunctional reenforcement patterns in the couple's interaction and replacing them with or accelerating more adaptive ones. When, for instance, Kathy invites and thereby reenforces her fiance's mind reading through her persistent hinting and indirectness, that behavior can be replaced by the rehearsal and shaping of a more open and transparent expression of her wishes and desires. Through the use of such interventions as modeling and doubling, perhaps accompanied by charting, this goal can be realized. Here, once again, the addition of a specific skill enriches the couple's interaction competency.

Or, a couple's interaction repertoire can also be enriched on a comprehensive basis, as in communications training. Time-limited and structured, such training has as its objective the overview and experiential practice of a broad range of communication skills. Yet each couple, or individual, can identify certain of those skills for special attention and development.

The storehouse of competencies proffered in communications training include skills in self-awareness and in other-awareness. One learns how to sort out and transmit one's sensory information, thoughts, feelings, intentions, and actions. Skills in empathy, in effective listening, in clarifying, and in feeding back and sharing common understandings can also be added. Such training also adds skills in negotiation, in conflict resolution, and in decision making, all of which place a premium on the couple's balancing of individuality and mutuality.

As Gurman (1978) has observed, communications training approaches have much to recommend them because of their very comprehensiveness. They include emotionality and intentionality in their set of objectives. This may account for some of their effectiveness, especially when compared with other more digital approaches that arbitrarily exclude such elements from attention.

Recent work of Bandler and Grinder (1976) offers further resources for enriching structured communication training programs. Their methods for adding and shifting representational systems can be included in training sessions, with the goal of augmenting partner's skills in nonverbal sensitivity. Becoming more attuned to auditory channels, such as voice tones and rates of speech, and more alert to visual messages, such as facial expressions and body positions, can enhance mates' ability to sense different levels and orders of messages. The actualization of these objectives can result in a marked increase in the couple's empathic resonance with each other, a sensitivity so crucial in effective listening.

In the recent past the marital intervention field has witnessed the emergence of a movement called marriage enrichment. Characterized by many different leadership styles, group compositions, methods, and settings, the movement exhibits considerable momentum, potential, and intrinsic value for extending intervention into the community.

The movement has been impeded, however, as one of its founders (Mace 1975) has observed, by lack of a clear definition of objectives. It lacks, Mace suggests, compelling meanings for such terms as enrichment, growth, potential, or improvement. Bantered about in the literature of the field, these concepts have lacked precise definitions that can guide the construction of program designs. Enrichment goals sound inherently right and worthwhile, but almost without exception, every article or volume describing such a program contains disclaimers about doing therapy, which, presumably, is the province of some other professional group. Marriage enrichment as an evolving field, it can be said, has been too diffuse in its focus and too modest in its claims.

The target of enrichment, it can be theorized, is the addition of communication skills. Moreover, enrichment, as the movement seems to interpret itself, appears to be directed to the surface structure of couple interaction. It adds to the couple's communication competencies both generic and specific skills. Aimed at the overt levels of the couple's communication, it nevertheless can claim impact on the deep structure, insofar as these covert reaches are analogically interconnected with the remainder of the interaction pattern. Either through indirect or transferred learning, enrichment, like other communication interventions, can interrupt and redirect dysfunctional patterns. Moreover, as we shall see later in an examination of other kinds of experiential group process, marriage enrichment, when it dares to do so, can converge directly on the deeper structures of marital interaction.

Enrichment then, is consistent with the broad social purposes articulated by Brodey (1967). He calls in the helping process for the active augmentation of skills which enable couples, and families, to be responsible (response-*able*) to the inevitable demands of change and adaptation. In his model, marriage can be viewed as a changing organism that has to operate in real time, continuously negotiating issues of change, stability, and control. Communication becomes the means through which partners change with change, making necessary adjustments to maintain stability while evolving variations to meet new conditions. Enrichment, in short, provides training and a degree of control in the process of adaptation itself.

If the therapy of the overt level is the addition of new interaction patterns, that of the covert level is the completion and resolution of antecedent ones. Especially when unresolved patterns bring about maladaptive fusions and displacements in the couple's current interaction, their power has to be broken. When the therapist finds a maladaptive overlap of one interaction field with another, intervention goals can properly be directed towards the antecedent unfinished business. In defining these objectives, the therapist may here, too, consider a number of important variables.

One such variable is the interaction models intrinsic to each partner's family of origin, but especially his or her own incomplete or unresolved relationship phases within it. No two family fields are exactly the same, and each one is extremely complex, placing stress upon the importance of an idiographic study of each mate's original interaction milieu.

The unfinished business of some partners clusters around relationship phases in which boundaries were transgressed. Such trespass occurs frequently in triadic interaction patterns, in which the growing child is made the scapegoat, the go-between, the focus of concern, or a coalition ally in the parents' implicit or explicit conflicts, disappointments, or unfulfilled lives. In overinvolved relationships, such as the parent-child pattern seen in Mark's family, a partner is infantilized, kept dependent and regressively helpless by the often well-intentioned guidance and nurture of one or both parents. A mate's developing selfhood may be trespassed upon by conditions of worth or injunctions that are placed upon him or her in the family network, but particularly by the parents. In order to be acceptable, or simply to get attention, a child may be forced to deny, distort, conceal, or suppress emerging aspects of his or her selfhood. More aggressive intrusion can occur at both the emotional and the physical level, in such overt actions as belittling, denigrating, accusing, blaming, name-calling, and nagging, or in outright physical abuse. Trespass can take place within the family network in explicit incestuous acts or, equally perniciously, in subtle relationship intimacies that sexualize interaction at a precocious or inappropriate level (Napier 1978). In each of these enmeshed patterns a person's intrapersonal and/or fitting parent-child boundaries are overstepped.

For some partners unfinished business has to do with their own trespasses. Their complicity in triadic entanglements, their aggressive or hurtful intrusion in the lives of others, the conditions of worth they have levied, and the emotional or physical abuses they have heaped reflect their transgressions in the family interaction field.

For other partners the antecedent family model is characterized essentially by relationship omissions. In rigid and disengaged patterns a partner can experience the absence or loss of emotional or physical resources which he or she needed. Such omissions can occur through inattention, neglect, or in the outright desertion or abandonment of the child. It was this lack of access to the parent that resulted in Kathy's sense of deprivation. The absence of models for imitation and of structures to depend on are the result of this neglect. In the parentification process seen somtimes in families, a child is stripped of his or her own position as a developing person and is drawn inappropriately and prematurely into the parental subsystem. Rescuing a parent, or the parents, by rendering care and helpfulness which is not really his or hers to assume, this partner feels deprived of nurturing and cheated from the spontaneities of childhood.

And, as before, a partner's unfinished family business may have to do with his or her own omissions. A lack of involvement and caring, of attention to the needs of family members, or of abandoning the family in some degree or another are the earmarks of this uninvolvement. An extreme form of this position is evident in the emotional cutoff identified by Bowen (1978). In an intrapsychic process of isolation and withdrawal, sometimes accompanied by actual physical distancing, a partner exudes a pseudo-individuation. Such extreme disengagement from the past often masks an undiminished hurt and rage at the disappointments, deprivations, or trespasses, that one has known. Continuing to locate the problem in the family of origin is to disown one's complicity in the breakdown and to foreclose one's ability to understand and forgive.

Finally, experiences of loss, through death and divorce, while not forms of direct omission, often result in unresolved relationship phases. These times of dissolution are imbued with strong feelings that can be denied or concealed, causing emotional constriction and fixation. Instead of completing the task of relationship termination, attempts are made to ward off disquieting emotions like grief and helplessness and to restore the lost object. Covert assignments and expectations are made on others to replace or fulfill the losses that have occurred in one's life.

Intrinsically associated with each of these many relationship states is a deep reservoir of feeling. In changing, alternating relationship phases there are especially high levels of intense emotionality. Thus, for Mark, as we have seen, his mother's original nurture generated strong feelings of security, stability, and confidence. With the onrush of a more differentiated relationship phase, new emotions have evolved. Now the mother's actions are interpreted differently, and behaviors which once evoked one set of emotions now produce new ones, feelings of intrusion and resentment. Joined too, with his emerging differentiation are feelings of self-reliance and self-confidence.

The dynamic of the fixation point, or of unfinished business, which figures so prominently in the therapy of displacement can be understood fundamentally as an emotional impasse. Feelings are blocked and left unresolved in their intensity. And the symptom of reluctance to experience or to complete this intensity is anxiety.

Bowen's (1978) concept of fusion can be amplified to embrace the interactional consequences of this emotional impasse. Fusion is indeed the contamination of intellect and emotion, as he asserts, but an underlying structure of the process can be identified.

When feelings are not contacted and undergone, a marital partner has disowned or denied his own emotional separateness. He or she is not fully, in that moment, emotionally differentiated, not fully angry, sad, tender, guilty, or compassionate in that discrete event of interaction. Failing to be fully there, fully differential in the feelings of the moment, the mate becomes anxious and vulnerable. Energy then goes into warding off the disowned or denied emotionality.

The partner, then, sensing this anxious emotional incompleteness and vulnerability, can also become anxious. He or she can become fused, responsible now for helping the partner avoid the disquieting emotional state. The second partner is thereby also rendered undifferentiated. Now he or she can no longer be emotionally open and separate. His or her genuine feelings cannot be expressed, lest they contaminate and overload the first partner's already high-pitched emotionality. The anxiety attached to the original mate's emotional block spreads diffusely through the interaction sequence and brings into being undifferentiated and unclear internal and interpersonal boundaries. Anxiety creates more anxiety, which in turn creates an impasse. Repetitive interaction sequences reflect the continuing avoidance and completion of primary levels of emotional closeness.

Thus, Mark during an interaction event senses his fiancee's feelings of disappointment or rejection and assumes responsibility for preventing the upswell of these emotions. In so doing, he inhibits his own feelings and wishes. Kathy, conversely, sensing her partner's mounting anxiety, his mixed emotions of guilt and resentment, takes responsibility on herself to prevent the further onrush of disquiet in him. She becomes guarded and restrained in her entreaties and requests.

Each partner intuits the amount of distance that needs to be maintained in order not to transgress the other's vulnerable emotional boundaries. The impasse, paradoxically, is grounded in each mate's sensitivity and compassion for the other, as well as for self.

The goal of therapy for the depth structure is the completion of relevant emotional states and interaction binds. More precisely, the therapeutic objective is the reduction of the anxiety level that is a natural consequence of unexpressed and undifferentiated emotional states. Enabling each partner to complete the feelings that were blocked in the family of origin breaks their displacement power in the present. Actualization of this objective establishes in the marital dyad the capacity for separateness that is the prerequisite for any genuine togetherness.

Since, as Bowen (1978) observes, patterns of interaction are always replete with emotionality, any long-term change requires intervention in this level. Permanent change frees emotional energies that have been impeded and dissipated in fusions, repetitive interaction sequences, interaction binds, and displacements. Short of such energy release, where indicated, therapeutic changes in the marital relationship can be short-lived and ineffective. The couple can relapse, returning to their former emotional level. They can even incorporate as facets of their maladaptive interaction some of the very interventions made in therapy.

It is worth noting that therapies of both the surface and the depth structures can and do reduce the level of personal and interpersonal anxiety. In some structured communication approaches therapists are quite sensitive to risk or anxiety levels in the design and execution of exercises. Couples are constantly given a chance to monitor their participation in different aspects of the program and the kinds of issues that they are prepared to handle. A program can progressively increase risk or anxiety levels and, through the practice of new skills, enable the partners to use these same competencies in the more open sharing of deep feelings and wants.

In the modeling, imitation, and rehearsals of some behavioral approaches (Liberman 1972) anxiety is progressively desensitized. In procedures like doubling, the therapist can emphathize with and articulate feelings and wishes that are being denied or distorted in the depth structure. In so doing, he or she can potentially reduce anxiety levels by enabling partners to express feelings that otherwise could remain hidden or disowned. A partner is enabled to hear the other's experience where previously there had been only fusion. As a partner rehearses new behaviors of emotional disclosure, he learns to experience the wide range of emotions that previously provoked anxiety and produced diffuse relationship boundaries.

It has been often asked how so many manifestly different marital therapies can accomplish equally productive outcomes. One hypothesis may be that the differences, at least in some aspects, are more apparent than real. Effective therapies impact on the couple's interactional bind by facilitating passage through previous emotional impasses. Whether the target of intervention lies at overt or covert levels of the interaction pattern, such therapies desensitize anxiety levels, enabling the couple to risk more, to share more, to differ more. Therapies of enrichment provide additional skills for coping with the anxiety. Therapies of completion provide resolution of antecendant emotional impasses that generated the anxiety in the first place.

Chapter 3

The Enactment

About a month after the earlier checkup Kathy scheduled a second interview for herself and Mark, this time for therapy. When the couple came for the appointment a few days later, Mark began by reporting that his and Kathy's relationship was becoming increasingly strained. A religious conflict, as he framed it, was erupting between them.

While he had been reared Catholic, his fiancee was Protestant. He had been accompanying Kathy to her church and its programs, he explained, and had grown to enjoy them very much. At the same time, he was beginning to feel led astray, implying that Kathy was directly or indirectly doing the leading. Furthermore, he was feeling more and more guilty, as if somehow disloyal to his own upbringing. As he told this story, Mark looked visibly stressed, turning at times with an almost apologetic look to face his fiancee.

As Mark related his view of the conflict, the therapist began to trace the current field of interaction. The manifest issue, religion, he hypothesized, was an analogue for interpersonal and intrapersonal process. He listened, then, not just to the verbal content of Mark's statement, but also to the underlying emotionality and interactional themes associated with his words. The therapist began to empathize with the deeper undertones of his verbal stream.

When he goes home for weekends or holidays, Mark continued, his mother questions him about his new church involvements. He is both troubled and angry about her queries.

The therapist recalls his earlier assessment of Mark. He is stuck at an impasse in his transition towards differentiated selfhood. Powerful emotional strivings pull in opposite directions at once. If he individuates, he risks feelings of rejection, loss of affection, and guilt in relation to his mother. If he does not separate emotionally, he risks feelings of resentment and loss of self-esteem.

In this issue of religion, I begin to hypothesize, Mark's displacement has reached an acute state. It occurs to me that he is projecting the two sides of his dilemma, his inner ambivalence about individuation, onto his fiancee and his mother. Kathy, in his mind, is associated with his tendency towards differentiation of self. His mother, at the same time, is symbolic of loyalty and continued enmeshment in the family of origin. The two women have become metaphorical images of his own internal split (Levitsky and Perls 1970). Having tried to delay, deny, or distort his passage to selfhood, Mark has now displaced his seemingly irreconcilable conflict outward onto Kathy and his mother. Inwardly torn, he now projects an impending rift between his fiancee and his parent.

I sense that Mark has reached such a high pitch of anxiety, that he feels impelled to take some form of action, including the possibility of terminating the relationship with Kathy. Norman Paul (1977) observes that divorce and separation often fall under this dynamic. An individual separates from the spouse as a (unrecognized) means of finding relief from the unbearable impasses, displacements, and symbolic reenactments in which he or she is living. Divorce permits a pulling back from intolerable intrapersonal and interpersonal entanglements. It can be, at the same time, a form of injustice and unbalancing of the relationship ledger to disengage from the spouse instead of facing one's own inability to adapt and change (Boszormenyi-Nagy 1973). At least one meaning of a developmental impasse is the unwillingness to suffer strong and disquieting emotions.

The task at this point is to create a therapeutic environment that can facilitate Mark's transcending, that is, going beyond his unresolved impasse. Since his client is coping with covert issues in the deep structure of the couple's interaction, the therapist wants to provide resources that will reach into these tacit levels, into emotionality as well as awareness. Long-term change can come in the resolution of emotional intensities connected with the interpersonal bind. The effective therapeutic design now will be one that can foster the completion of Mark's impasse, thereby releasing emotional fixations that are restricting the relationship between himself and his fiancee.

Thus it will be necessary to tease out (Goulding 1972) this deep structure, to explore Mark's impasse, his fixation points, and his subject-object assignments and symbolic reenactments. Effective intervention will confront him with an exact experiential replica of his current interaction field made up of himself, his fiancee, and his mother.

To accomplish these experiential interventions, the therapist draws upon gestalt experiments (Levitsky and Perls 1970), augmented by the use of other modalities, such as sculpting, psychodrama, communications, and systems. Applying these procedures should provide Mark with a model that duplicates his present life situation.

The cast of characters will be, as the enactment begins, himself, his mother, and Kathy. Others may be drawn into the environment as it unfolds. The therapist will observe the stimulus effect that these various personages have upon one another, their responses or reactions to these stimuli, and the interaction themes and outcomes that transpire among them. In addition, if other environmental elements flow naturally into the enactment, he will try to provide a metaphorical means for their representation and then observe the characters' responses to these stimuli.

The enactment, then, is like an externalized projective screen which makes internal process visible and immediate. It unearths underlying attitudes, emotions, and interaction themes. As it unfolds, it provides a vehicle for the ongoing assessment of Mark's intrapersonal dynamic and for testing the hypothesis about the displacement of an internal split. Exploratory and revelatory, the enactment can disclose previously hidden or unarticulated dynamics. It can be full of surprises for everyone present, offering new information leading to the formulation of new patterns, new goals, and new interventions in an ongoing interaction analysis.

At the same time, the enactment provides the therapist with opportunities for direct and immediate intervention into Mark's psychodynamic process. It would be his task to track the unfolding events carefully, to discern their probable meaning, and then suggest to Mark the next appropriate exercise or action. In an ever-recurring series of intervention loops, the therapist's function would be to observe the field of interaction, make interpretations, determine tactics, implement directives to his client, and then note the consequences of his interventions. The feedback received from each of these interventions would, in turn, set off yet another feedback loop. Step by step, the therapist would receive information, analyze it, and make a fitting input back into the enactment.

The therapist explained to Mark that it sounded as though he was experiencing some unfinished business with his mother over the matter of religion and that it could be worthwhile to work on that. He agreed. The therapist then suggested taking a look at one of the typical visits back home, since that seemed to be the time when the stressful encounters occurred.

This strategy takes its start from the concern presented by Mark. The issue, as he himself frames it, is brought into the therapy setting. The ensuing enactment will then focus on the actual encounter that is causing stress, more precisely, in an anticipation of such an encounter.

The inactive partner in the therapeutic enactment, in this case Kathy, would by no means be a nonparticipating observer. As she vicariously looks on, cross-encounter will occur as she empathizes with her partner's work. Mark's emotional blocks can be disclosed to her, along with the displacements that he is making. The enactment, therefore, can potentially clarify boundaries for her. It can provide her with a concrete and vivid embodiment of her partner's internal conflicts and the way they are displaced onto his relationship with her. At least, such is the operational hypothesis of the intervention design.

From time to time during the enactment, and certainly following it, Kathy's responses will be solicited by the therapist. As she empathizes with Mark's emotionality, his assumptions, and his expectations during the simulation, she can perhaps form a deeper understanding of his internal and interpersonal binds. Hopefully boundaries will be clarified for her, especially at the all-important emotional level, where interpersonal realignments can take place.

In the remainder of this chapter the therapeutic enactment will be presented. Actual verbatim transcript will appear first, followed by the therapist's running commentary on unfolding events. These remarks by the therapist will provide an insight into his actual thought process from moment to moment.

Therapist: You know, Mark, I believe it would be more productive for us to set up a simulated situation to work on this religious conflict rather than merely talking about it.

One of the most potent benefits of gestalt therapy is the principle of the now (Levitsky and Perls 1970). The process of enacting material in present terms gives an experience the impact of immediacy, and avoids the blandness and distancing that can occur in talking *about* contents and structures.

Mark: Okay.

Kathy: (Smiles).

Therapist: I'd like for you to role play your mother during one of these times when you're at home and she brings up the subject of religion.

This leads into the enactment by extending the tracking (Minuchin 1974) already done regarding the religious conflict. The enactment will attempt to replicate an actual encounter with his mother during one of his visits home. This serves to let the therapy process be directed to and relevant for the concern that the couple originally presented in the opening moments of the session.

The therapist directs Mark to role play his maternal introject (Boszormenyi-Nagy and Framo 1965). To do this, he will have to draw upon a host of images associated with his mother. Deposited in his mind as though recorded on tape is a configuration of images built up in countless encounters with his mother. Imitating her in the role playing, enacting her thoughts and feelings in fantasy, he will debrief this parental tape.

Mark: I'll try.

Therapist: See, what I'm trying to develop here is an opportunity for you to experience one of these encounters with your mother, so that we don't end up simply gossiping about her.

This is a modification of the no gossiping (Levitsky and Perls 1970) rule in gestalt. "Mom," that is, his parent should be there, so that she can confront him directly and so that his emotions in response can be aroused. If Mom is actually present, even as a fantasized portrayal of the introject, she can be addressed directly, and Mark's emotional process in her presence cannot be avoided (Levitsky and Perls 1970).

Just pretend to be her. Speak for her in the first person, as though you were she.

This directive to use first person language, "I" language (Levitsky and Perls 1970) reenforces involvement and immediacy and diminishes distancing.

How about your sitting here while you role play her (therapist moves a chair and motions Mark toward it).

This is metaphorical manipulation of space (Constantine 1978). Using an object, in this instance a chair, to represent Mom's place, is marking an individual boundary (Minuchin 1974).

I'll sit over here (therapist positions his chair at an angle to Mark's).

This is a step in the creation of an environment in which Mark's maternal tape can be teased out (Goulding 1972) and differentiated. This seating arrangement, a mini-sculpture, (Constantine 1978) portrays this symbolic differentiation process by means of an externalized spatial metaphor (Bandler and Grinder 1975). It also distances both Mark and Kathy from the maternal introject, thus facilitating increased objectivity in understanding "her."

Therapist: (To Mark role playing "Mom.") How is Kathy trying to get Mark to change his religion?

This question establishes the beginning of a fantasized dialogue (Levitsky and Perls, 1970), one of several gestalt experiments. They are experimental and exploratory, in that they are designed to catalyze intrapersonal and interpersonal process, rather than being rigid or mechanical procedures. The fantasized dialogue is limited by the fact that Mark's portrayal of his mother can contain inferences and projections that are untrue of her.

A conjoint approach (Satir 1967) in which Mark's mother were actually present in the interview would allow her to make her own direct feedback and correction of her son's image. It is still the case that even were the mother actually there, he would relate to her out of the same long standing mental set he brings to the enactment.

Mom: I don't know for sure that she is.

Therapist: What are you seeing happen?

This process question (Miller, Nunnally and Wackman 1975) asks Mark to document what he thinks are his mother's perceptions of him, what she's seeing and hearing.

In effect, he's describing his own behavior through his mother's eye.

Mom: Well, he was brought up Catholic all through grade school, all his life, and now he just . . . the more I see, he's probably losing interest in religion.

This is Mark's inference about his mother's interpretation (losing interest) of his behavior.

Therapist: What's he doing?

Again, the therapist asks her to document what she's seeing and hearing.

Mom: I can tell he doesn't like going to church, just by his actions.

Therapist: What's he doing? . . . Not going to church, or what?

The fantasized dialogue, once more directs Mark to describe his own behavior as Mom perceives it.

Mom: No, it's that he just kinda gets huffy when he has to go to church.

The use of "has to" connotes an external expectation.

Therapist: You mean, you say something about going to church and he gets huffy?

This process question requires Mark to describe his mother's actions towards him. It uses the categories of the interaction field to trace the interaction between Mark and Mom. With that mental framework in view, the therapist is trying to elicit and fill in gaps of information.

Mom: He gets like . . . it's boring, and he's not interested. And he goes to her church when he's with her. So it looks like it doesn't really matter to him what religion he goes to . . . or to what church.

Therapist: How do you feel about that?

This process question directs Mark to depict his inferences about his mother's feelings in response to his actions.

Mom: (Long pause). I tried to bring him up Catholic; and now, all of a sudden, he's changing.

The pause, as well as a heavy, labored tone in Mark's voice can be used to infer that these nonverbal cues indicate movement into his emotional process. Mark is beginning to feel the weight of the maternal introject.

At this point, the therapist might have used the gestalt procedure of sensory awareness (Levitsky and Perls 1970). This intervention would have directed Mark to be his voice, to converge on his tone and to express a stream of consciousness script for it (Simpkin 1972). This procedure could have guided Mark towards his underlying emotionality.

Therapist: I hear you saying that you feel that you're losing Mark.

In this reflective listening (Rogers 1961) the therapist empathizes with the emotionality contained in Mark's words and tone, tries to articulate it, and feed it back to him.

Mom: Yeah . . . kind of.

Therapist: "I've invested a lot of myself in you, Mark." And now you're seeing what you wanted for him changing. He's going another way.

Mark is fed a sentence (Levitsky and Perls 1970) about the attitude implied in his maternal introject. Mark must make the message his own by active participation and identification with it. A reflective listening follows next.

Mom: It seems like all this time hasn't paid off. He's resenting it or something.

Therapist: You mean, you made quite an investment of yourself, and not only is he changing, but he actually resents what you did. Or, seems to.

Mom: Yeah.

Therapist: I hear you saying your intentions were good, to bring him up Catholic.

Mom: From my viewpoint ... yeah.

The fantasized dialogue has enacted one interaction theme and its outcome: the mother's well-intentioned nurturance and guidance and her disappointment at the current result, her son's resentment.

Therapist: What other viewpoint is there?

Having marked the boundary (Minuchin 1974) of the maternal introject on the subject of religion, or more accurately, on the issue of nurturance and individuation, this question serves to enlarge the parental framework. It directs the maternal introject to attend to the son's point of view. It metaphorically begins to draw a boundary around the autonomous Mark, establishing his separateness, and thus facilitating movement towards differentiation of self.

Mom: Well, there's his, and that's where he's going now. He's doing what he wants. And all my training, I suppose hasn't paid off, to have him go the way I wanted him to.

This statement establishes and recognizes Mark as a separate self over against the mother. It is a beginning first step in the emotional transition from an overinvolved relationship phase with the mother to a more individuated one. Mark's depressive tone seems to represent the sadness that accompanies the termination of the former parent-child overinvolvement. But the therapist really cannot be certain what is being channeled through the tone.

Therapist: You didn't quite say this, but I got a sense that you were close to saying it: "It's not something that Mark wants to do. It must be Kathy leading him."

Again, the therapist feeds a sentence which articulates the maternal attitude during this interaction.

Mom: Or influencing him to some extent.

This statement contains a degree of projection in the classic sense, attributing to Kathy his own individuation tendencies. To the extent that his own tendencies remain covert and disowned, such projection is maladaptive.

Therapist: It would be hard to believe Mark would move this way without some kind of external influence. So it must be Kathy.

Mom: Yeah.

Therapist: Now, I'd like for you to be Mark and reply to your mother.

This directive creates a fantasized dialogue with a significant other, (Levitsky and Perls 1970), his mother. This procedure actually recreates the nuclear family, (Goulding 1972), at least the mother-son relationship.

Therapist: (Pulling up chair opposite the one Mark has occupied while role playing Mom). Why don't you take this chair and face your mother.

This procedure uses an object as a stand-in for the parent (Constantine 1978). This manipulation of spatial metaphors symbolically delineates boundaries even further, placing Mark opposite and thus clearly differentiated from the maternal introject.

Mark: It's everything I've learned. I've learned that just going to church doesn't give me anything, I suppose. Just something to do for an hour a week, and it's boring. I got into church and religion a lot when I first came up here. 'Cause back home the priest and the church just seemed really old fashioned. They talk about the same things every day, every week. It got to be like watching an old movie. You didn't pay close attention any more, 'cause you knew what was going to happen.

Mark's voice is more animated and forceful. The previous oppressive tone has vanished. This sensory cue probably represents a change in his emotional process.

And up here, when I first came, there were young priests, and they . . . the mass was completely different. And I really got back into it. And now, they've changed priests again, and I've fallen right back out of it. They don't. . . . In Kathy's church there was a change.

Therapist: What's Kathy's church like? Could you tell your mother.

This directive uses "church" metaphorically (Bandler and Grinder 1975), as the symbolic vehicle for emphasizing differences and for developing the implicit conflict, (Minuchin 1975) the anxiety, associated with differentiated, separate selfhood.

The therapist is listening associatively (Paul 1967), to the emotions and attitudes associated with

Mark's descriptions of "church." This is part of tracking the meanings of that analogue for him and his emotional response to that image.

Mark: I suppose . . . it wasn't so standardized. They . . . there was a more casual attitude, I suppose, a more friendly basis. They had a lot more singing and . . . participation from the people. Everybody would participate in the mass. You felt more a part of it. And in the Catholic religion all I was seeing was the priest standing up there and lecturing . . . and everybody else just sitting back and listening. I just got bored.

Mark's use of the phrase, "I suppose," reflected his work, his effort to sort out his thoughts and feelings on the subject. Such clarification of his experience and owning of it is a step towards autonomy.

Therapist: Let me feed you a sentence, to see if this is what you said; if so, I'd like you to claim it for yourself.

This feeding a sentence (Levitsky and Perls 1970), is intended to depict and feed back to Mark the interaction field portrayed metaphorically in his verbal content, that is, priests (the environmental press) lecture and Mark sits passively. The outcome of this interaction sequence is Mark's feeling bored and uninvolved. It is possible that in his mind priests and parents are unconsciously associated.

Mom, the stuff back home became boring. I take responsibility for the fact that I became bored.

And at first a new priest came up here, and I was pretty tuned in. But then a new one came in, and he became boring.

Taking responsibility (Levitsky and Perls 1970) requires Mark to own his feelings of boredom. This intervention draws a boundary around the emotion and facilitates Mark's integrating it into his own awareness rather than holding his fiancee responsible for it.

And at the other church I feel excited, like I'm participating. I feel involved. I'm not just listening. And I take responsibility for the fact that I feel more excited and more involved.

Mark: Nods.

Mark's nod denotes his active participation and claiming of the sentence fed to him.

Therapist: Could you tell your mother, "Mom, that's the way I felt, and that's the way I'm feeling now."

This directive requires Mark to express this differentiated experience to and over against the parent. It is a fantasized rehearsal (Levitsky and Perls 1970) of individuation, cutting through the anxiety associated with it.

Mark: I think I could.

It isn't clear here whether Mark is anticipating a more autonomous role with his mother or whether he is withdrawing from such direct contact.

I think the way Kathy comes into it is that she showed me something new. And if she'd never shown me anything new, I'd still be . . . you know. . . . I suppose she still resents . . . you know . . . feels resentful or hostile toward Kathy, just for showing me this.

Mark is here actively developing the concept supplied by an earlier feedback.

Therapist: Kathy is responsible for exposing me to the new possibilities.

The therapist feeds him another sentence to articulate his framework.

Mark: Yeah.

Therapist: Were you on the verge of

saying, "But Kathy is not responsible for my feelings, my excitement. She's responsible only for showing me the possibilities."

Mark: Um (nods). She's responsible only for showing me the possibilities, opening the door, so to speak. But I take responsibility for the feeling more turned on by Kathy's church.

In this remark an important intrapersonal boundary becomes clarified. Mark's own drives towards autonomy have been symbolically fused (Boszormenyi-Nagy 1965, Bowen 1978) with and projected onto Kathy and her church. Here, he differentiates more objectively between Kathy's actions in exposing him to her church and his subjective responses to her actions. He internalizes and owns his feelings which have given impetus to the former projection.

Therapist: Be your mother now (gesturing for him to return to "her" chair). What do you hear Mark saying, Mom?

Having, in effect, differentiated Kathy out of Mark's intrapersonal process by withdrawing his projection onto her, the stage is now set for an internal dialogue between the autonomous self and the maternal introject.

Mom: That is not. . . . Kathy had nothing to do with it, as far as he's concerned. And . . . that he's looking for something new.

He addresses the therapist as the go-between (Bowen 1978).

Therapist: How do you feel about what he said, Mom?

Mom: I suppose I can see his point.

Here the internal dichotomy (Boszormenyi-Nagy and Framo 1965) is beginning to close. The maternal introject is extending and reframing itself to understand the autonomous self.

Therapist: Could you tell him what his point is?

This instruction to say it directly (Levitsky and Perls 1970), requires the maternal introject to make direct and immediate contact with the son. It increases emotional intensity and anxiety and to that extent creates the possibility of resolving the conflictual impasse (Bowen 1978).

Mom: That he's bored and looking for some changes, or something new. Or at least something to keep him interested in religion.

He once more talks to the therapist. He may be avoiding contact with his mother even in this anticipatory rehearsal. Or he may simply be maintaining the established go-between pattern of the interview.

Therapist: Mark, is that what you said? (motioning for him to take the opposite chair). Did your mother understand you?

Mark: (To "Mom" chair). I'm not really looking for another religion. I'm just looking for. . . . I would take the Catholic religion if it was exciting, if it was, you know, how it was when I first came to school.

This manipulation of physical space by moving him back and forth between the two chairs sculpts and makes visible (Constantine 1978) the internal dialogue, the metaphorical differentiation, between the autonomous self and the enmeshed self.

Therapist: How do you feel about that, Mom? (again directs Mark to "Mom's" chair).

Mom: What's so different . . . so exciting . . . from ours?

Therapist: What does Mark say?

This rapid, back-and-forth exchange pits the two sides of Mark's ambivalence over against each other. The fantasized dialogue, by juxtaposing them, is designed to effect a reconciliation, a more integrated functioning, that moves beyond the impasse (Levitsky and Perls 1970).

Mark: It's more involved, keeps people involved.

Therapist: You're having a hard time letting go, aren't you, Mom?

At this point in the dialogue, Mark seems to be stuck. The parental introject resists accommodation to the autonomous self.

Mom: Yeah, I can't see any other . . . I was brought up this way all my life, and I can't see any other way.

Therapist: You know what I'm hearing?

Listening with the third ear (Boszormenyi-Nagy and Framo 1965) to the words, "all my life," the therapist draws a parallel (Paul 1975) with the way "Mom" described Mark's upbringing. And a pattern of intergenerational transmission (Boszormenyi-Nagy and Spark 1973, Bowen 1978) forms in his mind. He suddenly sees Mom caught in an impasse in her own individuation in differentiating from her upbringing. The therapist infers that she would then be emotionally threatened by her son's reactivation of the anxieties associated with her own unfinished business (Paul 1970). His movement towards autonomy symbolically reminds her of her own incomplete development.

Let me feed you a sentence, Mom: "I was brought up Catholic, and if I stand by and sanction your becoming something else, it's as if I'm being disloyal to my upbringing."

This is a probe (Minuchin, 1974) of the therapist's hypothesis.

In the language of transactional analysis, Mom enjoins Mark not to individuate—"Don't be separate." (Goulding 1972). She thereby remains faithful to all her invisible loyalties (Boszormenyi-Nagy and Spark 1973) to her own family of origin and its Catholic connections.

Mom: Um hum. (Mark looks very introspective).

Therapist: Were you ever bored, Mom?

Mark: I don't know. I can't answer that.

With this remark, we have reached the limits of fantasized dialogue and rehearsal.

Therapist: I'd really encourage you to ask her that sometime—maybe talk about this whole business of religion.

Here, the therapist is coaching (Bowen 1978) Mark to talk directly on a one-to-one basis with his mother. This could provide him with an occasion to research some of the intergenerational transmission dynamics we have been hypothesizing (Bowen 1978).

The work in this session has helped Mark rehearse some of the intense emotionality that has been implicit in his encounters with his mother and which probably will occur again. In an actual encounter with his mother Mark can check out firsthand the fantasies and speculations that have taken place in the enactment, and actually experience himself saying some of the things that have been rehearsed in the therapeutic enactment.

Mark: (Laughs).

Therapist: I can surely imagine where she could be coming from. It's as though . . . if she endorses or sanctions your changing, she's being disloyal to her Catholic origins, to her parents, her priests, her history. She may very well have engaged in the same struggle you've been in, and she chose to be loyal.

This intervention reframes (Bandler and Grinder 1975) Mark's perception of his mother.

Mark: (Smiling, looking at Kathy).

Therapist: What's your smile saying?

Mark: Looks as though she's really not too involved in all this . . . I don't know . . . I just . . . I never looked at it this way before.

Therapist: How are you looking at it now?

Mark: Well, I just always thought that my mom was old-fashioned, you know, and wanted everything her way. Maybe it's not like that at all. She's just trying to . . . by not letting me go, she's just trying to hold up her end by keeping me loyal. Like you say, if she lets me go, then she's being disloyal. She'd feel like she's not doing something.

The reframed (Watzlawick, Weakland, and Fisch 1974) relationship enables Mark to view his historical encounters with the parent in a whole new light. The intergenerational dynamic posited in this reframing is probably a more faithful account of those events than a view of the mother as just old-fashioned and traditional.

Mark is moving to a new and in

many ways more transforming relationships phase with his mother.
He is rejoining her as a fellow
human being who has suffered her
own hurts and struggles (Goulding
1972). Some of her unfinished relationship business she has projected
onto Mark. For him to see her conflict, and the reasons behind her
injunctions to him, is to feel empathy and understanding for her.

Therapist: There seems to be a kind
of implicit understanding of where
your mother's coming from. You
can really understand.

Mark: Yeah.

Therapist: You can understand the
pressure she's under, because
you've experienced the same thing.

Mark: (Looks sad and teary).

The emotional process of indi-
viduating evokes both relief and
sadness—relief that the anxiety of
the impasse is finished, sadness for
the lost relationship, and, in Mark's
case, for the mother who is left
alone with the pain of the family
projection process (Bowen 1978).

Therapist: Kathy, where are you
with all this?

This question actively solicits the
partner's response (Paul 1967).

Kathy: Well, it helps me understand
a lot.

Therapist: What?

The therapist wants to clarify interpersonal boundaries.

Kathy: Well, I see now that I wasn't responsible for the conflict he was having with his mother over church.

Therapist: How's that?

This is a procedure of repetition (Levitsky and Perls 1970), to bring Kathy's empathtic responses fully into awareness.

Kathy: Well . . . his feelings about my church were . . . they were his, and he can't blame me for them.

Therapist: But, you see, he felt guilty for feeling them.

Kathy: I know . . . and I can see the kind of pressure that his mother was putting on him. I think I knew sometimes when I . . . when I wanted something for Mark . . . that's why I didn't push.

Therapist: Why not?

Kathy: Because I knew how much pressure it put on him.

Therapist: But you see, he couldn't disagree with you because he had his mother's face on you.

This metaphor articulates the interpersonal displacement.

Kathy: You mean I reminded him of her.

Therapist: When you expected something and pushed . . . it's as if Mark had to learn how to disagree comfortably with you. Mark, I really hope you'll have that talk with

In the final analysis, it is the external expectations and the anxiety of disregarding them that has precipitated the impasse.

your mother. You could probably
get some stuff going that we
haven't even touched on.

And come back in, if you like, after you've seen her, and we can debrief what happened. Or bring your mother in with you.	This leaves open the possibility for a later coaching session (Bowen 1978) as Mark does homework on his relationship with his mother, or for a conjoint session with her present.

This enactment has demonstrated the theory and practice of experiential intervention in the clarification and modification of intrapersonal and interpersonal process. The couple's presenting concern about religion was taken as a metaphor for an underlying intrapsychic conflict within Mark, a developmental impasse which was being displaced into the interpersonal relationship. The enactment was created to replicate the interactional field between Mark, his fiancee, and his mother.

Using experiential procedures, the therapist sought to evoke tacit attitudes and emotions, to assess points of impasse, displacement, and boundary diffusion, and to facilitate the completion of unresolved individuation and rejoining processes within Mark. This modification of internal emotional ambivalence resulted in the clarification of interpersonal boundaries, the withdrawal of displacements, deeper empathic understanding between the partners, and greater tolerance for difference and separateness. This increased differentiation of self creates the possibility for a more adaptive interpersonal system.

Change in the Therapeutic Process

During the course of therapy, for the couple and therapist alike, the perception of what needs to be changed will itself undergo change. For change is a multi-faceted process. Stating their original concerns in therapy, the couple will say far more than they are able to know. And, paradoxically, they will know far more than they are able to say. The couple's original articulation of their problem will reflect a grasp of certain facets of their relationship bind. At the same time, in voicing their concern, they will know things, however intuitively, that they are unable to comprehend in words. Certain facets of the problem lie outside their ability to express.

The therapist, too, upon hearing the couple's initial description of their problem, will have a preliminary grasp of certain dimensions of the relationship. In many respects, those originally presented symptoms and concerns, as analogues, will provide a nucleus of the pattern to be unearthed during therapy. Observing this initial framework of the problem, as the couple views it, will provide clues to the depths beneath the symptoms. But as the therapy evolves, deeper dimensions will be disclosed, both as they relate to the presenting issues and as they interconnect with aspects never perceived in the original problem definition. Things will not remain as they initially appear.

The experiential therapist, therefore, operates with a cascading conception of knowledge as therapy proceeds. At different stages in the therapeutic process the therapist forms a persepective on certain facets of the interaction pattern. Each perspective, in turn, feeds into the next in succession. Gradually, and sometimes abruptly and unexpectedly, the therapist grasps elements and connections in the extraordinary depth which makes up the relationship pattern.

This cascading perception of change can be observed in the interviews with Kathy and Mark, considered now in retrospect. For Kathy, initially, the presenting concern is twofold, one, to get to know her fiance better, and two, to improve the relationship. She states these needs in a rather low-key fashion, not so much as problems but as opportunities for growth. The therapist, realizing that there was much more to be disclosed on both these subjects, nevertheless accepted them as presented. Moreover, in the final outcome of the checkup, Kathy would need to be satisfied in the accomplishment of these aims.

It can be inferred, on the basis of evidence now available, that in articulating her original concern Kathy knew more than she was able to say. She was aware of a reticence in her partner. She knew that the negotiation of a decision, like doing a checkup, was a stressful occasion for him, and thus also for her. She knew that she had to proceed delicately, in what we know now to be a fused manner, lest he withdraw or, even worse, lash out. She knew that she had best propose the checkup to him in a low-key manner, had best not come out and say all she knew, lest he hesitate and balk. The nucleus of the entire relationship pattern was revealed in the decision leading up to the checkup.

At the same time, there is a sense in which Kathy did not know why she had to relate this way with her partner. Why, we may infer her to have been asking, is it necessary to relate to Mark in this manner? To say it somewhat awkwardly, she knew more than she was able to say, and she said more than she knew. But there were facets of the pattern that Kathy knew she did not know—thus, her wish for the checkup. Something, she probably did not know what, had to change.

The therapist, at this point, also inferred that there were facets of the relationship that Kathy wanted help in understanding. He did not know, could not yet know, what they were. But there was, he surmised, an implicit request for assistance in clarifying depths which she did not presently grasp.

Kathy's concern to improve the relationship, it can be inferred now, was related to her need to understand her fiance better. No doubt already experiencing considerable stress in the relationship and not knowing how to transcend it, she was seeking some external facilitation. The relationship fusion and the huge expenditures of emotional energy required to maintain it were already beginning to place the engagement in jeopardy. She knew that their interaction on occasion came to a virtual standstill, to an impasse of hinting, hesitating, and indecisiveness, at best, and to name-calling and uproar, at worst.

She probably knew, but was unable to articulate, some of these interaction facets. But there were other ingredients of the impassable bind that lay beyond her comprehension, which required the external, objective evocation by the therapist. As to this need, then, she had said more than she knew, knew more than she was able to say, and knew that there were some facets which were hidden from her grasp.

As the checkup proceeded, the therapist began to form a perception of interaction elements to be changed. Kathy's distorted expression of wishes, Mark's concealed feelings, and his propensity for mind reading all came into focus as dysfunctional and incongruent communication patterns. From a behavioral perspective, one partner's observable actions served as cues for the other's reciprocal reaction. These, the therapist determined, could be changed by the enrichment of communication skills. These debilitating facets could be altered either in the direct and immediate interruption of dysfunctional exchanges coupled with the modeling and shaping of new competencies, or in comprehensive training in a repertoire of skills.

Over the therapist's initial perceptions has now flowed a new wave of knowledge and understanding. Being more concerete and specific, this newly formed perspective can serve as a more reliable basis for apprehending patterns and planning strategies of change. It provides a more empirical basis for defining the concerns originally stated by Kathy.

Each perspective in the therapist's evolving knowledge of the couple is based on interaction loops between couple and helper. Every step of the way the therapist listens and observes, traces and sorts information, forms patterns, determines goals of intervention, designs strategies, and feeds that internal processing back into the therapy system in some manner. Each cascading perspective emerges from a series of interactions between the observing therapist and the observed couple.

Having formed a perspective on the couple's overt interaction, the therapist moves on to an exploration of deeper structures in the relationship. Inquiry is directed to the potentially more stressful facets of interaction. The couple's capacity for handling difference being such a critical and distinguishing mark of couple adaptedness, the therapist moves into this area. How, the therapist probes, do the partners handle differences? That investigation, it turns out, reveals some of the most stressful facets of Kathy's and Mark's interaction. He sometimes eventually resorts to name-calling, she to uproar and self-denigration. This finding strongly suggests that in the important task of balancing separateness and togetherness the couple is encountering difficulty. If that condition is not altered and ameliorated in some way, the risk of further disorganization and even disintegration in the relationship is high. The therapist's perception of what needs to be changed has gone through a further modification.

The therapist's previous perspective on the couple feeds into the newly emerged perception. The couple's incapacity to balance individuality and mutuality in the relationship represents an exaggeration of difficulties found in the surface structure. Kathy's inability to be differentiated in her intentions, Mark with his emotions, can lead to an exacerbated state of conflict. Not being able to go beyond the limits of their communication skills, the pair falls into a bind.

When the experiential therapist finds reified and homeostatic patterns in the surface structure of the relationship, he or she raises questions about the deeper levels in which they are grounded. He or she wants to know what more primary interaction patterns have broken down, have been left incomplete or unresolved, so that they contribute to the lack of differentiation in one or both partners.

This inquiry into facets anteceding the relationship itself is directed to each partner's personal development, especially within the family of origin. The overall quality of that model, reflected in clear, enmeshed, or disengaged relationship patterns, may shed light on a partner's interpersonal interaction style. The model of intimate relationships emulated by the parents may well have bearing. The partner's own relationships within that family system could be pertinent, especially those that are unresolved or incomplete. For the experiential therapist, it is not that any of these facets necessarily have to prove to be relevant in formulating the couple's pattern and devising a change program.

Investigation of Mark's family of origin disclosed a highly enmeshed model, of Kathy's a highly disengaged one. Of particular importance in Mark's development, the therapist perceived, is a continuing unresolved relationship with the mother, one moving from protracted overinvolvement toward one more individuated. Still in process, Mark is caught in the throes of intense, ambivalent emotionality. In Kathy's history the therapist perceived pronounced rigidity, especially with the father, leaving her with incomplete needs for closeness and stability.

In the formation of the therpist's perspective on these antecedent facets of the couple's relationship a number of parallels were noted. These findings led to a hypothesis of displacement on the part of both partners, each projecting into the relationship with the mate unfinished business from the past. The present became a symbolic reenactment of concerns originating within another field of interaction.

The therapist's perspective of the couple had, by now, been greatly expanded, and yet all the orders of data were unified and interconnected. Homeostatic mechanisms in the surface structure were grounded in the breakdown of antecedent interaction patterns in each partner's personal development. Hidden away in the deeper structures of the relationship were processes that lay outside the partners' awareness. Yet the therapist inferred that Kathy, in making her request for the checkup, had wanted an excavation of these depths whose structures and dynamics she was not able to know or express.

In seeking to make a match between his own perspective and that of both Kathy and Mark, at the conclusion of the checkup, the therapist determined that a communications training group would be a suitable recommendation. The rehearsal and modification of communication skills in a subsequent interview would be another suitable design. The subject of Mark's lingering stress with his mother had been broached, but not to an extent that the therapist could suggest work on it without provoking a skew between his perspective and the couple's expressed need. Also, elements could be disturbed that might be resolved through primary processes of family and personal development.

When the couple later appeared for an explicit therapy interview, the perception of change was altered once more. Mark's obvious stress and his fiancee's apparent helplessness signaled that intervention had to be directed to new and deeper levels in the relationship. The therapist functioned within the framework of Mark's perception of the problem, which was a religious conflict placing him in a bind between his mother and his fiancee. The therapist related this new wave of information to patterns and therapy designs previously formulated. The hypothesis was made, in this emerging perspective, of unfinished business between Mark and his mother. The overt religious conflict and triadic process were viewed by the therapist as analogues for an unresolved developmental transition from an enmeshed to a more individuated personal state. Associated with that impasse were a host of mixed emotions pitted against one another and inducing intense levels of anxiety.

The therapist elected to explore this hypothesis within the context which Mark himself had established, namely, visits back to his family of origin and encounters with his mother. Taking that anticipated event as the starting point, the therapist proceeded to create an enactment which brought the troubling situation into the therapy session. The goals of that simulation were to provide an experiential milieu within which Mark could rehearse the anxiety-provoking encounter, could face the disquieting feelings connected with it, tease out any hidden assumptions and decisions, and set the stage for an actual person-to-person meeting with the parent. Closely united with these goals were the clarification of intrapersonal and interpersonal boundaries between Mark, his fiancee, and his mother. Within that triadic pattern, inferred the therapist, existed considerable fusion and displacement.

Viewing the enactment every step of the way as an experimental exploration, the therapist attempted to intervene with procedures that made visible, audible, and concrete each emerging element of the encounter. The interaction field in its intrapersonal, interpersonal, and triadic facets became more fully revealed. Then, unexpectedly, the entire sequence gets reframed, the therapist inferring an intergenerational transmission process that could account for the binding and guilt that Mark was experiencing. Feeding that inference into the enactment created substantial change for him. As he put it, "I've never looked at it like that before."

Change In The Client Couple

Change in the couple's interaction is a many-faceted process. Each of the following statements encompasses certain aspects of that change, yet none fully accounts for it.

To declare that Mark's change is both cognitive and emotional is partially true, yet those two concepts are inadequate to explain what has happened. To say that his behavior has been modified is accurate, but insufficient. His tendencies to conceal feelings and to remain opaque have been replaced with at least the practice of more transparent communication. That his emotionality has been altered is also true, but only a partial account of the change. That he now frames the relationship with his mother and his fiancee differently is true, but such alteration of perception is insufficient to explain the change. A whole series of events has been reinterpreted, perhaps in ways that account for the facts better than his previous view. The mother is not just old-fashioned and traditional, but loyal and bound to her upbringing. That Mark is more individuated, having confronted an anxiety-provoking situation forthrightly, is true. That this encounter has clarified intrapersonal and interpersonal boundaries is a partial explanation of the change. The breakup of fusions and displacements is likewise an account of the change that has occurred.

Kathy's original aim, to know her fiance better, has been fulfilled, at levels way beyond what she was able to state initially. But this knowledge is not simply a matter of understanding, though it includes that. It is, instead, knowledge in the deepest sense, an encounter with her partner's emotionality, with his antecedent history which has formed the base of the present impasse.

Such empathic knowing is practical and relevant in her relationship with Mark. Encountering the workings of her fiance's mind permits her to know that the threat which almost undid her engagement was brought on by a deep, long-standing internal struggle. It brought her close to the injustice of a situation in which her fiance could be on the verge of solving an internal struggle by ridding himself of her and what she symbolically represented to him. Such applied knowledge can create in her an acceptance and understanding which defuses the frustration, helplessness, and resentment associated with the earlier stalemate. Mark, for Kathy, is reframed, no longer just the frustrating mate who cannot negotiate, but a person whose patterns of interaction are meaningful within a developmental context.

Chapter 4

The Narrow Passage

PROLOGUE

Keith and I were hurriedly making our way through a narrow basement corridor in an old building. The walls were made of brick covered with a plaster of cement, and in places this covering had chipped away, leaving a ragged, neglected appearance. A thin patina of dust and grime was all about.

We were frantically seeking a way out. I held Keith, my thirteen-year-old son, by the arm and was leading him. I felt impelled to escape more for his sake than for mine.

From time to time we came upon another, more narrow passageway off to our left. As we approached each one, my spirits soared in anticipation. Around the next corner would be the passageway that we could follow out. But at each opening we were confronted by the same scene, a narrow hall no more than ten feet long extending to the outer wall of the building. At the end of each side passage was a small window covered with iron-cage-like bars. Looking out these portals, we could see other, equally aging and ugly buildings.

Panic welled up inside me, for I began to fear that we were not going to be able to escape this underground prison. With this, I waked.

After waking, I still felt panicky and trembled. I knew immediately that this was an important dream, if for no other reason because of its intense emotional impact on me. It could, if I chose to work with it, provide me with a way to make contact with dimensions of my present experience that otherwise could go unheeded.

A Dream Hypothesis

For the therapist of experiential persuasion the dream is a pathway to the depth and complexity of intrapersonal and interpersonal process. In the present chapter we shall examine the nature of the dream and its use in therapy. The case example to be demonstrated here is not, strictly speaking, couple- but family-oriented, but the principles to be discussed and applied are essentially the same for both therapeutic settings.

In the previous chapter we saw how the therapist, using experiential interventions, created an environment to confront the client with an exact replica of an anticipated event in his life situation. Using metaphor, sculpting, gestalt experiments, and other representational methods the therapist enabled the client to tease out, make contact with, and modify covert elements of fixation, displacement, and symbolic reenactment. This therapeutic process facilitated a movement towards personal individuation and clarification of boundaries between past and present, between self and partner.

When Mark finished the enactment described previously, he shook his head, as though waking from a trance or other sleeplike state. He exclaimed, "Wow! That's like being in a dream!" Experiential methods evoke covert and subsidiary elements of experience and leave the client with a sense of having made contact with dreamlike material.

The dream, in many respects, is the corollary of a therapeutic enactment. It is, however, a spontaneous product, whose creation occurs without facilitation, when the directed thoughts and activities of conscious life are quiet. Dream language is figurative, concrete, and fantasylike. Its imagery, like the metaphors of a therapeutic enactment, represent feelings and tendencies that have been forgotten, ignored, or repressed. Such images are symbols which originate in association with and which represent covert elements in both the surface and deep structures of the dreamer's life situation. They stand for and provide a medium for making contact with such components as resisted events and impasses; feelings or personal traits; unavilable persons and unresolved relationship phases; unknown aspects of a situation; and unknown facets of the self (Polster and Polster 1973). They open the dreamer to covert elements of which he or she is unaware. Contacting, experiencing, and working through these hidden elements can clarify and realign intrapersonal and interpersonal systems.

The hypothesis that every component of fantasy material is a projection of the dreamer is basic to the use of dreams in marital therapy (Perls 1970). The term *projection,* in traditional usage, refers to an individual's attributing to other persons feelings and attitudes which properly belong to the self, but which have been rejected or disowned (Henry 1956).

Projection, as it is used in dream analysis, refers to an individual's objectification through spontaneously generated fantasy material of some field of interaction of which he or she is a part. In this concept the dream is a symbolic enactment of an interactional drama. The self in a field of interconnected forces becomes the focus of the dream, and the dreamer replicates in imagery his or her characteristic responses within that field, his habitual assumptions about the actions of others, his own feelings and intentions in the event, his preoccupation with certain themes, sequences, and outcomes, and his perspective on the past, present, and future course of these interactions. Often, the dream represents an impasse or anxiety-ridden transition in the dreamer's life.

The Unraveling Process

One of the most effective methods for using fantasy material in marital and family therapy is a dramatic enactment of the dream plot. Whereas in the therapeutic enactment examined previously, the interactional field had to be created and teased out through experiential procedures, in the dream enactment the task is one of unraveling the interactional environment that has already been represented in fantasy.

The enactment procedure requires the dreamer to recount his dream in the first person (Simkin 1972). As in the facilitated enactment, this method brings the dream work into the present and gives it the impact of immediacy. The use of first person language facilitates involvement and owning of dream elements as parts of the self in the field of interaction. The dreamer enacts, experiences, and integrates (Perls 1970) the dream elements rather than merely talking about, analyzing, or gaining insight into them.

The partner is present during the enactment and can empathize with and cross-reference material and experience. As intrapersonal fixation points and displacements are disclosed, the partner can begin the process of differentiating personal and interpersonal systems and their interconnections. Usually, the partner can amplify and clarify dream symbols and other elements of the enactment. Of crucial importance is the partner's firsthand involvement in intense emotional process. Such immersion serves to clarify covert levels of interaction.

Following the first person, present tense narration of the dream, the dreamer is asked to assume the identity of some symbol (Simkin 1972). This exercise requires the client to identify with the symbol, whether animate or inanimate, and to personify it in the first person. The client is directed to give voice to the symbol, enacting a script for it. Later, the client is moved to a second dream element, then to a third, and so on, each time entering into the symbol with active imagination.

The therapist who is facilitating this opening up process converges on whatever experiential element emerges into the foreground at the moment, on the basis that each new element is a natural and spontaneous creation. Neither therapist nor client can know in advance where the development of each new element will go, nor how the various elements will eventually interlock in the general pattern. But therapist and client stay with each symbol and its enacted representations until all its implications are explored, or until a new element arises into the foreground.

For example, in connection with the development of some symbol the client may make an unwitting gesture or body movement. If it is abortive or incomplete, the therapist may direct the client to exaggerate (Levitsky and Perls 1970) the movement. Thus, the body language that has arisen obliquely and perhaps unconsciously is converged upon, contacted, and brought into the enactment. The tone of voice, a tear, a grimace, and other nonverbal cues are often emergents that disclose tacit but critical facets of experience. They represent the continuum between awareness and other representational channels in intrapersonal process.

Drawing upon the rich repertoire of experiential interventions, the therapist can facilitate exploration of the dream. Each procedure is an experiment (Levitsky and Perls 1970), a potential catalyst of psychic process. No experiment is automatic and mechanical. None guarantees the unraveling and integration of the fantasy material.

The interaction that takes place between client and therapist in a dream enactment is far more tentative than that which occurs in the treatment of more overt material. In many respects, the entire enactment is an exploration and assessment of covert elements. Therapist interventions are designed, therefore, to facilitate this discovery process. The therapist's task is one of attending to the unfolding auditory, visual, and spatial portrayal of symbolic process, to the action that emerges into the foreground, and then feeding back a procedure to amplify and develop that action.

The enactment becomes a stage upon which a drama unfolds depicting the present existence of the dreamer (Polster and Polster 1973). Therefore, as the enactment progresses the therapist begins to look for patterns (Fagan 1970) of interaction. He or she begins to trace the various interlocking elements in the dramatic field: the cast of characters; the environment within which they interact; the plot that transpires among them; and the themes and outcomes of their various interactions.

The conceptual model of the interaction field guides the therapist's creation and direction of the dream reenactment. The framework afforded by the model can be applied to the analysis of interaction patterns as the re-creation unfolds. It provides a cognitive map for tracing dream symbols and the analogues they represent during the evolving of the therapeutic event. The relevant categories of analysis in the model are, to review them here:

1. The attributes of the environment in which the characters interact.
2. The stimuli which this environment places upon the characters.
3. The responses of the characters to these stimuli.
4. The stimulus effects which the characters exert on one another.
5. The responses of the characters to these reciprocal stimuli.
6. The themes and outcomes of these stimulus-response interac-

tions and their unfolding development. As in the feedback
model of interaction, a character's action is met by a reciprocal
stimulus from another character, which stimulates a further
and perhaps different response in the first, and so forth.

Once certain symbols have been amplified and the rough con-
tours of the drama begin to take shape, sculpting provides a means
for projecting intrapersonal reality into external space, thus establishing a correspondence between dream imagery and spatial analogues (Constantine 1978). Physical objects, other persons, or
fantasized metaphors can be positioned to represent the environment of the dream. Likewise, such stand-ins can represent the
various cast of characters, or parts of the self, that interact within
the environment.

For example, one husband in a couples group was helped to
create a life space sculpture by positioning portable chairs to
represent the diverse claims on his time. Manipulating the chairs
and interacting with the realities they represented, he explored his
role as husband, as father, and as professional.

The dreamer, in molding and touching the various components
of the sculpture, can make contact with his or her sensory continuum, with information stored as kinesthetic, musculomotor
memories (Constantine 1978). As he or she moves about in the
sculpture, such action can represent actual interaction between
symbols, both intrapersonal and interpersonal. He or she can make
the rounds (Levitsky and Perls 1970) among the various metaphors, expressing, through words or touching, the feelings and
intentions regarding each one. Each stand-in can be contacted or
avoided according to the degree of anxiety or comfort associated
with it.

Gestalt games of fantasized dialogue (Levitsky and Perls 1970)
can be used by the therapist to enact the stimulus-response sequences between symbols. The client can be directed to become,
that is, give voice to some element in the environment and talk to
(act upon) some other element. The effect of that original action
can be observed in the second symbol, and the client can then be
instructed to enact a response for the second. Or a symbol standing
for some character (significant person) in the dreamer's life can

address the dreamer and the impact be noted. The dreamer, in turn, can be instructed to reply to the first speaker. As these symbolic sequences are enacted the therapist can track themes and outcomes. Points of anxiety, impasse, and unfinished business can be identified.

At points in the dream enactment the therapist can make direct and immediate interventions. He or she can direct the client to stay with (Levitsky and Perls 1970) some feeling or intention, to confront it fully, to take responsibility for it and to own it as a part of himself. The game of reversal (Levitsky and Perls 1970) enables the client to plunge into some latent or underlying tendency by playing it out. The excessively inhibited person becomes the exhibitionist; the timid becomes the assertive; the aggressive becomes the cooperative. Exaggeration (Levitsky and Perls 1970) instructs the client to enact an extreme expression, either vocally or through body movement, of some incomplete or underdeveloped emotion or tendency.

Frequently, the dream enactment teases out unfinished business from the past, especially from the family of origin. After much unraveling, often standing revealed in the dream's cast of characters are parents, siblings, grandparents, and other significant personages. Disclosed in the interaction patterns of the dream enactment are themes or unresolved relationships and incomplete events from the family of origin. Often revealed in the themes of the dream are the dreamer's struggles to restore lost relationships, to correct them, to master them, to atone for them, to seek retribution for them (Framo 1975). Standing revealed as though it were only yesterday, are feelings of resentment associated with memories of injustice and exploitation, feelings of sadness from an unmourned loss, of guilt from a denied transgression, of affection for a gratitude never expressed. Such emotions linger as unfinished fixation points.

Often disclosed, too, are existential decisions the dreamer once made and which continue to color his or her style of life (Goulding 1972). Such lingering decisions have the effect of arresting the dreamer's development. He or she remains stuck in the interpersonal system in which some decision was made, for example, a decision not to be close or one not to separate. Changing this decision, this life position, is fraught with great anxiety and risk for the dreamer. For it affects not only himself or herself, but all those who have a vested interest in keeping one in a particular place in the field and whose own positions are maintained by one's staying there. An existential decision to change can induce stress that can ripple through a potentially wide field.

Often, the unfolding of the dream through enactment discloses the overlap between past and present. Parallels between the family of origin and present relationships become manifest. Revealed in the dream and its enactment are similarities between one's parent and one's spouse, as well as the manipulations of the present to maneuver a spouse or other members of the immediate family into becoming symbolic surrogates for past relations. Made transparent, too, are the multitude of ways that the past is symbolically reenacted in the present.

It is at this point that the dream enactment really beings to clarify marital or families boundaries, especially at the crucial emotional level. The spouse or other family members are able to experience and understand intrapersonal and interpersonal dynamics that have long been operative, but which have remained hidden and covert. Patterns of projection, the transfer of internal states into interpersonal interaction, can also be traced. Covert displacements, manipulations, and repetitive interaction sequences can be empathically encountered and clarified.

Once the boundaries of the interpersonal system have been clarified and differentiated, therapy can be directed to the intrapersonal subsystem. Unresolved relationships and unfinished events can be reenacted in the therapy session. Through games of dialogue (Levitsky and Perls 1970) the client can be directed to reconstruct an encounter with some significant person or persons. Particular attention is given by the therapist to intense emotions and to areas of anxiety and avoidance. Indicative of an emotional impasse, such points can be approached by therapeutic experiments with the procedure of rehearsal (Levitsky and Perls 1970). The client is directed to anticipate an actual encounter with a significant other, to cut through the high levels of anxiety and emotionality associated with such contact, and to say those things that have been avoided, concealed, or distorted. The original unresolved relationship is brought into present immediacy and intensity, and the impasse is confronted.

Even though the confrontation is conducted in fantasy, it is often preparation for a real life encounter with the person in question. Such rehearsal enables the client to discover and to integrate various feelings and attitudes *vis a vis* the other and to move beyond the point of fixation and emotional immobility.

When an actual encounter with the other occurs, perhaps in a conjoint therapy session, perhaps back in the parental home, the client has already rehearsed the intense, disquieting emotions associated with that contact and is better prepared to cope with and complete the unresolved relationship or event.

A SIMULATION

When I waked from my dream narrated earlier, I was filled with anxiety and panic. It was still so vivid, so close, that I decided to work on it right then. While it is usually beneficial to have an external facilitator in the enactment of fantasy material, in order to overcome areas of resistance, avoidance, and impasse, it is possible to unravel and to integrate one's own dream (Polster and Polster 1973).

I decided to reenact the dream again in my mind, in the present. I would identify with each image, in effect, personify each image, and speak for it. I would, if necessary, have the symbols address each other, thus enacting themes of interaction among them. I would use my active imagination to work with the dream images until I evoked the personal and interpersonal concerns and plots hidden away within them.

What follows is a simulation of my work on the dream. In actuality, my emotional and symbolic associations took place very quickly. This simulation, then depicts a greatly slowed-down version of what transpired, although the elements of interaction are as they were experienced. The detailed and rigorous presentation of the dream work here will demonstrate the practice and possibilities in the enactment of fantasy material.

I closed my eyes and began:

The Corridor: I am the corridor. I am a narrow hall in the basement of a building. I am gray and dingy. I am dimly lighted, and then only with light coming from small windows high in the wall. I am the basement of the house here. I am not old, but I look old. My walls are made of concrete cinder blocks, and are slightly damp.

The corridor was a rich symbol for the physical environment in which the dream was set. My family had recently moved to a small town in rural Wisconsin, and had bought and moved into a large, country-style house with basement walls and lighting literally like those represented in the dream. Associated with the image were feelings of depression, depicted in the gray and dingy adjectives associated with it.

These characteristics attributed to the environment reflected, in part, raw sensory input. These were objective perceptions of an actual basement. Yet these raw sensations were fused with my subjective state at the time. My processing of objects "out there" was colored by own depressed emotional state. The gray quality I associated with my physical environment was a subtle blend of objective sensations and internal emotionality projected onto them.

The Corridor (continued): I stand in such stark contrast to the house in San Antonio.

This thought emerged into the foreground of my mind, amplifying the original dream images. The house where we were now was such a stark contrast with the one where we had been.

We had been living in San Antonio, where we had built our dream home, sparing no cost or effort to make it exactly what we wanted. To us, it was beautiful, with Mexican tile floors, a planted courtyard, wide expanses of glass letting in much sunlight and above all, a sunken living room with a tall antique white fireplace at one end and a large span of glass overlooking seven live oak trees at the other.

As my thoughts went back to San Antonio house, feelings of grief and sadness came over me. I missed it so! I remembered the Sunday when we had decided to move. As I had walked through the living room which had been the site of so many good memories, a deep feeling of sadness had welled up inside me. I went into the bedroom, fell across the bed, and cried. I didn't want to give it up.

But I also realized that the two houses, one gray and dark, the other light and bright, were core metaphors, standing for larger associations. The rural house represented our new environment in general, both in its physical and cultural attributes: old, turn-of-the-century buildings; cold, bitter winters; a dearth of shopping outlets, restaurants, and other social amenities. My feelings, in connection with these images were ones of lack and deprivation. The Southwestern house, by contrast, conjured up images of San Antonio: limestone hills, broad skies and breathtaking sunsets; shopping centers, dining places, and everywhere the pervasive presence of urban cultural opportunities.

So, the dream juxtaposed two polar opposites, the now and the then, the gray and the bright. Moreover, it suggested movement, a transition, from one setting to the other.

Thus, the dream disclosed through fantasy my underlying perceptions of the new environment, the attributes I ascribed to it, and its stimulus effect on me. It also revealed my emotional reaction to the environmental stimuli: depression, deprivation, and disappointment.

I was already in contact with a basis theme of my dream, and could have gone into a more conscious reflection. Fortunately, I did not, but pressed on instead with my self-directed gestalt experiments.

Keith: I need rescuing. Dad has me by the arm and is trying to get me out of here. He's trying to rescue me.

In this personification, the dream introduces one of the cast of characters interacting in the drama, my thirteen-year-old son. The script I spoke for Keith voiced my perception of him at the time. It amplified my perception of the stimulus effect of the new environment on him.

I miss my old neighborhood. I miss my simulation club.

In san Antonio he had been happily involved in a variety of activities, a simulation club, a hobby shop which he frequented often, a neighborhood where he had lived nearly six years, with many friends, and ample free play.

I hate this place. It's just old buildings, no hobby shops, nothing to do.

Now, he was isolated. There were no hobby shops, no clubs, no friends. He stayed in his room withdrawing into solitairy board games. He appeared to lack initiative in breaking into the new environment.

I'm helpless. I need rescuing.

The impact of the new milieu on Keith, then, left him isolated, withdrawn, depressed, passive, and helpless.

Get me out of here. Send me back to San Antonio. Do something, Dad! Feel guilty, Dad!

This part of the dream enactment introduces the stimulus effect that one character, Keith, has on another, me.

Keith's state has implications for me. I feel responsible, obligated to do something. I also feel guilty, guilty for uprooting him from his past and placing him down in this new and miserable situation.

The enactment is beginning to open up the underlying interaction field of my current life situation: the contrasting environments, and especially the impact of the new one on me and on my son. It is also disclosing the stimulus effect of Keith's state on me, and my response to that stimulus.

Frank: I am holding Keith by the arm, leading him along.

This dramatic action in the dream reflects my response towards Keith. I feel responsible and guilty and want to take some action.

I had been "leading" Keith even

before we left San Antonio. I had tried to mystify (Laing 1965) him into thinking about our new home the way I wanted him to, thereby trying to obscure the facts about it and to minimize and deny our loss. I tried to instill positive images about the new town: the outdoor recreational opportunities we would have; the great north woods with its snow-covered hills suited for cross-country skiing; the beautiful fall colors; the apple orchards.

But my efforts to coerce him into seeing the advantages of the new town failed. When Keith made occasional remarks that showed his disappointment, I did not really listen. I discounted such comments, hoping that time would change his perceptions and feelings. Moreover, he felt betrayed and resentful about all my mystifications.

Keith: Feel guilty, Dad! I want to punish you, Dad!

The Side Passages: I lead off from the main corridor. I may be your way out.

When time did not take care of my son's progressive depression and, if anything, he became even more withdrawn, I became anxious and worried. I felt even more responsible. I tried to replace what Keith had lost, to make it up to him. We tried to locate hobby shops and simulation clubs, making frequent and bracing trips to Minneapolis. But they were not to be found, and even if they had been, they were not the same; they could not replace the friends and ties that had been lost.

Keith became even more depressed. He began writing letters to his friends back in San Antonio.

The metaphor of the side passage represented all the false starts I had made, all the actions and counteractions that had transpired between me and Keith—my mystifications and manipulations; my initiatives to replace the lost elements in his life; my solicitousness. The outcome of all these interactions was a blind alley.

The bars: I am the hard cross-bars at the end of each passageway. I block your exit. I am your prison.

All of my actions, my leading, were blocked. I could see no alternative.

The Buildings in the Distance: I am the old buildings here. Everytime you think you've found a way out, you're blocked, and you look out and see more of me. I'm omnipresent. You can't escape me.

I feel the restraining press of the environment. I feel trapped. I feel helpless. I feel panicky.

All my efforts to pretend, to suppress, to gloss over, to wrench some meaning out of the present, had come to naught.

Frank: I feel so helpless.

Having no power to change my life situation inevitably plunged me even deeper into depression. And, of course, the effect of my overinvolvement with Keith was to condition in him even greater helplessness and depression.

Frank; I can't just find another job someplace else so quickly. Besides, we just moved here.

I thought of leaving our new town, but I knew that would take time and planning. I could not make it happen in time to solve my immediate problems.

I was filled with anxiety, and panic, and desperation. I was indeed in a narrow passage, and it was entrapping me.

With that feverish pitch of emotionality, I had waked.

Then, as so often happens in experiential work, a new feeling emerged into awareness. It had been there all along, submerged, the inevitable outcome of this frenzied drama. I was furious, at first, with Keith:

Frank: (to Keith). Damn you, Keith! Damn you for heaping all this guilt and pain on me!

I vented my rage on the object of all my overinvolvement and the source of all my concern, and with that, all my helplessness, my guilt, depression. Because of him I was suffering the anxiety of this impassable situation.

But then, my rage turned to its proper object, myself:

The Enraged Frank: (to the stuck Frank) You're killing yourself, and you're killing Keith. It's futile trying to rescue him. He's got to do it himself.

A part of me was able to look at my bound-up self and to see the futility, the maladaptedness, of the impasse.

Frank: (to Keith) I can't save you. You'll just have to get on with coping here—or perish. I'm just making you and myself shriveled wrecks.

I was able to clarify the consequences of my overinvolvement, rendering my son ever more withdrawn and depressed, more resentful and punitive.

Frank: (to Frank) That sounds harsh and cruel, but that's the way it's got to be.

I actually experienced myself pulling back, getting out of Keith's way. It was a movement, a differentiation, that I knew was right, yet I had a deep sense of abandoning him.

There was a fleeting internal split between the part of me that knew what had to be, and was adaptive, and the part that felt disloyal and cruel, but was ultimately maladaptive.

I had made a deep-seated, existential decision and felt a great sense of relief. I knew that the dream, and the enactment of it, had been a turning point. It had come, and none too soon. From out of my own depths had emerged the missing resource, the rage to change.

My life situation was reframed. To pull back from my efforts to rescue my son felt so wrong. But it was so right. I had to force myself to start acting on this new framing of the interaction. And I was able to do so primarily because of the emotional support that had been evoked and gained through the dream revelations.

EPILOGUE

I shared the dream and my decision with Alice, my wife, who had been for weeks a spectator to this futile maladaptive struggle. My depression, guilt, and anxiety had inexorably spilled over to her. More confident than I regarding Keith's coping, she had listened to and accepted my suffering and had been caught up in the abortive, strenuous trips to the Twin Cities. When she heard my decision, I sensed her implicit acknowledgement of its essential rightness.

As for Keith, with me out of the way, he did fine. He formed some deep friendships, got involved in a youth group, became an avid tennis player, and in general, came to enjoy our new location.

ENACTMENT AS RITUAL

The dream, in many respects, is like a ritual of adaptation. It gathers up all that has gone before in some transitional situation, frames the impasse with all its relevant emotional intensity, and provides some hint, some prospect of the way through.

Among the Indians of the American Southwest the sandpainting is a ritual which mediates the resolution of inner conflict by reestablishing a harmonious condition between the self and the surrounding environment (Villasenor 1963). Using such natural materials as sand, corn meal, flower pollen, or powdered roots and bark, the shaman creates a symbolic tapestry which mediates metaphorically between inner reality and forces in the environment.

So too, is the dream and its enactment a rite of passage. A spontaneously generated internal drama, the dream uses concrete sensory images to portray the self, in its many aspects, coping with some life situation. Working with these symbols, opening them up and amplifying them, the therapist creates a living sand painting, an enactment, which depicts an environment, a cast of characters, the impact of the environment on these characters, and their effect on one another.

Using metaphors of sculpting and other symbolic stand-ins, the interactional field among the characters can be made explicit and visible. Patterns of interlocking action can be explored, traced, and analyzed. Points of fixation, impasse, and displacement can be identified and interventions made to facilitate movement towards more adaptive relationships. With the spouse or other family members present, empathic understanding and clarification of intra- and interpersonal boundaries can be accomplished. More adaptive differentiation and alignment of individual, marital, and family systems can be established.

Chapter 5

The Experiential Group

In the couple therapist's storehouse of methods one particularly efficient and promising approach is the experiential group. This intervention design will be examined in this chapter in considerable detail.

For some therapists the multiple couples' group is the preferred, if not the exclusive, method of choice. Among such helpers the format for group interaction can vary from therapist to therapist. In chapter two the time-limited, highly structured design of the communications training group was discussed briefly. Its purpose being the enrichment of couples' communication skills, it provides a series of carefully planned exercises for practice and skill development. Other groups are more informal and less tightly designed, but nevertheless draw upon long-standing principles of group dynamics. These latter formats provide settings in which couples can discuss and mutually explore their separate and common concerns. Sometimes, through direct and immediate encounter among themselves, participants discover factors contributing to marital stress and rehearse new patterns of relating.

The General Design

The design of the experiential group is centered around the enactment of some concern, event, or situation in the life of a couple or individual partner. Group members share in the creation and development of the interaction field and in the exploration and learning that grow out of it. The enactment becomes a stimulus that generates a host of dynamics that spread throughout the group as a whole.

The interaction situations or issues that can be enacted are virtually unlimited. In the case example to follow the enactment centers on a wife's visit to her family of origin during the previous weekend. The simulation for another couple re-creates events of the previous evening, when the entire family dines at a local restaurant. In this second case the wife, observing what she considers to be obstreperous behavior in her children, feels abandoned by her husband in restraining and managing them. As the enactment unfolds, she becomes aware of feelings of embarrassment. She becomes concerned about what people at nearby tables must think of her for having such unruly children.

Suddenly, it is not the onlookers at adjacent tables who are peering at her, but her parents, and especially her mother. She has reverted to another field, her childhood family. Displacement has occurred, and what started out as the replication of a recent social situation shifts to another time and place. At that point, her nuclear family is re-created with its themes of interaction and its unfinished outcomes.

The enactment, then, can begin with the present, as this one did, and trace its origins into the past. Or it can start in the replication of some past milieu and project its influence into current relationships.

The enactment requires an organized set of procedures for regulating an essentially evolving process. Thus, in creating and developing the interaction field the therapist draws upon a multitude of interventions taken from a variety of therapies. From gestalt, communications, systems, sculpting, structural, transactional analysis, and other approaches are drawn those procedures that can most fittingly catalyze and facilitate the enactment at a given moment. Being guided by the frame of reference of the person or couple whose enactment is being created, the therapist uses group members for stand-ins and doubles, manipulates physical spatial patterns and arrangements, directs fantasized dialogues, asks process questions to channel communication, and in general, applies an intervention that keeps the enactment evolving. Each instance of intercession seeks to make audible and visible some aspect of the client's experience lying in the foreground at that moment.

In the writer's experience, clients respond to this approach, for they sense that if the therapist is going to be of help, it is inherently sound to re-create the conditions that are causing stress. For the couple who has just undergone a miserable dinner out the previous evening, it seems right to them to replay that incident and to get the benefit of the therapist's and group members' perspectives on it. In that replication they hope to discover a better way of handling the situation, to rehearse new patterns, and to change.

As the enactment unfolds the therapist does not know from one moment to the next exactly where the action is going. This means that information has to be gleaned, quickly interpreted and organized into meaningful patterns, a fitting procedure chosen, and action fed back into the enactment—all without interrupting its development.

The therapist's function while the simulation is transpiring, then, consists of a recurring series of interaction or feedback loops. Data are traced, patterns discerned, procedures selected, and actions taken, time and again. With each new cycle the therapist must once again observe and interpret the consequences of his or her actions on the evolving enactment. Thus, while appearing open-ended and fluid, the creation and development of the field are organized and carefully controlled.

Like a thematic apperception protocol, in which a client reveals himself or herself in the narration of a story, the enactment is created by the group member who is disclosed in the very act of creation. The simulation requires the creator to make visible and auditory his or her inner experience relative to the event or situation that is being replicated. Thoughts, feelings, images, memories, and assumptions are all projected outward, given embodiment, and dramatized in action. The group member's frame of reference towards the field of interaction is progressively externalized and objectified.

The simulation, then, becomes an ongoing source of exploration and discovery of the group member's interaction pattern in the event or situation under review. The therapist can trace not only overt levels of communication and behavior but underlying elements of the deep structure as well. Evoked by the dramatization can be such covert and tacit dynamics as interpersonal fusions, triadic process, diffuse and rigid boundaries, shifting and incomplete relationship phases, and emotional impasses, any one or all of which can be dispaced into the event or situation in a maladaptive way.

Approaching the simulation with an attitude of sustained tentativeness, both therapist and client can anticipate and be prepared for the unexpected and the unpredictable. New nuances of feeling, new shades of meaning, and new frames of reference may surface where least foreseen. The serendipity which so often accompanies the excavation of depth can and does occur.

The exploration and learning that take place in the total group following the simulation are likewise grounded in established dynamics, many of them drawn from multiple-family therapy (Laqueur 1972). Group participants learn through analogy, seeing and hearing in the simulation dynamics much like their own and observing how others are working these matters out. A group member may undergo a cross-encounter, an empathic resonance, with some intense emotional state that emerges during the enactment. Another group member, or a cluster of participants, may identify with some figure or condition in the dramatization. The group as a whole may gain understanding of a wide array of family processes by having experienced these dynamics concretely, first-hand. Basic principles of adaptive functioning can be extrapolated from the simulation, such as, for example, how to extricate one's self from triadic interaction in one's family of origin. These and other dynamics of learning in the experiential group will be examined following the presentation of the case example.

THE STIMULUS ENACTMENT

Bev, a member of a couples' group, announced at the beginning of a session that she would like to work on an experience that had been severely upsetting for her. The previous weekend she had driven back to her home town to, as she put it, take care of a crisis that had arisen in her family. Such trips she felt compelled to make whenever she received word of trouble in her childhood family, a fact that caused no small amount of consternation for her husband, Jim.

As he put it, "Whenever one of 'em calls or sends word that things aren't going well, she just has to go. Never mind where that leaves me and the kids." Jim left no doubt that he thought it worthwhile for his wife to look at the matter in the group setting.

Other members of the group acknowledged Bev's need to work on what was obviously a crucial issue for her and her husband, and they yielded the time to her. The recognition of pressing and urgent concern for an individual group member or couple was one pricipal criterion for deciding an agenda for the session at hand. Besides, by now all participants realized that the work done by one member or couple becomes a concrete resource for the learning of all.

The therapist, wanting to ground Bev's work in an experiential enactment, elected to replicate her family of origin with a sculpture. By re-creating her family and simulating the interaction within it, the therapist wanted to provide Bev with an exact model of her family of origin. Then, by moving about in that field of interaction she could be confronted by her feelings, thoughts, and actions within it. Hidden assumptions, attitudes, intrapersonal states, and roles could be teased out, and where she wanted, Bev could rehearse and decide upon new patterns of relating within her family of origin.

For the therapist and other group members looking on and engaging in the simulation, the enactment would make visible and concrete the total field of interaction. They could see and hear information that could be fed into the enactment for Bev's sake, bringing to her awareness experience that might otherwise remain denied, distorted, or concealed. At appropriate and strategic points, other participants could assist in the simulation, doubling or standing-in for some member of her family, role playing in some interaction sequence, or simply, but importantly, providing support and encouragement to Bev as she enacts the event.

The enactment proceeds thus:

Therapist: Bev, I'd like you to sculpt your family. Pick members of the group to represent, or stand-in, for the members of your childhood

The directive to sculpt requires Bev to make visible her perception of the family interaction field. Stand-ins represent and provide an intro-

family who should be in the sculpture. You're free to choose whom-
ever you like for whatever reason.
Take each stand-in and position
him or her in the sculpture where
you want.

duction to the cast of characters in
the model. Her positioning of the
stand-ins potentially can yield data
on such interaction themes as distance and closeness within the
family, as well as the general orientation of the *dramatis personae*, that
is, whether they appear basically to
be turned toward the family system or away from it. In her positioning of stand-ins, and the
manipulation of physical space inherent in that action, Bev will
provide a map of the family structure. As she objectifies her internal
perceptions and images of different
persons and their relationships
among one another, she will
provide both explicit and tacit information on such configurations
as dyads and triads, on enmeshed
and rigid boundaries, on coalitions,
or on emotional cutoffs. For other
members of the group this visible
model can demonstrate and make
evident some of these processes of
family structure. The sculpture becomes an embodied specimen of
boundaries, coalitions, and other
structures. It serves, consequently,
as a vehicle for exhibiting and
learning basic dynamics of family
process.

Bev's selection of group members
to represent members of her family
also has potential revelatory
power. Of course, her choices may
be entirely random. But the probability is great that in some instances her preferences will be

based on psychodynamic factors. Something that someone has said, or how he or she sounded or appeared at some time or another in the group process, may evoke a subjective state inside Bev. This transference having occurred, Bev may then choose that individual as a suitable object to stand-in for someone in her family group. He or she, in effect, reminds her of some trait borne by the family member being represented. Later, the enactment may evolve to the point where Bev actually engages in some form of interaction with the stand-in, using him or her vicariously to complete unfinished relationship concerns with that family member.

The use of this displacement phenomenon when and if it occurs can serve later on to enrich the therapeutic potency of the enactment.

The direction given to Bev to sculpt is very open-ended. Specific instructions could have been given to give special attention to body postures or to facial expressions. The therapist could, moreover, ask her not to talk while she is creating the sculpture, thus forcing even more her manipulation of these visual representational systems. Electing not to call her attention to these informational channels leaves room for her spontaneous portrayal of them. She may, that is, without realizing that she is doing so, depict postures and expressions that contain significant disclosures. (Print media cannot capture these nonverbal visual channels nor, for that matter, auditory messages of tone and speech rate. The therapist can in the verbatim only interpret these messages for the reader.)

Bev: (Proceeds to choose members from the group and to position them in the sculpture. She and the participants exude a general air of fun and playfulness. The exact features of the sculpture will be described for the reader as the enactment unfolds.)

Therapist: Tell us, please, who these people are. Just give us their names and ages.

This directive can be varied. Group members can be asked to make inferences regarding the stand-ins, that is, who most likely represents whom in Bev's family. The therapist, however, instructs an observer to document his or her perceptions leading to the inferences. Sometimes, an observer's evidence, a nonverbal clue, can call a previously hidden element to Bev's attention.

Bev: OK. This is my father, who is sixty years old (she points). My eldest brother, who's thirty-five, Rob (walks over towards this stand-in and again points). My next brother, who's thirty-four, Dick (walks towards him and points).

The three stand-ins are positioned side by side about three feet apart. The father figure is centered between the other two, with the oldest son to his right and the younger to the left. The younger son has his right hand extended, gripping some object, like a glass.

This is my sister, Pat, who's exactly eleven years to the day older than I am.

This is my brother, David, who's in Pennsylvania. He's twenty-eight. (Points toward him.)

Pat is seated at a desk about five feet and slightly outside a right angle to the older brother. She is stooped over the desk, looking down. When introducing Pat, she touches the desk. David is standing about fifteen feet outside the sculpture, looking towards it. He is positioned at an angle behind and beside the older brother.

Therapist: Good. (To the other group members) Please feel free now to walk around in the sculpture. That's what sculpture is, three-dimensional and solid. Please note what you see.

This instruction specifically directs observers to use their senses to see the visual cues.

Group Member: What do you mean, "Walk around?"

The instruction given is not always heard, for one reason, because people attach different meanings to the same word. This is an opportunity to clarify directives, to make certain everyone is operating on the same wavelength. A fundamental principle in an enactment is: slow it down! There is always far more going on, far greater depth, than can be attended and processed. The seemingly most insignificant cue can contain extensive material worthy of excavation.

Therapist: I mean literally, walk around. Look at the sculpture from different angles. Face the stand-ins. What do you see?

Again, the therapist can direct observers to pay particular attention to facial expressions and body postures. But to do so might disrupt their spontaneous perceptions. The more specific directives can be given later.

The use of participants as obser-

(Group members mull about within sculpture.)

Therapist: (to Bev) Are the body positions and facial expressions of the stand-ins right, or are there some you would want to change in any way?

Bev: (Looks at the sculpture. Reflects.) Dick is right, with his arm reaching out like that. (Goes over to Rob, the older brother.) You're kinda confident (said to this stand-in). (Moves over to the father stand-in.) You're kinda sloppy (group members laugh). Slump your shoulders. (She then proceeds to place the hands of the father stand-in in his pockets.) And you're kinda weak (to the representative of the younger brother, Dick).

Therapist: (To group.) All right. If you'd like to walk around a bit more, to take a look at these latest shapings of Bev's, please do so. (A few participants walk around, looking at the sculpture once more.)

Therapist: (Noticing that Bev herself is standing off to the side, so that it is not clear whether she is simply admiring her modeling efforts or

vers taps the wealth of perceptual resources present in the group. This pooling of observers greatly expands the therapist's individual perceptions. These collective capabilities reflect the enormous therapeutic potency of a group.

Now the therapist is calling attention to these visual cues.

In speaking, Bev has violated the directive. Yet she provides valuable information in the form of interpretations. In effect, she has assigned to each of the stand-ins an image, which reflects her composite recollection of the many personality traits of these male members of her family. At the same time, by molding these characteristics into the stand-ins, for example, the father's hands in his pockets, she has indicated some of her visual cues regarding their actions in the family network.

This directive now calls the visual cues to the observers' attention.

This is a highly important directive, eliciting information on her position and general orientation in the family structure.

whether she is part of the form.) Where are you in the sculpture, Bev? Are you in place? And if you are not, could you put yourself in the sculpture.

Bev: (Pauses for a moment, as if deciding. Then, she takes a place facing her father, about six feet in front of him, with her arms outstretched as though embracing the entire cluster.)

So the final form of the sculpture looks thus:

David
    Rob   Father   Dick
Pat   Bev

Therapist: (To the group.) Okay, what do you see? What are some of your most obvious observations?

This question begins the process of collecting the group's perceptions.

Female Group Member: I see competition.

Therapist: (Interrupting) I hear that as an *interpretation* of what you're seeing, making meaning out of your perceptions. But document, first of all, what you see that leads you to draw that conclusion.

Often, group members are impelled to go past their sensory input to the formation of thoughts, meanings, and inferences. Therefore, this directive to document is filled with considerable training implications. It teaches the process of documenting interpretations with sensory data (Miller, Nunnally and Wackman 1975).

Female Group Member: Well, their position . . . one on each side of the father, I guess. And . . . um, I don't know, maybe the way they're standing and the way they're looking. It just looks to me as if they're trying to outdo each other.

Listening to her remarks and looking over the properties of the sculpture, at first, the therapist thought this group member was projecting. He could not see evidence leading to an interpretation of competition. Nevertheless, he accepted her perceptions, realizing that she could be picking up some cue that I was not. Besides, one of the benefits of this process of pooling perceptions is the consensual validation of evidence on the part of everyone present. The group, in other words, contains the wherewithal of a radical empiricism, in which judgments can be immediately noted and corroborated by others present.

Should the group member be, in fact, projecting, she is doing so under the stimulus of the sculpture before her. Thus, the enactment has the potential of cross-encounter, evoking in other participants some internal concern or memory that can later be worked on in the group.

Second Group Member: I see David standing way outside the sculpture.

Therapist: What do you think that could mean? Now, I'm asking you to interpret what you see.

The therapist is now sanctioning interpretations of visible clues.

Second Group Member: It could be geographical. He could be living at some distance. Or it could be psychological . . . somehow out of the family, looking on.

Third Group Member: Or both. He could be outside the family in spirit as well as physically someplace else.

Therapist: Stay with that.

Third Group Member: Well, he's got

two brothers, and it's a male dominated family.

Therapist: Why do you think that?
Document.

The tendency to interpret is almost
an involuntary tendency. Seeing
this, the therapist immediately
blocked her and called for sensory
evidence.

Third Group Member: Because, um ...
she's (pointing to the figure of Pat
at the desk) kind of passive, sitting
down. And there are three men
here. Maybe he removed himself
from that situation. Maybe he
didn't want to have to compete ...
just go away and let them have it.

This is another interpretation
based on a visual stimulus, Pat's
being seated. This cue, of course,
does not in itself necessarily connote passivity in Pat.

Again, the therapist records the
fact that another observer has
picked up the competitive element.

Therapist: What about it, Bev?
Why's David out here in the sculpture?

Believing that the pooling process
has gone far enough, and that it
now needs Bev's input, the therapist asks this question. Bev can interpret for the group, making use
of the perceptions and thoughts of
observers where helpful.

Bev: (To Third Group Member)
You're right. He's living in another
state, but it's a purposeful removal.
He left home at age nineteen to go
into the service. He comes home
and visits. But he keeps the family
distant because he saw what was
happening. So he got out. He left
me. He was the child. And when he
got out, I caught it next.

Therapist: So that the pressure ... I
got a sense of pressure. Is that
right?

The therapist wants to check out
his understanding of such words
as, "caught it" and "got out."

Bev: Right.

Therapist: So the pressure bypassed these three (gesturing to encompass the father and other two sons) and converged first on David and then on you?

Bev: (Nods assent).

Therapist: What did David escape?

This question begins to probe interaction themes. Certain interactions took place that resulted in the outcome of David's leaving. What are they?

Bev: My mother was a very dominant, powerful woman. She dominated the family. She dominated my father and all my brothers . . . and everybody. My sister's been in psychotherapy because of her hatred for my mother.

Group Member: Why is Pat seated?

This member documents (seated) and then asks Bev to interpret. This suggests, at least for this one participant, an accommodation to the distinction between sensing and thinking.

Bev: She's having emotional problems, as I said. I feel everybody's kinda dismissing her, abandoning her. She's kinda out of it.

Therapist: We're getting more into the family's dynamics now. But before we do, is there anyone else who wants to share a perception?

Group Member: Bev's standing in front of the father and . . . looking back at him and the brothers. It's like she's saying, "Look at me. Be concerned with me."

Bev: (Smiles and nods agreement. Continues to look at male figures before her) Dick (looks and motions toward the brother described as weak) could do no wrong in my mother's eyes. Rob (looks at the oldest, "strong" brother) could do no wrong in my father's eyes. Years ago, when we were growing up, it was "Dad's boy," "Mom's boy."

Bev is documenting that in the family myth there were alignments between parents and children.

Therapist: Rob was dad's boy.

Bev: Um hum. But that's reversed itself now.

Therapist: Why was Rob dad's boy?

This probes the interaction between Rob and the father, that is, Rob's characteristics that pleased the father.

Bev: He was until this last conflict.

Therapist: You mean the conflict that upset you last weekend.

Bev: That's right. Rob is strong and self-sufficient . . . a real go-getter. He doesn't have a lot of education, but everything he does seems to turn into money. He has a talent for money matters. And he's always shown that characteristic of a go-getter. He's a mouther. He talks.

Therapist: So Rob is a go-getter, and Dad is passive.

This reflection simply marks the contrast between the two.

Bev: He's very passive, but he was always proud of Rob's behavior.... (reflecting). Okay, (as if she just made contact with something) maybe he ... suppressed feeling....

Therapist: Your father?

Bev: Yeah . . . I've always thought that, you know, Rob could do no wrong. Rob was always a good boy. Maybe because he was the eldest son. That might have something to do with it, but I really don't know. And Mom had to mother Dick, because he was introverted . . . and didn't talk, like Rob. Rob has a natural gift of gab that Dick does not have. He's more retiring. And so he gets his feelings out in his drinking. He got married. It didn't work out. He's divorced . . . and has three daughters. He's failed . . . a black sheep type failure.

Bev appears to be trying to figure out why Rob was such a favorite in the father's eyes.

Note the parallel between Dad's suppressing feeling and Dick's taking out his emotions in drink. Also, the sharp contrast she draws between the two sons is interesting, one vocal and outgoing, the other restrained and introverted. In the family interaction Mom mothers, presumably nurtures, the more passive son, Dick.

Dad actually sounds, as presented by Bev, more similar to Dick, yet his favorite is Rob.

The interaction theme, mother nurturing the more passive son, is noted and simply put away, pending further data.

Therapist: Does he (pointing to the stand-in for Dick) have a beer or drink in his hand?

This interprets the stand-in's outstretched hand, holding something.

Bev: I picture him becoming an alcoholic.

Therapist: Who mystified him with this black sheep image.

The group was familiar with this concept, mystification, from a previous session. In this process, as described by Laing (1965) one family member attributes a characteristic to another and then subsequently invalidates or disqualifies any action manifested by the other that appears to countermand the attribution. Moreover, the person being mystified into the image or role eventually is seduced or coerced into accepting the attribution as being a part of his nature or existence.

Bev: I don't know. He's quite a bit older than I. He was old when I was born. It's always been that way. I can't say how it got that way.

The therapist thinks that Bev has exhausted her ability to make sense out of this part of the family myth.

Therapist: OK, let's go back a bit. What was the pressure that converged on David?

Bev: David was . . . there were four of them, very close in age. David was born . . . he was the baby of the family. My mother babied each of us. Her youngest always got babied.

Therapist: What does that mean?

The question is intended to surface the specific actions that were signified by this verb.

Bev: Oh, they were the special one for a while, until the next one came along. And there wasn't much time between Rob, Dick, and Pat. And after David there were four years

The interaction sequence connoted by the word, "special," is not clear. Inferences drawn would have to be speculative.

... I had another brother who died at birth. And when he died, my mother converged back on David even stronger. Then I came along after eight years of his being the spoiled one. There was a lot of competition. I remember him (sic) getting yelled at, and hit, and shooed off in the corner all my childhood. I played on that in my childhood. My brother and I would get into a conflict, and I'd run to Mommy, yelling, "He's beating on me." And he'd get sent to his room or spanked or something. I played on that all my childhood. I really used him.

Again, the meaning of, "converge," is not clear. The exact meaning of the interaction theme is obscure.

Note the appearance and parallelism of "competition." Only now, at least in this interaction sequence, one sibling triangulates the mother into an explicit conflict with another—or, more accurately, uses her favored position in an alignment with the mother to exert control of David.

Bev documents the presence of triadic process in her family, that is, two members going through a third to cope with a conflict. This concrete case material can be used directly by the therapist for demonstration and explication of triadic family process. Group members may also use it indirectly, in vicarious and analagous learning.

Therapist: You used David?

Bev: Yeah, I did.

Therapist: Then, when he left what pressure fell on you?

Bev: Well, it wasn't right after he left. He left, and about a year later my mother died...a year and a half later. And then all the family pressure fell on me. When my mother died, everybody had somebody else. I mean, Rob was married; Dick was married; David was engaged. My sister was with my mother

The interaction sequences during the mother's death are becoming more transparent. Everyone had someone else for emotional support. The inference can be drawn from the data at hand that Bev felt alone and emotionally isolated.

when she died, and she lost her cool completely, went hysterical in the hospital. Through the whole funeral . . . that whole ordeal, she was sedated. And a close friend took care of her the whole time. She couldn't talk. I was twelve, and I felt like nobody cared what happened to me. I was going through just as much as they were, yet no one responded to my needs.

I was expected to take care of preparations, as far as the house . . . I was expected to manage the meals . . . I had to take care of all that. All that responsibility fell on me. I was only a child, and I resented them all for doing that to me.

It is not clear who did the "expecting" in this series of interactions. It appears to be, implicitly, the remainder of the family system. Yet Bev feels precociously pressured into responsibility (I was . . . a child). The connotation of the sequence is that someone, by failing to be responsible, forced Bev into being prematurely overresponsible. Someone, by omitting proper response in what appears to be a disengaged way reciprocally violated Bev's boundaries as a child and drew her into inappropriately adult behavior. The outcome was her feeling resentful, an emotional response fitting to the violation of her boundaries.

Therapist: How old were you?

Bev: Twelve. They just forgot about me in the shuffle.

Therapist: Is what happened last week almost a reenactment of what happened when your mother died . . . and afterwards?

The therapist is probing the parallelism between her earlier report of having to go home to solve a family crisis and her having to take over at the time of her mother's death. Is there a displacement, or at least replication, in the two events?

Bev: It's almost the opposite. Then, they forgot me, because . . . It was like I wasn't important enough. But now, they corner me into squabbles. And I don't want to be in that role. I don't want to be the mediator of all their conflict. In their bickering they stick me in the middle.

"Cornered" is the perfect metaphor for one caught in the middle of triadic process.

This is rich material for group learning. The mediator or go-between is assigned, usually tacitly, the task of helping the other two persons in a triangle to resolve their implicit or explicit conflict.

Therapist: Whom are you talking about?

Bev: These three (points to father, Rob, and Dick). They're having a conflict between the three of them, between Dad and the other two.

And they're all . . . when I went home last weekend, they all shouted at me, "He's terrible. He's doing this or that, and he's terrible. And he's not doing anything about this or that. I'm mad at them for that."

The therapist starts to work out a patterning process. Earlier, he noted the fact that while the father is himself passive, he favors Rob, the go-getter. This suggests an identification process on the father's part with this trait in his son. It is as if the father, lacking or not having actualized this characteristic, nevertheless admires and rewards it in his son. The other son, Dick, is described essentially, by Bev, as possessing attributes like the father, that is, passive and weak. At a preliminary level, the conjecture can be made that the two sons, with their respective traits, reflect an internal conflict within the father. Here, the therapist simply formulates this conjecture, to be tested against forthcoming data.

Therapist: And what are you supposed to do about it?

Bev has described the actions of other family members, the three men. This question probes what her reciprocal response is supposed to be, that is, what they expect her to do, what output back into the system.

Bev: They expect me to fix everything.

Therapist: Like your mother did.

Note the parallelism, in her use of the phrase, "fix everything," between her mother and Bev. The mother, when she was alive, played this role, and now it has fallen to the daughter.

Bev: (Looks surprised. Reflects momentarily.) Probably.

This sudden, unexpected discovery is the essence of the teasing-out process. In this case, Bev is taken unawares by the similarities in the roles played by her and her mother. Such serendipity is the hallmark of the experiential enactment, one of whose chief functions is the exploration and unearthing of deep and covert elements in the interaction pattern.

Therapist: When someone has a gripe against someone else, you go to Mom, and Mom fixes it.

This statement summarizes and feeds back the interaction script.

Bev: Pretty much so.

Group Member: Are they living at home now?

This seems an extraneous question at this time, almost defusing the emotional level Bev is undergoing. Since that stress has been escalated, for Bev and perhaps for the group member as well, this question provides a means for pulling back. Anxiety is too intense.

Bev: Dick's divorced, and again, no money except . . .Dad didn't want him. . . . Dad feels that when we go, we should stand on our own two feet and do it ourselves. Um. . . . He also thinks that Dick's a failure. He doesn't say so, but he thinks it.

The therapist notes that she is interpreting her father's subjectivity here. But her manner indicates that she is not merely mind reading, but has some objective evidence, perhaps in remarks Dad has made to her or to others about Dick, what he thinks. Such gossiping, it has been established, occurs in this family.

Rob's very self-confident, but Dick doesn't approve of what Rob's doing. They're fighting.

So Dick, the failure, can criticize Rob, the go-getter.

My family's in a hassle over the money my grandfather left all of us. And they're fighting, and it's very ugly. And if I had my way, I'd . . . if I could go in there and say, "This is the way it's going to be. I'd just . . . "

Probably without realizing it, Bev has just role played her "fixer" behavior. Her tone has an aggressive, authoritative demand to it.

It's not so much between us, but between us and our cousins. But it's turned into being between us. The problem outside becomes a problem inside. And Dick believes Rob's just doing it to get more money. And because he's always resented Rob's ability to be good at things and to make money . . . where Dick's never had any money, because he's always failing and can't hold a job.

The competition seen by some group members in the sculpture is now confirmed.

And that's part of the conflict, too.

The parallel, implicit though it is,

Pat is getting married in November. She's mentally unstable, and she met this man in the hospital who is just as mentally unstable as she is. And Rob says, "If a man doesn't have a job, he's got no right to get married. This guy's just a lazy, good-for-nothing bum. I don't trust the man she's going to marry." And Dick says, "You can't do anything about it, so you might as well help her along. At least she'll be happy this way."

And my Dad's goin, "Yeah, you might as well. I don't like him either, but we can't do anything about it." Daddy's the kind of guy . . . you can't fight city hall. And that's all that Rob does is fight city hall, that type of person.

Therapist: I sense that you have some concerns with your family as a whole, as well as with individual members in it.

Bev: Yeah.

Therapist: With whom are you most upset, now that you're back from last weekend?

Bev: I think I'm most upset with my father.

Therapist: Would you tell him.

between the man who is to marry Pat, who does not have a job and is denigrated by Rob, and Dick, who also can't hold a job, is apparent. Rob's covert attitude towards Dick is analogically implied.

Dick intuits the implicit denigration (the black sheep metaphor with which he has been mystified) and appears to identify with Pat's proposed partner.

Bev has spontaneously broken into dialogue for the characters. This is a good time to move into a more direct and immediate style of enactment.

So her father's identification with Rob has to do with the fact that his elder son can assert himself while the parent cannot.

This question will begin to concentrate the enactment in relationship impasses that are most pressing for her.

The therapist directs her to send

Would you go over to him, face him, and tell him.

Bev: I'm most upset with you, because you're not doing anything. You're not acting like a father is supposed to act . . . and take care of his problems. You're willing to let me take the brunt of it.

I know you're lonely, even though you won't remarry, even though we'd all like to see you get remarried. Because it would take care of some of your loneliness. It would give you somebody to talk to.

her message to the father. This procedure can facilitate confrontation of feelings in the present.

Bev's message to him elaborates on themes she developed earlier, when reviewing the time of her mother's death. Only now she is more specific concerning the one who is neglecting to act, namely, the father. He is failing to act where his action is required. His disengagement causes the pressure to spill over to Bev.

For the group as a whole, this case material offers a vivid demonstration of a disengaged boundary. By omitting involvement, the father falls short of action that is demanded in the situation. When one person falls short of a fitting response, someone else has to step in to take up the slack, to fulfill the missing family functions.

This borders on fusion, in which Bev senses and assumes responsibility for her father's emotionality, his loneliness. Also, she becomes enmeshed with him by overresponsibly advising and giving solutions. The probable effect of the message on him, however, is not one that Bev really intends. At the covert level she is communicating her lack of confidence in his ability to arrive at his own solution, or, if he can, to act upon his convictions. Once more, Bev is acting out the "fixer" role that she so much dislikes yet continues to fill.

Inasmuch as this role is one that once was filled by the mother and now by Bev, the daughter has been parentified. The function which fell upon her as a child and which she still fills is that of the parent. It is as though the father, in his abdication, covertly injoined Bev, "Take care of it. Be the mother. Be my wife surrogate."

I feel like I'm just a dumping ground for your problems. And your being unhappy with Rob and with Dick, and with your own unhappiness with the entire situation. . . . You're just dumping them on me and expecting me to take Mom's role and fix it all.

This case material, once again, affords rich teaching illustrations of the parentification and injunction process. Probably no one ever openly said to Bev, "Be the parent." But the forces of interaction in the family, the boundary configurations, combine ever so efficaciously to put her there and keep her there. At the same time, she complies with the role, the injunction. She both conspires with and resents the external charge and expectations. She is system maintained and system maintaining (Minuchin 1974). Being the fixer, she rescues her father in his passivity and thus also helps him avoid its consequences.

A preliminary conjecture occurs to the therapist at this point, that Bev's mother had also cared for her husband in this manner, too. And the mother is Bev's model. That is, the therapist wonders whether the parental couple, in their marriage, had modeled fusion and enmeshment. The one, being passive, reenforces the other in being active and overinvolved.

Therapist: Would you now come and stand beside your father and speak for him. (She moves over). Role play him and reply to what you just heard Bev say.

This directive continues the fantasized dialogue. Bev, drawing upon a host of images and memories of the father, can role play this significant person in her life.

Bev: You can't fight everybody, Bev, (she addresses the place where she previously had stood). I'm not lonely. I'm doing just fine. I've got the farm and my animals, and I don't need to get remarried. Your brother, Dick, just doesn't have it. I wish he'd get out on his own. And Rob's just so self-centered. He's concerned only about himself. I don't know how his wife puts up with him. You can't fight it all like this. You just gotta let go, and things will take care of themselves.

(She stops and shakes her head) He wouldn't say those things. If I threw that at him, he would evade it and talk around it . . . and talk about everything else.

Bev in this statement ascribes new properties to her father. He is not just passive, but evasive. The therapist infers that she also means that he is elusive in saying what he really thinks and feels. If so, this is another form of disengagement.

Therapist: Would you come over here and be yourself (motioning her toward her place in the sculpture). Respond to what you just said.

Bev has distanced herself from the direct contact, and this directive will help to put her back in it.

Bev: But Daddy, you gotta take a stand. You can't let everybody walk all over you like that. You've gotta stand up . . . tell 'em when something's wrong. There's no excuse for not fighting if something's wrong. You can't just pretend it's not there. You can fight city hall

Now Bev attributes more images to the father. He's walked over. He pretends and avoids issues.

Once more, Bev uses parallel metaphors. Rob fights city hall, which suggests implicitly that he asserts himself to effect change in his en-

and solve the problems. You can't just avoid them. (Her voice has an urgent, insistent quality, as though she's lending him emotional support.)

vironment. Dad, in contrast, pretends that problems do not exist, avoids them, becomes resigned to them.

The impact on Bev appears to be, as disclosed in her tone of voice, disappointment and frustration. The thought crossed the therapist's mind that Mom must also have felt disappointed in her husband's recessive style.

And if you had remarried, you wouldn't feel the need to drag me into these things. You wouldn't feel the need to have me come home, leave my family, when honest to God, I don't want to come home.

One can literally see and hear Bev's ambivalence beginning to surface. Forces of change and individuation are pitted against those of stability and enmeshment. Feelings of autonomy alternate with those of loyalty, feelings of resentment with those of guilt. In one breath Bev is saying she wants out, and in the next she is telling her father what to do. She is out; she is in.

Bev's struggles here afford the group a strikingly vital depiction of changing relationship phases and the emotional intensities that accompany them. She is suspended in a vigorous transition whose outcome is yet uncertain.

Therapist: Would you tell him why?

This directive facilitates her further articulation and elaboration of the forces of differentiation.

Bev: Because all I hear when I come home . . . all I hear is complaint, bitching back and forth. I wish I could be like David and just get up

She reverts back to the disappointment and pain. Then she swings back into individuation. Her feelings of frustration and futility are

and leave you all. If it's going to be so petty and little . . . just stay that way, because I don't care.

evident here. Not only is she embroiled in trying to rescue the family, but her efforts to do so do not work. From a patterning standpoint, the father who draws Bev into overinvolvement in his passivity, can in that same inertia frustrate her every effort to change him. As Fritz Perls puts it, "Under-Dog always wins." This seemingly paradoxical statement recognizes the fact that Top-Dog, who is Bev with all her pushiness and moralizing, will be defeated and chronically thwarted by the one she tries to rescue. In his excuses, delays, and avoidances, the father remains passively resistant. It is Bev, then, who gets bent out of shape. The father expresses any latent resentment to her indirectly, without ever really appearing to be angry.

Group members can see in this sequence the tandem and reciprocal nature of interaction.

In her final remark, "I don't care any more," can be heard the underpinnings of an emotional cutoff. She could indeed walk away, as David perhaps has done, but all the unresolved feelings and incomplete relationship phases would go with her. She would remain as bound to the family as ever.

Therapist: Why don't you?

The blunt question confronts her with the fact that she has decided for the role she is playing. It also redirects her attention to the forces of homeostasis.

Bev: I'm just tired of it and....

She reverts to the emotional consequences of her position.

Therapist: You didn't answer my question.

The therapist confronts her head-on with her decision (Goulding 1979).

Bev: What?

The emotional intensity seems so high that Bev is in a trancelike state. Here, she virtually has to concentrate her attention to hear the question.

Therapist: Why don't you just leave like David?

The therapist continues confronting her with the fact that she has decided to stay, that there are loyalties and obligations she is fulfilling by staying. Also, in meeting those obligations she does not have to suffer certain feelings and consequences that would otherwise ensue.

Bev: Because I . . . (her voice is low. She hesitates.)

Therapist: Tell him.

Here the therapist intentionally forces her to confront the anxiety head-on and to go through it. This enables her, in rehearsal, to express herself in a congruent and differentiated way, with the fusions and enmeshments and anxieties sloughed off.

Bev: Somebody's got to do it around here. And nobody's getting off their dead ass to do it. . . . so I can't just let you all fight. You're my family. And I can't just let this continue. I just can't let everybody sit

Now she sounds angry, and that feeling is often an intermediate step towards differentiating.

The power of her enmeshment and loyalty is evident here. "I can't" also

back and be unhappy. I can't just sit back and let you fight amongst yourselves. I just can't.

Therapist: Who told you you couldn't?

Bev: I dunno. (I don't know. Said very rapidly.) My mother.

. . . (reflective) I don't know how she did it, but she did (her voice sounds sad, her speech rate slow). My feelings of guilt, if I don't. . . . She reached my feelings (contemplative, probing tone).

Therapist: (to stand-ins) Why don't you have a seat. Pull up a chair and sit where you are in the sculpture.

(to Bev) Tell your mother....

Bev: (interrupting the therapist) I don't know the way you did it. The way you brought me up is a . . . (pauses) all my feelings, every time I did something wrong . . . as a child. I was doing it to make you unhappy . . . (her rate of speech slowing down).

translates, "I won't." This latter position connotes a decision for which Bev is responsible.

This is an informed probe. This question is designed to personify the injunction that has been levied on Bev to rescue the family.

Her quick reply suggests initial ignorance on the matter. Almost as quickly she makes contact with the source of the injunction. The power of the enactment as an exploratory medium is once more evident here.

This instruction lets the individuals serving as stand-ins relax, yet still be in place if needed. It seems now that most of Bev's work will be with her mother and father.

This directs her into present-centered encounter.

Her pauses, searching for insight indicate exploration and work.

Implicit in Bev's remarks is the feeling of guilt, in response to her mother's blaming her. The interaction theme seems to be one of the mother's imputing (interpreting) a malicious intent to her daughter's actions. There is no data indicating what those actions were.

Therapist: What are you in touch with right now?

Bev: Deep down inside I know . . . my mother had a saying. She always said that when I misbehaved or didn't do my share of work (her speech rate is picking up rapidly) . . . cause I was considered lazy or irresponsible as a child.

The phrase, "had a saying," suggests an interaction theme of some duration. In it, certain actions of Bev's were interpreted by the mother as lazy and irresponsible. Having had the image laid on her, mystifying her, Bev evidently complied with it and is now struggling against it.

Because Pat worked so hard, and when I didn't do my work . . . My mother was sick all the time. She'd had a stroke. She had diabetes, and heart problems. And she always said, "You're lazy, and you're gonna drive me into my grave!"

Heavy stuff this is! The mother, ascribing to herself ill health and evidently wanting her daughter to help, sends other-directed messages to Bev, blaming her and impugning her as lazy. In effect, she holds Bev responsible for her own well-being.

Therapist: Did you?

This simply probes whether Bev does in fact feel responsible for her mother's death.

Bev: I don't know. I wish I could have known her as an adult (her voice becomes quivering).

Therapist: Would you tell her that. Let's put her here (I place the mother figure in imagination behind Bev in the sculpture.)

The therapist senses the emergence of sad, tender feelings in Bev towards the mother. These, too, should be said directly.

Positioning the mother figure was an unconscious act on the therapist's part. But inadvertently, he placed her where he had her in his mental map of the family structure. Since Bev's place had been so defined by the maternal model, then the mother, too, belongs in front of and responsible for the entire family system. Since she is deceased, she is behind Bev but still using her daughter, as perhaps she did while alive, as a parental surrogate. It seems right to the therapist to place the mother behind the child whom she had parentified, and who is still filling her function. For all practical purposes, the deceased mother is Bev's alter ego.

Bev: I wish I had known you as an adult, because maybe I could have understood your behavior and your feelings. But I didn't. I was only a child (Bev is now talking slowly, through a trembling voice). I don't think my behavior, looking back now, was so unusual for a child. You expected me to be a full-grown woman at ten. You expected me to run the household and do the dishes . . . and the cooking, and the cleaning, and the ironing, and the laundry.

She is deciding here against the mystification, that is, that she was not lazy but normal for her age.

She recites these chores almost like a litany, as though that very ceremonial pace were an analogous channel for the repetitiveness and drudgery of the duties.

And I wanted to be a child. And you didn't give me a chance to be the child I wanted to be, by pushing me into all these responsibilities (her tone is a mixture of sadness and resentment).

The sense of being trespassed upon, of having her childhood boundaries violated, is obvious in this remark. Here, too, is further evidence of the parentification process.

And you left me when I probably needed you most, the most I've ever needed you. I was only twelve,

An inference of Bev's grief and sense of abandonment is probable here.

but . . . (she pauses). There's something I should throw in here. My sister was having emotional problems. She was living in another town at the time. The minister there called my mother to say she's in very bad shape. And Mom thought she could fix it . . . if she went there, she could fix things.

The parallelism in the use of "fix" is additional evidence of an intergenerational transmission process. The mother emitted the behavior now being acted out by Bev.

So my brother, Rob, and his wife and my mother all drove over there. And while she was there she had a heart attack. My sister was driving the car and . . . they drove her to the hospital. And she died minutes later. And Rob and Pat had been in a very emotionally involved religious group, and they had been at church with her when she had her first heart attack that night. And Rob told me later on that Mom, during the service, had prayed to God that He would take her and leave my sister, so that my sister could get better.

This is chilling in its impact, with respect to its implications for Pat. The effect on her of her mother's "sacrifice" would be extreme guilt, as though she was responsible for the parent's death. And Mom, it was disclosed earlier, sent messages to her children that they were driving her to the grave. It is hard to see how Pat could survive these interactions without severe emotional trauma.

And I feel like she chose my sister's life over mine . . . and disregarded me as a child who needed a mother.

At face value, Bev's literal interpretation of her mother's sacrifice, if it is that, borders on the irrational. She may be speaking as the child, with the child's imagination and as the child could experience the death, as the choice of one sibling over another.

Therapist: Would you tell her that.

This draws her back from talking about the incident to reexperiencing it.

Bev: I feel like you deserted me and left me sitting there when I needed

Her feelings of deprivation can be inferred here.

you most growing up. And I feel like you placed Pat's life as more important than mine. I know, at least I think I know, you did it because you thought I could always manage and that I was strong like you . . . and dominant and aggressive, and that I could pull through. Well, I did, but I still wish you'd been there.

An ambivalence is evident here. On the one hand, Bev (and the mother) is strong and self-sufficient, but on the other she wants care and concern.

Therapist: Are you tired of being the parent?

Bev: Yeah (an emphatic tone). I'm tired of playing mother. I'm tired of taking care of everybody. I'd like to live my own life, just take care of myself (her voice contains a pleading quality).

Once again, the two sides of the decision and individuation process are apparent, with at first an emotional self-affirmation followed almost alternately by a whining plea for permission.

Therapist: To have the freedom of the child.

Bev: I never had a childhood. I mean I was always the favorite, the baby, and all of a sudden I wasn't anything. I was taking care of everybody else . . . I'm the most important person in my life. And I've never been able to do that . . . and that's caused me problems in every relationship that I've ever had. Because I mother people. I mother Jim (Points to her husband). I mother the kids, do things they can do for themselves. I fight the urge to mother them, but I do it anyway. I know it. I've worked on it ever since I became aware of it. But it's such a natural role for me to fall into. I automatically. . . .

Now Bev is beginning to draw the interpersonal implications of her behavior. In these statements can also be heard the power and durability of the deep structure. She has been so long in this pattern, so impelled by it, that she cannot alter her actions even when she wills it.

Therapist: What do you do?

The therapist wants her to describe the actions denoted by the verb, "mother."

Bev: People come to me and dump all their problems on me, and I fix them if I can. If somebody needs something done, I'll do it. I make sacrifices that I don't want to make, but I make them because I feel it's my responsibility . . . to do it, to take care of them, if they need somebody. That's my role in life (resigned, helpless tone).

The parallel with her mother's sacrifices is evident in these remarks. She is truly her mother's daughter, imitating her model in so many ways. The therapist wonders, in a fleeting thought, whether Bev, too, like her mother, ever fantasizes some kind of ultimate sacrifice, an illness or even death brought on by her overresponsibility and other people's apathy. In the language of transactional analysis, that would be the logical way to cash in her brown stamps or resentments (Goulding 1972).

Therapist: Would you be your mother now and respond to you, to what you just said to her.

Bev: I don't know what she'd say. I never really knew her. The years that she was there she wasn't really there. We were poor, and my mother worked. She worked from four in the afternoon until midnight. I never saw her. I don't know her as a person. I know her as the figure I have in my mind. I wanted to know her and love her as a person. Even at the funeral I cried, but not really, because I didn't know what I was losing.

Therapist: I want to share something with you, to let you try it out. I got a sense that when you were over

This is feedback to check out inferences about the similarities between Bev and her mother.

here talking to your father, that
your mother was over here.

Bev: Yeah, she pushed him. Yeah
(her tone is decisive). If you don't
push, you don't go anywhere.
You're just content to stay put. But
she pushed him. That's why they
fought all the time when I was a
child.

So Mom is the source of the declaration about initiative. She pushed
her husband, who in turn pushed
his oldest son and admired his success. The parents' explicit conflict
was projected onto the children.

She pushed him, and he didn't like
to be pushed. And he doesn't like it
when I push him. He hates my
pushing, generally.

She draws her own parallel between the mother's pushing and
her own, and the father's resentment. This is the first confirmation
that inherent in the father's passivity was resentment.

When I take on the tone of my
mother and yell at him, because
he's not doing something, he reacts
like he did with my mother. He'll go
outside and work . . . or he'll . . .

This information confirms the inference about avoidance and unavailability.

Therapist: How do you feel about
that?

The therapist wants to hear Bev's
reaction to her perception of the
father's leaving (his visible action).
What does she think and feel. Since
the past is so much displaced on the
present, he hopes to discover more
about the past by observing the
present.

Bev: I don't know. I feel that when I
tell him things . . . and express
things that are for his best . . . I feel
he won't get up and do it unless I
push him.

This is a tacit assumption, that she
knows what is best for him. His
reaction to that assumption,
though probably never expressed
openly, only in passive acting out,
would be resentment.

It hurts when he just leaves and

The therapist infers that Bev's

goes outside and shuts me out. I don't like that. (Long pause.)

mother was at this point, too, feeling shut out and alienated from her husband.

Therapist: Part of you wants to be a child and part of you comes on as a parent.

This is an attempt to delineate the two sides of Bev's internal split. Perhaps the stage can be set for a fantasized dialogue between these two warring tendencies, in the hope that integration can come about.

Bev: I don't want to parent anybody else. I want to be self-centered and selfish. I do. I really do. I really want that. But I feel like I can't let myself go to be that way, because that would be wrong. I would feel guilty. It's hard to bring these two together.

Bev labels the forces of autonomy as self-centered and selfish. Erick Fromm (1947) has an excellent discussion of selfishness and self-love, but Bev probably could not hear those concepts if the therapist shared them. This split she has to work out for herself.

Therapist: Hey, let's change the pace here. I'd like to set up a dialogue between your selfish self and your mothering self. That was the selfish self that just spoke. Come over here (a position to one side of the spot where she has been standing in the sculpture) and face the mothering self over there (a spot about four feet opposite and on the other side of her location in the sculpture).

This is a deliberate use of the label, "selfish," since that is the image that is at the forefront of her mind for the moment. The therapist expects to start there, but to see the image change and evolve. It may not. But in the experiential approach the therapist intervenes with a procedure addressed to the manifest phenomenon, not knowing what will happen next. This approach allows for spontaneous surprise and discovery.

This mini-sculpture within the larger one represents the internal split within Bev herself. It depicts a shift in orientation from interpersonal to intrapersonal concern.

Would you repeat to the mothering self what you just said.

This instruction to say it directly creates an internal encounter between the two components of the self.

Bev: (facing the "mother" self) I want to just take care of me. I want to quit all this stuff of trying to fix other peoples' stuff, mothering them.

Her tone sounds perfunctory and stiff. The dialogue, it seems, feels unnatural to her.

Therapist: Would you come over here now (motions to the "mother" spot) and reply to the selfish self.

Bev: If you just care about yourself and are selfish, then you *should* feel guilty. And that's not good, to feel like that. That's not a good person. And you want to be a good person, don't you?

Therapist: Would you please come back over here and reply.

Bev: But I'm tired of being that, and . . . I don't wanta have to take care of everybody else. And I'm tired of being that kind of person. I want to be self-centered. I want to live for me. I don't want that guilt laid on me (her tone is insistent and demanding, and with her right hand open she pushes out).

Now she sounds more emotionally into the dialogue.

This visual cue embodies her pushing the mothering self back. If so, that very metaphor represents a movement towards an internal boundary realignment. She is, symbolically, forcing the guilt-inducing component back and thus exerting greater space for her "selfish" self.

No more! When I . . . I don't want

This is virtually the script of inter-

the guilt laid on me that I'm being selfish. That's unfair to me. I don't owe anybody anything. And I don't want you to tell me that I do, and make me feel guilty when I do the things I really want to do.

action patterns in Bev's family of origin. Someone, especially Mom, enjoined Bev to assist in parental responsibilities and to feel guilty if she did not. Not to perform these precocious obligations and, instead, to pursue the pleasures of childhood was selfish. So now Bev carries this parental injunction, and a host of recorded sayings and imprinted images that deposited it, around in her head. She still tries to fulfill its obligations and feels guilty if she does not. With her mother's death, it was inevitable that the family system would expect and even exaggerate this role function into which she had already been inducted.

Therapist: Come over here now, please (I motion her to a place midway between the two selves). I'd like you now as yourself to look at the selfish self. Could you describe how she is a selfish person.

In effect, this puts Bev in the adult vantage point, looking at both sides of the split (Levitsky and Perls 1970). It also sets the stage for her to integrate the two. For now, it will permit her to observe her selfish self, describe her actions in it, and evaluate it for herself. *She* becomes the assessor, not the parent.

Bev: (Looking at the selfish spot) Being selfish is just thinking of yourself first . . . of not coming through for your family and friends . . . when they need you. Just thinking of yourself, not taking care of anybody who needs you.

These are the very thoughts she has about her parents. Her father does not come through when the family needs him. The mother died just when Bev needed her. It is not that Bev has not come through for them, but that they have not come through for her . In fact, paradoxically, her parentification reflects her rigorous attempts not to escape but to fill the voids in the parents' omissions.

As indicated before, her thinking concerning the mother seems unreasonable and irrational, but perhaps it is not. For the inference can be drawn that the mother, prior to her death, was charging her daughter to step into the parental system and to take up slack there. It was as though she was asking Bev to rescue her in her overwhelming situation, which included chronically ill health, but perhaps more. Having to mother her mother, she felt deprived of a mother's nurture.

Therapist: Do you think Bev was this way when she was little?

The therapist affiliates with the adult Bev in a discussion and appraisal of her childhood self.

Bev: I was to an extent. I didn't do the dishes real well. I did them, but I complained because I didn't wanta do them. I'd go to my room, and instead of cleaning it, I'd read a book. And when Mom would get on my case, I'd get it together and start doing it. But I was . . . I would rather . . . I did the work every Saturday morning. Mom puttered around and didn't get anything accomplished. Then I had to do it.

So the child did assert herself, disregarding the injunctions, yet also setting herself up to feel guilty.

Here is confirming information regarding the mother's falling short of adult performance.

Therapist: I'm hearing how much Mom was like you. Are you saying Mom is selfish?

This reflection creates a paradoxical reframing of the mother, not as one always practicing what she preaches, but as falling short like Bev.

Bev: She was sick, I guess. I didn't realize how sick she was. . . . But she did putter. Instead of cleaning the house until it looked clean, she'd clean out three drawers, so that they were clean inside. But no one ever saw the inside of drawers. And I'd come back from confirmation class on Saturday morning . . . I'd just hope and pray that when I got there she'd have the house clean. And I'd get home, and she hadn't even started. She'd been on the phone, and maybe cleaned out one drawer. Then I'd have to jump in and do the whole thing.

Therapist: As I listen to Bev tell this story, I get a sense that she felt she was doing a whole lot of things for this family . . . even though she thought she had the right to be a child. As I listen to her, I hear her saying real loud and clear, "I was really trying to help out."

Bev: (Bev nods. She gets tears in her eyes.)

(At this point a group member gets up and walks to the mother figure's place in the sculpture. She faces Bev.)

Group Member: (speaking for Bev's mother) Bev I was struggling, too. I was sick, and I felt all the responsibilities on me. I was just trying to find a little peace, a little spontaneity in my life. I felt the way you're feeling now.

Bev steps in to take up the slack in the parent's deficiencies. There is a similarity between the mother and father, with respect to apathy and ineffectiveness, each in his or her own way.

Affiliating with her as a neutral onlooker and addressing the child as some objective third party, distances her from her childhood self and enables her to view herself differently. It is not the therapist but Bev, the adult woman, who finally has to demystify her bad image and accept herself as a contributing, if anything, overresponsible girl.

This is a classic role playing procedure from psychodrama. Group participants were aware of the process and felt free to use it as a contribution to the enactment. It requires the interpretation and articulation of some aspect of events that have transpired. Bev can participate in the offering and can accept, alter, or reject it.

Bev: (Nods. Reflects, tears still in her eyes.) But I can't go on.

The therapist infers that her assent reflects empathy and understanding with her mother. She could identify with and understand the source of her parent's frustration and overwhelming sense of responsibility. Bev has and is experiencing it now.

Therapist: To whom is that said?

Bev: To my father . . . all of them (waves at the entire cluster).

Therapist: Say it again. Stay with that.

This directs her to repeat and take responsibility for this new position.

Bev: (to her father). Daddy, I'm not your wife. Stop telling me about all the things that are wrong. Quit confiding in me. I can't . . .

Therapist: Do you mean can't or won't.

The latter verb is the position of the active agent owning the position she is espousing.

Bev: Won't. I know you're lonely. And I know you have lots of problems. But I can't . . . won't . . . come in here and fix 'em. (She pauses, as though letting that message settle). Dick (she walks over and faces this stand-in), you'd better get your act together. I know you've made a lot of mistakes and . . . but if you don't quit taking it out in the bottle, you're going to become an alcoholic. You'd better . . .

Therapist: Where are you right now?

Bev is slipping back into the mothering role, and the therapist wants her to contact that impulse.

Bev: My God, I can't stop, can I? (She laughs. Many members of the group laugh.)

This immediate contacting, awareness, and interruption of maladaptive interaction is the essence of experiential therapy. Bev has been confronted with an exact replica of her interaction pattern, except that now she is more in touch with some of its underlying sources and dynamics. More importantly, she realizes that, paradoxically, what seems so wrong is really so right. To differentiate from her former role function, which she experiences as deserting her family, is in fact the most adaptive act for herself and for them.

In some of the discussion and wrap-up which followed the enactment a number of issues were clarified for Bev and Jim, her husband. Jim for the first time, was really able to understand and be sensitive to the deep sources of his wife's dilemma. Of particular significance, he had heard and seen some of the intense and complex emotionality that kept her bound to this script. Both Bev and Jim realized that all of his efforts, made in a variety of ways, to force his wife's individuation from her family of origin were of no avail. Only she, finally, could accomplish that. She alone could cut through all the painful suffering, the resentment, the guilt, the sadness, that differentiation demands.

Light was shed, too, on Bev's mothering tendencies with her husband and children. Now, the couple realized, when and if Jim falls short in certain relationship functions, becomes disengaged, his behavior reciprocally draws Bev into her overresponsible pattern. Acknowledging the consequences of his behaviors, like Bev's father, on other members of the family, Jim expressed the intent to be more involved. Bev, in turn, can be more adept in catching herself moving into overresponsible attitudes and feelings and pull back. Now she knows that to act on these impulses is, though it seems self-contradictory, maladaptive for everyone concerned.

GROUP DYNAMICS

The experiential group offers a wealth of resources and opportunities for change that simply are not available in the therapy of a couple alone. It will be the purpose of the present critique to isolate these various factors and to examine the merits of each.

Stand-Ins and Role Players

The contribution that different group members make to the creation and development of the enactment is no small element. To be willing just to stand in as a representative of some absent family member is to lend help in a common growth-enhancing endeavor. Sometimes the mere fact of standing-in places a group member in such situations as lying on the floor and being stepped on or being verbally abused face-to-face, and the willingness to undergo such acts for another is a sacrificial offering of oneself. For the stand-in the enactment is but a simulation, but it is not without risks. Anxiety is escalated, and the stand-in's consent to have it so is a major value in the whole enterprise.

When the stand-in involves himself or herself even more, the self-giving is heightened. To bring one's self more deeply into the enactment entails such actions as role playing the family member one represents or, at a minimum, to share what one experiences as the stand-in at a given place or position in the simulation. For instance, the individual who stood in for her brother, David, in Bev's sculpture engaged in the following exchange with her:

David Stand-In: Just one thing occurred to me. When this role playing started I asked a question to Bev about David. She seemed to put him out of the role playing altogether and . . . I felt that. I felt left out throughout the whole thing. Until the very last part, when you began sharing some of your feelings. I felt I wanted to get close to you then. I didn't want to be so far away as Pennsylvania.

Bev: (Long pause, contemplating) That makes me wonder if that's how he does feel. If he feels like he's part of the family, but he's not. . . . I don't know, maybe it would be a good idea for me to . . . I don't know if I could handle the confrontation . . . That's a hell of a lot of stuff . . . But he would be the easiest person to express my feelings to.

Therapist: Are you likely to see him anytime soon? I'd really encourage you to talk with David person-to-person, and share some of these things. It'd give you a chance to learn where he really is in all this.

The therapist recommends a person-to-person encounter between Bev and her brother, so that they can begin to clarify their relationship. The enactment is the simulation and rehearsal of feelings and attitudes that can then be channeled into direct family encounter. The enactment can, however, clarify and alter boundaries and decisions that have remained hidden and covert and thus establish the basis for a deeper, more meaningful meeting between family members. Bev's being able to empathize with and understand David's emotional cutoff, if it is that, creates the possibility of a more congruent and conciliatory encounter with him. Having in the enactment come in touch with her own tendencies to flee and give up, she can identify with these same inclinations in him.

An even deeper form of engagement by a group participant occurs in the actual protrayal of the family member for whom he or she is substituting. In such role playing the group member takes part in the simulation by acting out his or her experience while the action evoles. As a general rule, in this writer's observations, the systemic forces in the interaction field go a long way toward defining that role for the actor. For that reason, the player's performance becomes a useful source of information and feedback for the individual whose family model is being depicted.

For example, in Bev's enactment had there been someone portraying the mother, that actor would no doubt have been drawn into the constraints and pressures of the role. Experiencing the father's withdrawal and apathy, she probably would have felt quickly drawn into overresponsibility. Feeling overwhelmed, resentful, and tired, the actor would inevitably project those feelings into the simulation, that is, would have acted them out. Seeing that representation of her mother, Bev might more readily have come to a point of empathy, understanding, and identification with the deceased parent. It is not uncommon for an actor during an enactment to undergo kinesthetic changes while fulfilling a role, suffering a headache, a knot in the stomach, a dizziness, under the impact of the systemic forces. Role playing, to repeat, can be sacrificial.

A role player's performance can be specified, his or her characterization heightened, and the benefits of the portrayal more focused by the giving of basic directions and cues. Thus, Bev, after sculpting the stand-ins in her enactment but before engaging in dialogue with them, could describe the role that each is to depict. In doing so, she projects her inner images and memories into the actor's portrayal. Such explicit directions tend to define the roles and to keep them as true as possible to the actual family model. Otherwise, actors can act out of their own scripts, thus skewing the simulation, rendering it less useful, sometimes disrupting it.

Such specific directions can be seen, in our case simulation of Bev's family of origin, in her telling the stand-ins how to look. She was doing no more than describing their overall body demeanor. Characterizations of lines, attitudes, and feelings were not even included. Yet even in her almost fleeting mention of adjectives like "strong," "sloppy," and "weak," she projected a highly relevant set of inner images. Her directions themselves become disclosures useful in the unfolding enactment.

The more removed the enactment becomes from the client's governance, the less concrete and beneficial it is. Thus, to guarantee that the field is not diverted by doubles and role players, fantasized dialogues can be employed. As Bev, for example, converses directly with significant members of her family, she projects her own inner images and memories of them. Her protrayals are grounded in countless instances of encounter.

To be sure, such simulated conversations are not without their pitfalls, too. The fantasized portrayals that flow out of the client's mind can be based on projections, on fears, and on unrealistic anxiety. Properties can be ascribed and depicted for others that might not hold up in the direct encounters of the conjoint session.

Be that as it may, it is those inner images, those parent tapes for example, with which the client inwardly contends. It is those internal images and the subject-object interactions that generated them that place a client like Bev in her binds and impasses. It is in confrontation with those specters that her disquieting and seemingly impassable emotionality is aroused. Role players and stand-ins, even when cued in their portrayals, can be more removed from these real internal figures.

At the same time, the alter ego or doubling function in the simulation can be a highly useful contribution on the part of a group member. This, for this writer, is the best use of role playing. For a group participant to perceive or intuit certain feelings, thoughts, or intentions on the part of some family member and to feed those discrete bits of information into the enactment can be quite productive. This was evident in the contribution of the double who role played Bev's mother ever so briefly. This group member was sensitive to certain feelings in the situation of the mother and gave voice to those emotions at a time and place when they could be heard. Elements in the interaction field that otherwise might have remained hidden, outside Bev's frame of reference, were made transparent. In fact, they afforded a major breakthrough in the enactment.

The doubling function, thus, does not require the portrayal of a total role, with the pitfalls that can ensue from that. It does allow for the recognition and depiction of elements in the field that need to be made manifest—intrapersonal thoughts, feelings, and wants, or interpersonal themes and outcomes. Doubling enables the simulation to remain under the control of the client's frame of reference, with distinct and pointed excavations made from time to time. Features of the deep structure which lie outside the client's purview can be surfaced. If the double's offering does not fit, or if it needs modification, the client is free to work with it as he or she wishes. Then the enactment returns to the client's control.

Encouragement and Support

Another major contribution of group members to the simulation is encouragement and support. As Bev stated this aspect:

Bev: I felt a lot of . . . I feel really comfortable with the people in this room. I really feel like I . . . like you said (to therapist), it was a high risk situation. And granted it was. But the people in here made me feel like it wasn't such a big risk. I had a real good feeling. I felt good. I could look around the room, and I could see people smile at me. And that encouraged me enough to continue, because . . . a few times I would have backed out, and just walked away. But everybody seemed to have eye contact, you know. They reassured me that, yeah, it's okay to go on. I appreciate that.

Group Member: Thank you for doing it. I learned so much from it.

Bev: I'm glad I did it. I fought tears

through the whole thing. In a lot of
ways I can hide things.

Therapist: Is that part of the role?

Bev: Yeah.

Therapist: Could your mother hide
tears?

Drawing an inference on the basis
of all the previous parallels.

Bev: She cried to get her way. And I
can do that, too, if I want. If I want
to cry.

Therapist: You didn't want to draw
out the tea and sympathy?

But you got a lot of empathy.

In effect, Bev is saying that during
the enactment she was deliberately
trying not to elicit sympathy. Like
her mother, she implies, capable of
evoking support by inducing guilt
in others.

But the therapeutic benefit of the group is not only for the one
who works. To be sure, considerable energy and focus go into
participants' sharing in the making and opening up of the simulation. The enactment, in turn, spills over to other couples and
individual partners present in the group. Some of these factors are
likewise worthy of examination.

Cross-Encounter and Tuning In

In the process of cross-encounter, as Paul (1968) calls it, a group
member's ability to empathize with emotional states in his or her
own life is catalyzed through a resonance with similar feelings that
are present during the enactment. A listener, bathed in some
highly charged moment or theme in the simulation, suddenly has
evoked in himself or herself emotions that have been forgotten,
denied, or concealed.

Cross-encounter, technically speaking, occurs when some repressed group participant comes into an empathic reverberation

with a feeling state in someone taking part in the simulation. The stimulus person may be the client in the enactment, or it may be someone else in the cast of characters.

Often, the feeling state and the memories and events associated with it are not sorted out initially. But a pervasive sense of sadness, of loss, or of smoldering resentment, to cite but a few possibilities, may linger and even swell in the listener as the simulation unfolds. Later, at the individual's request and with the group's consent, the aroused emotions and the events and situations that produced them can be explored. The therapist, in responding to the group member who has undergone the cross-encounter, may elect to listen associatively (Paul 1967), that is, not only to the overt content of his or her remarks but to nonverbal cues that can represent the underlying feeling states. Or an entirely new simulation can be established to work on this group member's newly surfaced experience.

If cross-encounter, strictly speaking, has to do with empathic emotional resonance between two or more group members, tuning in, as Laqueur (1972) defines it, refers to the recognition and identification of similar situations. This dynamic can be seen in the response of one group member to Bev's enactment:

Female Group Member: I can see that Bev's really been through a lot (pause) My Mom and Dad are getting a divorce now. The last time I was home my Dad came up to me, and he . . . what he said was, something like, "You're not doing anything to help us." I don't remember exactly what he said, but he made me so mad.

Therapist: So you're having some of the same kind of stuff as Bev?

Reflective clarification.

Female Group Member: Yeah. He made me so mad, and I said, "I'm not coming home!" He said some-

Tuning in to situations and interactions can include cross-encounter, the evocation of kindred feelings.

thing about coming home more often to help out, or something. And I could see how she (Bev) . . . I've been feeling a lot of that pressure, too. I, ah . . . I love both my parents so much.

Second Female Group Member: My parents are going through a divorce, too, right now. And I kinda see where you (to Bev) . . . that's how I feel. Me being the youngest, I'm really getting drawn into it now. I love both my folks too and I can't just sit there and look at my father and say, "Leave me out of this." I can't say that. I know I have to do it for my peace of mind, but I can't.

Therapist: He wants to talk with you about your mother?

Reflective clarification.

Second Female Group Member: They both do. She wants to talk to me about him. (Pause) He realizes now . . . like my Mom . . . well, my oldest brother is the only one that lives in the town that my folks do. And they both use my brother. And my Dad knows that my Mom's doing that, and he told my brother, that . . . that he's not supposed to bring any messages between the two of them. That if they're going to have anything to say, they're going to say it. Yet he still keeps on using my brother.

She has recognized and identified with the triadic process in which the parents project their conflict onto her and her brother.

Therapist: What do you think they want from him?

The therapist infers a perverse triangle in which each parent breaches the generational boundary and enjoins a son or daughter to coalesce with him or her, tacitly, against the other.

Second Female Group Member: They're both using him against the other.

Therapist: Do they know that?

This probes her perception of the covert nature of the intergenerational complicity.

Second Female Group Member: Do they realize what they're asking? I doubt it.

Therapist: It's the type of thing where you know you're feeling something, but you're not quite sure what it is.

The coalition that is being induced is, as Haley (1967) observed, denied or tacit. The injunction is rarely, almost never, voiced at the overt level, yet through a host of implicit relationship channels it is influenced into being.

Second Female Group Member: You know, . . . like you want . . . I don't know how to put it into words. So, instead . . . My Dad's real lonely, and so I feel this obligation to go home. And my Dad . . . I think that's it. He's just so lonely, and I'm his only daughter. I don't know how to say it.

She is visibly trying to sort out her feelings, her position in the triangle.

The triadic process is possible in part because of her fusion with her father. Sensing his emotional state, she feels responsible to care for it, to do something for him

Therapist: You're doing pretty well. Let me feed you a sentence, and you say whether it fits. "I sense my father's loneliness, and I want to be available to him emotionally. But it's almost as if I'm supposed to join in a coalition with him, but I'm not supposed to comment on it or check it out."

This feedback, almost an abstract definition of triadic process, nevertheless accurately describes her state. It is literally, therefore, a tuning in to a common family situation and identifying with it.

Identification

Closely related to tuning in but of a slightly different nature is the dynamic of identification and the identification constellation (Laqueur 1972). In this process a group member or members identify with a common family situation or function. Thus, in Bev's enactment the role of the parentified child was noticeably and markedly conspicuous, and others in the group who have experienced that position might rapidly identify with her and with one another.

Usually coming from large families and often female, the parentified child has been drawn prematurely into adult responsibilities. The person doing the inducting is frequently the mother, who, like Bev's parent, herself felt overwhelmed, deprived, and resentful and appeals to her daughter for help, for rescue. The daughter feels obligated, and guilty if she does not comply, but she also feels intruded upon, deprived, and resentful. Like Bev, she alternates back and forth between periods of loyalty and guilt and ones of deprivation and anger.

Though it did not happen in connection with Bev's enactment, group members who have known the parentified condition can rally together, share common experiences, help one another, and thus come in out of an isolated and seemingly hopeless condition.

Often, the working-through process includes intergenerational discovery and understanding. In person-to-person research with members of their respective families, members of the identification constellation frequently learn how and to what extent the adults who parentified them were likewise parentified. That learning filters throughout the entire constellation.

The enactment affords countless occasions for identification and for the learning that can come about through this process. In Bev's enactment certain group members might identify with different figures in her cast of characters. Some might put themselves in Bev's place, with her go-between and pseudo-parent bind, others with the mother and her sense of desperation, others with the father in his apathy and helplessness, and still others with David in his emotional isolation. Sometimes the identification can take a paradoxical twist. In this, group members align themselves vicariously with character traits or themes that are missing or undeveloped in themselves and their situations, just as Bev's father sided with his oldest son's assertiveness and drive which he himself did not possess.

One of the more dramatic instances of identification in the author's experience took place during a young woman's simulation of her family of origin. It illustrates the almost unlimited variety this process can take. In her sculpture the woman had placed herself, alongside her husband, in a triangular pattern between her mother and father. As the enactment developed, the dominant theme was her impatience with her parents' marriage. Her father she had sculpted as a workman down on one knee with his shovel, totally preoccupied with his task. Her mother she molded sitting in a chair, absorbed in the writing pad and pencil she held in her hands. She dramatized virtually no intimate exchange between the two, and she desperately wanted to do something about that void. She dialogued first with her mother and wanted to know how this parent could tolerate so sterile a relationship. But her real complaint, it turned out, was with her father. Plodding away ceaselessly at work, at home he was, as she said to him in a fantasized dialogue, like a hermit.

Wanting to develop this metaphor, the therapist instructed her to go over into a corner of the room and be the hermit, which she did. Down on both knees, head bowed, and arms extended downward towards the floor, hands clasping each other, she appeared almost in supplication. One group member sensed the figure's plea for understanding and recognition and doubled with that message. At that, the woman empathized with the father's contribution and devotion to the family, albeit expressed in the only ways he knew, in loving acts of providing. But he could not, would not, did not know how to, express the warmth and intimacy she expected.

Suddenly, the whole group riveted to the father stand-in, who was now bent over, face in his hands, sobbing. "I haven't cried in so long," he muttered through his weeping. A somewhat reticent but well-liked member of the group, it was common knowledge that he had spent most of his life in hard work in a kind of stoic, rural setting. In almost instant recognition of what he was experiencing at that moment, the heroine of the enactment went over to him, sat in his lap, and held his head while he wept. Others in the group were visibly moved.

In almost uncanny dynamics of identification and displacement, she had selected this particular group member to represent her father. Perhaps it was something he had said, how he said it, how he looked, her knowledge of his background, or a combination of these aspects that provoked her choice of him. For whatever reason, as the enactment progressed his identification with the father increased and evoked a cross-encounter with his own sadness and repression.

Delineating the Field

A major benefit of the simulation and the group's use of it is the delineation of the field of family interaction (Laqueur 1972). Concepts of family process are made concrete and given embodiment. They come alive and take on practical relevance. Participants can see, hear, and feel the interlocking forces of interaction.

In Bev's enactment, for instance, a wide array of family dynamics are exemplified. Demonstrated in that one scenario are all of the following: systems and subsystems; boundaries of the clear, enmeshed, and disengaged kind; fusions; triadic and dyadic patterns; parentification; binding and injunctions; impasses; intergenerational transmission; the projection of marital conflict; the lack of differentiation; and relationship phases.

Amplification

Once members of the group have personally observed and undergone the full impact of situations and events in a simulation, those elements can be amplified and elaborated for further learning. Having encountered family dynamics that are analogous to their own, participants are able and willing to give them full discussion. They usually want to learn all that they can from these case situations, so that they can apply them in their own lives. And the internalization that follows is usually grounded in both emotional and cognitive aspects.

For example, most of the participants who encountered Bev's

enactment were aware of triadic relationships in their own families. Wanting to develop the full implications of this common situation, then, the therapist explained:

> There's a message for all of us in this situation. When we're at home in our family of origin, or when someone from it contacts us by phone or letter, and we sense that this person wants to gossip about some other member of the family, there are some steps that we can take that are functional for everyone concerned.
>
> You know how it happens. Dad wants to talk about Sis, or Grandma wants to talk about Mom, or an aunt wants to talk about her niece. Sometimes the unspoken expectation is that the person hearing the gossip will convey it to the third person in the triangle (several group members nod their heads).
>
> When we sense ourselves being induced into this state of affairs, we can say something like, "Hey, you know, I sense that you've got some strong feelings about so-and-so. Why don't you talk them over with him, or her."
>
> Or we can handle it the way one family therapist did in his family. His mother was communicating to him her displeasure with his sister, at which point he began to agree and even to exaggerate his sister's faults until the mother, shocked, came to her daughter's defense (laughter in the group). He then called his sister and suggested that she find a better way to relate to their mother. As he put it, "I have given them back to one another to work out their problem" (Guerin 1972).

Modeling

Another form of learning that can be extrapolated from the simulation occurs through the use of modeling (Laqueur 1972). During the enactment, participants are able to see and hear behavioral cues and sequences that they themselves can integrate, rehearse, or emulate.

When Bev tells her father and her brothers to take their grievances to one another and not to her, group members are able to recognize the triadic process and to pinpoint specific steps for extricating oneself from it. When she sends messages to her father directly, observers can experience the emotional pain and intensity that such confrontation evokes. They can see and hear the rehearsal of person-to-person congruent communication.

The reaction to such modeling may be that of the member who said, "I can't say that to my father. I just can't." Her reaction may be valid for her, but it is based on the clear recognition of adaptive behaviors that have been exemplified to her. She adds, "I know it is best for my own peace of mind, but I just couldn't." Her problem now is not that she does not know what to do, but that she dreads the prospect of imitation. Modeling provides a demonstration of, sanction for, and cues to new action in the family.

The Humanizing Dimension

These many different factors in corporate learning, taken as a whole, add up to what may be the principal advantage of the group, its humanizing quality. Perhaps the *sine qua non* of mental stress is the pervasive sense of being different and alone. Couples (or individuals) may feel isolated in their thoughts, their feelings, their problems, or their fantasies. In this state of alienation a couple may feel like failures, their condition, they believe, unacceptably peculiar and shameful. As one marital partner expressed his thoughts toward the termination of one couples' group:

> When we first came into this group I really felt different. I honestly believed that most of you were coping with life . . . were managing your lives relatively well. I felt totally alone in some of the things we were going through. But when I got in here and heard some of the things some of you were going through, I realized that you were . . . that we weren't really all that different. I didn't feel so bad, so left out.

The experiential couples' group, in the simulations and shared dynamics it affords, can open up for couples the rich complexity and depth of family process. It can facilitate a communal awareness among its members, therefore, that everyone is more simply human than otherwise.

Chapter 6

The Teachable Moment

CASES IN POINT

Across from the young, female student therapist sits a hostile couple on the verge of separation. Observing live behind the one-way viewing glass, the supervisor notices that the trainee looks visibly stressed. She continues to interact with the partners between their bickering and vituperative remarks to each other, but she plainly is not doing the work of which she is capable. Following the session, she joins her peers and the supervisor for a postinterview wrap-up and consultation. She staggers towards her chair, half-joking, half-serious, and exclaims, "Whew! I just wanted to run out of there the whole time!"

A male student therapist sits across from a husband who is just beginning to feel stress in therapy, just becoming aware of his own complicity in the marital conflict. The therapist, as the supervisor and peers note from the adjoining booth, spends much of the session trying to explain to the husband, to get him to see, what it is he is doing that precipitates marital tension. A tall, drawling Texan, the husband leans forward and sideways as though straining to get the therapist's explanations. Yet for reasons perhaps known all too well to himself, the husband never quite gets it, but he does succeed in keeping the therapist expounding. It was no surprise to the supervisory group, then, when the therapist said afterwards, "Boy, was I doing all the work in there tonight!"

A male therapist, usually quite innovative and adept in his interventions, is virtually immobilized in his work with one family, especially by the father. "The way he just sits there so stolidly just intimidates the hell out of me," says the therapist to the supervisory group.

A fourth trainee, Bob, is doing premarital therapy with a couple in their late twenties. Their engagement, which has lasted for some time, has been quite stormy. It has become increasingly evident that a contributing factor clusters in some way around the female partner's unresolved grief associated with her father's death some three years earlier. Then, too, she has expressed concern about a good bit of unfinished business with him prior to the death.

As the supervisory group consults with Bob concerning strategies for forthcoming sessions, both he and others see the importance of her completing so much pertinent antecedent material. A valid intervention design, everyone concurs, would be the client's engaging in a fantasized dialogue with her father, which Bob would direct. Anticipating that prospect, Bob declared, "Oh man, that's kind of scary." He was just getting into experiential methods of intervention. "I don't want to muck her up," he exclaims.

In a somewhat different vein, another student, Carol, is anticipating her first therapy session to be viewed by her peers and supervisor. Since any or all of some ten students and four supervisors can observe her work, that prospect bothers her, as she shares in the strategy seminar prior to the sessions of that evening. "It kinda bothers me to think about all of you looking in," she declares, which sounds strange, to say the least, coming from an experienced psychiatric nurse with faculty teaching status.

In an individual supervisory session with the first female student, the one panicked by the splintering couple, the supervisor listens to her recall of feelings from the therapy interview. Listening associatively to her remarks, tuning in to her subdued tone, and attending to her facial features which once again show stress, the supervisor focuses on her wish to flee. As they talk, tears come into her eyes, for unexpectedly, her memories go back to another time and place, to the period in her life before her parents' divorce. Their alienation lasted for years, she recalls, and through the whole time leading up to the final rupture each enjoined her into coalitions. Caught in the middle, wanting desperately to keep them together but helpless and impotent to do so, she had gone through a protracted interval of pain in her life.

Sitting opposite her warring clients, she was flooded once again by these same feelings. Feeling obligated to keep them together and helpless to stop their faultfinding and verbal abuse of each other, she becomes emotionally fused. She loses her usual objectivity and becomes enmeshed, feeling overresponsible and impotent at one and the same time.

Following the male student's standoff with Big Tex, as the client came to be called by the student group, the session is reenacted. The supervisor, himself a slow-talking Texan who gets into the character, role plays the husband. As he acts out the role, the supervisor exaggerates the client's demeanor, egging the therapist on in his futile explanations, almost teasing him. Finally, after so much, the student throws up his hands and shouts, "Oh, to hell with you!"

This angry outburst out of the way, the student makes contact with another situation in which he felt constrained to make somebody else gain insight into his behavior. The scene shifts to his family of origin, in which he, the younger and brighter of two brothers, is enjoined by his parents to see to it that the older sibling toes the mark in school and in other activities. He had been as squashed by the elder brother as he had by Big Tex, which had served only to impel him to try harder. Fused with his client, the student symbolically reenacts an old and unfinished family obligation. His objectivity and differentiation in the session is lost.

In a group supervision session the third student, who has been intimidated by the father in his client family, moves from that figure to his own paternal parent. His father, who had immigrated years earlier from another country and who thus had been cut off from his family of origin, runs an ethnic restaurant specializing, ironically perhaps, in his native cuisine. Like a scene from the musical, "Flower Drum Song," the rift between the very Americanized son, the trainee, and his impassive, traditional father seems unbridgeable. He is as cut off from his parent as his father is from his. Beneath the apparent cultural differences lies a disengaged relationship between father and son.

He resolves during the group meeting to make person-to-person contact with his father during his next visit home, and subsequently does so. Following that encounter come short stints working in the restaurant. Like his father, he prepares the dishes of his ancestors with the same adroitness and flair that he brings to therapy. Having rejoined his family and taking pride in its heritage, on at least three occasions he demonstrates his culinary arts in the supervisor's home, much to the latter's pleasure.

Hearing Carol, the psychiatric nurse, declare her apprehension about being viewed in therapy, the supervisor directs her to make the rounds of her peer group and mentors. She addresses each person present, stating her comfort or anxiety with each, but zeroes in particularly on a female supervisor. Instructed to go over to that supervisor and to double as her, she does so. She pauses, collecting her thoughts, and then smiles. Then she says, speaking for the supervisor, "Carol, I'm not here to criticize you. I really want to be of help."

Asked by the supervisor in charge where or when she had experienced criticism while performing, she begins putting together an enactment, without being directed to do so. She pulls up a chair, sits in it, and begins to sew. "I'm about eight years old," she says, "and I'm just learning how to quilt." She quilts away.

Then she gets up and stands over the chair and says in a stern voice, "Carol, if you don't watch what you're doing, you're going to get that seam crooked." Guess who I am now," she said to the goup, smiling. Having broken the fusion with the female supervisor, it was as if she performed with abandon.

Following her therapy session that night, in which she had been equally relaxed and flexible, the supervisor remarked to her in passing, "Hell of a good quilting party!"

Bob, the student faced with the troubling prospect of directing his client's resolution of unfinished grief, will be the subject of the detailed case example to follow.

Common to all the training cases cited here is displacement on the part of the student into the therapeutic system. Unfinished business from another field of interaction, in each instance from the family of origin, intrudes into the therapeutic situation. Some person from the client group ceases to be a client, and a fusion occurs. Whether that fusion is generated by some objective characteristic of the client, some appearance, some mannerism, some tone of voice, some function in the family system, or whether it originates out of some subjective state in the student, or both, cannot be readily ascertained. Nor is it necessary, in the final analysis, to trace the subject-object interaction provoking the displacement.

Once the transference assignment is made by the student, or the student complies with one made by the client, boundaries become slurred. The client is experienced as the fighting parent, the stubborn brother, the impassive father; or a supervisor is given the specter of a critical parent. Past and present become blurred. Events transpiring in the therapy session become symbolic representations of unresolved or incomplete relationship phases from the past. Emotional intensity is heightened, and the student reexperiences the mixed feelings that, in another milieu, bound him or rendered him at an impasse. He or she is as blocked in the therapeutic system as in the earlier network of relationships. The range of options available to the therapist becomes severely restricted.

The Supervision of Displacement

Professional literature on the supervision of displacement is virtually nonexistent. In books and articles the issues that cluster around this topic are usually framed in different categories.

The subject is frequently treated in terms of the relative importance in the training experience of personal growth and therapy versus case management and strategy (Liddle and Halpin 1979). Fundamentally, the issue arises out of therapy orientations themselves, some systems recognizing and coping with displacement in the therapeutic process, others discounting it or dismissing it so far as supervision and case planning are concerned.

Bowen (1978) and his associates (Guerin and Fogarty 1972) recognize the role that fusion and displacement can play in the therapeutic process. Their approach, in effect, realizes the possibility of displacement but attempts to counteract it by encouraging trainees and supervisors alike to work on the continuing task of individuation. In family voyages and the ongoing research of one's own family one is continually learning how to move in and out of many kinds of relationships with objectivity and without becoming emotionally fused. This unremitting process of differentiation acts as an inhibitor of displacement in therapy.

To be developed in this chapter is the thesis that displacement, *when it occurs in the therapeutic system*, represents one of the most teachable moments in the supervisory and training process. The subject to be examined here is an all-important element in couple therapy, namely, the training of the one who is the designer and director of the therapeutic process.

As one method of investigating the phenomenon of student displacement in the therapeutic system and the supervision of it, the author frequently asks trainees to write up an episode as thoroughly and as soon as possible after it occurs. Thus, access is afforded to the student's experience in the incident as well as to the supervisor's. This approach represents a corrective to a mode in which the entire process is interpreted exclusively and one-sidedly from the supervisor's point of view.

The account which follows, then, was recorded by the trainee within hours of the time when it took place. Begun shortly following the supervisory group in which it occurred, it was completed later the same evening. The student's handwritten narrative, thus, relects an immediate preservation of firsthand experience.

Presentation of this supervisory record here, then, will take a new format. In the column to the left will appear the supervisor's internal awareness as the episode unfolds, to the right the student's. Thus, the interaction flow between the supervisor's experience and the student's can be traced in moment-by-moment self-interpretation by each. What the supervisor sees and hears, the patterns he forms, the interventions he makes and the reasons for making them will all be presented in his first person narrative. Intermingled with that recital of evolving events will be the student's own narrative, his perceptions, his thoughts, his feelings, his intentions, and his actions.

CASE EXAMPLE

Student: My gestalt experience is one that I will never forget. What I will do here is reconstruct my experience as it occurred. It all started with my fear of using gestalt in an actual session with some clients.

Supervisor: Bob has been working with a couple whose engagement has been fairly stormy. The female partner's father died about three years earlier. In the previous few minutes the entire team of trainees and supervisors has concurred with Bob that his client probably needs to do some experiential work to complete her unfinished relationship and her grief with her father. As we talk further about creating an intervention design in which he would direct his client through a fantasized dialogue with her father, he abruptly says:

Student:"That's kind of scary."

Supervisor:"What's scary about it?" I mentally frame an anticipatory interaction field of Bob and his client, and I hear him responding to that field with a feeling of fear. I want to hear how he is framing it, interpreting it, thus evoking fear in himself.

Student: Frank has asked me what it is that makes me feel scared. I answer by saying, "I don't want to mess anybody up."

Supervisor: Bob frames the interaction as one in which he acts and by that acting can cause harm to his client. I infer that he ascribes power to himself in the therapist's role, in this case in a very active, directing function.

Student: I am thinking of an article about how gestalt can be dangerous to the client if it is used wrong or if the person doing the gestalt doesn't know what he or she is doing.

Supervisor: I do not really have any reliable evidence at this point, but I conjecture that displacement could be going on in Bob. Whether it is or not, an appropriate supervisory design at this moment is to have Bob simulate an imaginary encounter with his client. I want him to rehearse the anticipatory situation in which he directs his client through an experience. This approach replicates the interaction field in which he is feeling fear and gives us a chance to walk through it together. If there is displacement, the enactment will tease it out. If there is not, the same simulation will let him practice being direct and authoritative. I and the other members of the team can coach or double where indicated.

I get up and put two chairs face to face, thus sculpting the interaction field metaphorically. Then I motion Bob into one of the chairs. "Bob, I'd like you to be the client that Bob is messing up. Could you give us a stream of consciousness of what's happening to you. How is Bob messing you up?" By starting with the client in the field, I am attempting to elicit information about the effect of his action, his direction, on her. I can see and hear what she's sensing, thinking, feeling, wanting. As he projects himself onto the client he is messing up, I can, in effect, observe the consequences of Bob's action.

Student: I believe then that Frank asked me who I had messed up. He told me to talk to that person.

Supervisor: Bob and I have different recall of this sequence of exchanges. But I do remember having him be, first of all, someone whom Bob has messed up.

Student: I respond by saying that I thought I had messed up my brother, my twin brother, Rich's life. I did this by always being superior in anything I did. I can feel myself choking up. It is a feeling that is very hard to explain.

Supervisor: Since Bob is fairly round-cheeked and bearded, it was easy to see the flush that came into his face, the tears in his eyes, and the raspiness in his voice.

Displacement is confirmed, and the relationship, the past interaction field that is entering into Bob's experience, has to do with his brother, Rich. It is clear, too, that in Bob's mind to be active and direct with his client is to reenact symbolically his superiority with Rich. I do not know what behavior on his part goes into his self-interpretation of superiority. But I do infer that that behavior, whatever it is or was, somehow messed up Rich, whatever that means.

For now, I simply want to articulate

and thus catalyze Bob's superior self-image. "I don't know if this will lead anywhere or not," I said, "but I'd like to feed you a sentence." I like to offer interventions like feeding a sentence experimentally, tentatively. If Bob participates in it and wants to claim it, fine. If not, I am ready to move on, letting his frame of reference serve as the outline of the enactment.

Student: I say, "Fine." I am feeling strong and confident. I like the feeling.

Supervisor: "I've always been Top-Dog, Rich," . . . Bob starts nodding and now crying more openly.

Student: I feel like my world is coming apart. Tears fill my eyes. I feel myself losing control.

Supervisor: "Do you want to go on?" I ask Bob. I do not want to press on, if his emotionality and stress have become intolerable.

Student: Frank asks me if I want to go on. I say, "Yes, I do." I feel a strong desire to go on. The pain is here, yet a good feeling is also present.

Supervisor: I assume that considerable experience is being represented through Bob's tears. Using the sensory continuum, I direct, "Be your tears. What are they saying?"

Supervisor: Bob remembers this instruction differently.

Student: Frank tells me to talk to my tears. I respond by saying that my tears are saying, "I'm sorry, Rich.

Bob, nevertheless, follows the directive and even goes beyond it, having his tears, that is, that portion of himself address his brother directly. The message being channeled via the tears is the feeling of remorse. Bob can recall specific instances in which his superior attitude has inflicted pain.

As I tune in to Bob's tone, I hear a note of contrition in his voice, as though now he is Under-Dog imploring his brother for forgiveness. I direct Bob, "Would you get on your knees and tell Rich these things." I want him to embody his pleading position.

Supervisor: Fritz Perls' apt saying, "Under-Dog always wins," crosses my mind here, because I see Bob feeling deep and painful regret and guilt. With that paradoxical reframing of the interaction, I now see Rich in the chair, looking down at his penitent brother.

I say to Bob, "Would you now be Rich and stand in this chair, looking down at Bob." I want to sculpt this new field in its present form. I wait for him to assume this position before proceeding. I want to see where he is experientially, once in the chair.

I'm sorry I've messed up your life. I'm sorry if my being superior has left you second best . . . has caused you pain. I can remember instances where I have caused you pain."

Student: Frank has me get on the floor and be Under-Dog. I look up and get a real feeling of what Rich might have felt. I can't remember what I say at this point.

Student: Frank has me stand on a chair and be Top-Dog talking to Under-Dog. As I get into the chair I suddenly feel like I have been here before. I look down, and Rich's face is right in front of me. "I'm not Top-Dog, and you're not Under-Dog," I say to Rich. "I'm no better than you are. I have never been, and I never will be. We are equal. I love you, Rich. You've helped me out so much in my life. You've always been there when I needed you, and now I want to help you."

Supervisor: Bob gets into the chair, but instead of becoming Rich, he reverts to being himself in that position. He spontaneously begins to address Rich directly.

Supervisor: "Be Rich now. What does he say?" I ask.

Student: Then I am Under-Dog again. Under-Dog responded by saying, "I understand. And I love you and feel equal to you." I have a tremendous feeling hearing Rich say that to me. I felt as though a big weight had been taken off my shoulders.

Supervisor: Bob looks visibly pleased and relieved.

Student: I say to Rich, "I hope you're not going to school just to keep up with me. I want you to do what *you* want to do. I want you to be happy."

Supervisor: I sense that the fusion of the displacement has been broken, clarified. His brother's face is no longer on that of his client. The painful memories and feelings of remorse associated with Rich have once again been placed in that field, that milieu. Now I want to ascertain where Bob is as he once more confronts his prospective role as an active therapist. So I instruct him, "Now, Bob, I'd like you to be yourself and talk to your client about the upcoming session." I move up two new chairs in order clearly to delineate a new field of interaction, the present one.

Student: Frank tells me to be myself now and talk to my client. I respond by saying to her, "I was afraid to do gestalt with you because of the chance of messing you up, like I thought I had done to my brother. I'll still make some mistakes, but my real concern is to help you."

Supervisor: "What does the client say?" I ask him. "Come over here and be her." Bob moves over to the client position.

Student: (as Client) "I know you might make mistakes," I say as the client. "But I am willing to take that risk because of the strong desire I feel from you to want to help."

I then go back to my chair and say, "That makes me feel like a million bucks." I knew (reverting to the past tense as he starts wrapping up the summary) right then that I would be able to do the gestalt work with my clients. I also realized that the reason I was scared to do it in the first place was because unconsciously I had put my brother's face on my clients and was afraid of messing them up like I thought I had messed him up. I now realize that I did make mistakes with Rich and that I'll make mistakes with my clients. But the important thing is I want to help people. I'm ready to do it. I know I can.

Bob did conduct the fantasized dialogue between the client and her father. Through it all, through her intense emotionality, a mixture of sadness and disappointment and anger, he remained firmly in control and unanxious. Throughout the remainder of his training program he became steadily bolder and self-confident, a therapist able to assume the leadership responsibility that was his.

Displacement, to summarize, places the therapist at the point of an impasse in the therapeutic system. Fused, unable to differentiate between the present situation and some past or extraneous one, a host of old emotions aroused, the therapist almost cannot continue. Or should he or she try to press on, therapeutic effectiveness is diminished.

Experiential supervision begins by placing the trainee in the interaction field that has him or her bound. Using all the repertoire of experiential intervention, sculpting, gestalt, systems, communication, the supervisor walks the student through that field. At a minimum the simulation helps the student rehearse the situation, identify the points of stress, and practice new procedures to move on. If, however, displacement is unearthed, the simulation enables the trainee to go to that time and place, that milieu, in which his or her own unfinished business has occurred. Once there in imagination, reliving that earlier set of interactions, the student can complete relationship phases, redecide old family roles and scripts, and go through the painful emotionality that has come back to haunt him or her.

Experiential supervision, by way of no small secondary gain, models the very types of procedures that the student himself or herself is learning to acquire. The capacity to imitate these competencies is greatly increased by the trainee's having experienced them firsthand. They are not, then, merely cues to be recognized from afar and then emulated. They have been guidelines in an experience that has mattered in one's own life. One has heard them and seen them and undergone their consequences for oneself. One has stood where the client will stand.

CRITIQUE

In a fairly recent publication Haley (1976) devotes an entire chapter to the subject of training in family therapy. In this writing, as he so often has done in historical analyses of the field, he sharply delineates many of the crucial issues in supervision and the making of the therapist.

Taking it for granted that supervisors operate on basic premises about the nature of therapy and training, Haley proceeds to lay out in polar extremes two approaches, one labeled *Orientation A* and the second *Orientation Z*.

Extremes, of course, are like straw men, easily pushed over in their very inflexibility. Haley's polarities will be utilized here, not for the worthless exercise of knocking them over, but as a framework within which to conduct a critical discussion of the issue of supervision and displacement. The polarized propositions of Haley's two orientations will be examined from the vantage point of the experiential supervisor.

Personal Growth Versus Problem Solving

One of the first lines demarcating the two orientations lies in their respective emphasis on personal growth versus problem solving in training and therapy. In Orientation A, says Haley, the trainee is encouraged to enter personal therapy on the assumption that this experience will enable him or her to learn what the human mind is all about, to become a mature and developed individual, and to be an expert therapist. A supervisor of this persuasion would tend to emphasize the personality and personal problems of the student therapist. He or she might bring students together and ask them to simulate families, not only as a way of learning about relationships but also to understand themselves better. Encounter and family sculpting techniques are sometimes employed. In some cases, Haley contends, this group experience could comprise the entire training experience, the supervisor never actually observing the trainee's therapy. From the viewpoint of this Orientation if a student has difficulty with authority figures in therapy, he or she would be encouraged to understand how he feels about such personages and to resolve that personal problem.

Standing behind this training approach is a view of therapy as education and enrichment. If symptoms or problems are brought to the therapist of this persuasion, he or she is likely to leave the details about them unexamined and to focus, instead, on the general background of the client. Often, such a therapist will attempt to persuade the couple or family that what they want is really something different from the complaint they bring. The treatment approach is interpretive and experiential.

The supervisor in Orientation Z, by contrast, focuses on helping the student solve the problems he meets in therapy. The student grows by success in performing that task, and the supervisor's objective, therefore, is to help him or her function well. This supervisor operates on the belief that therapy cannot be learned by reading about it, hearing lectures about it, seeing others do it, though that can be valuable, or having discussions or case conferences. It is learned by doing therapy face to face while guided by a supervisor at the moment the process is happening.

The economical way to do such training is a group. Students become a team in which their exposure to cases is increased via live observation of one another's work, and in which the supervisor's guidance is made available to all. Within this group approach, however, the supervisor's functions are consistent with the underlying therapeutic system—planning strategies, giving directives, guiding students to solve their therapy problems. If a trainee is having difficulty handling an authority figure in therapy, the supervisor provides specific ways to deal with such clients.

Thus, supervision in Orientation Z is consistent with its underlying therapy approach, in which the therapist is a problem solver. The problems of the client, in this persuasion, are taken as presented. Getting clients over the specific problems they bring to therapy is the task in focus.

The experiential supervisor, and here the author speaks for himself, concurs with Orientation A in the importance of personal growth. He would very much encourage students and their partners to engage in such experiences as the structured communications training program and, following that, an experiential couples group. The former not only can enrich the trainee's own intimate relationship, but also facilitate the acquisition of skills bearing on therapy. The highly structured exercises of the communications training group require the student to become very adept in sorting out elements of self-awareness, for example, to discriminate between perceptions, interpretations, feelings, and intentions. He or she has to learn to recognize styles of interpersonal communication, those in which partners mind read or interpret the subjectivity of their partner, as contrasted with a more open, self-disclosed style. In asking process questions in the course of the training group, the student develops skills with enormous applications to the tasks of therapy. Finally, in those exercises where he or she has to observe and provide feedback to other couples, there can be an increase of competencies which transfer directly to the therapy situation. The training group, thus, is an enrichment experience that adds skills critical to the implementation of the communications mode of therapy.

The experiential group, aside from helping trainees and their partners clarify boundaries and patterns in the deeper structures of their relationship, can help students increase the range of human situations in which they can operate with objectivity and a lack of fusion. The goal of the experiential group is not just self-understanding, although students and their partners will learn to recognize unclear and rigid boundaries, triadic process, parentification dynamics, injunctions and decisions, and other elements of the deep structure, in their own lives and in others'. The objective is differentiation, that is coming close to these highly charged family dynamics and learning how to function within them without becoming anxious, fused, overinvolved, or disengaged.

The experiential therapist would find it difficult even to think in Orientation A's terms about personal therapy for the student. He would not have the pathology bias implied is such an outlook. Therapy for therapy's sake would never be recommended to a student in this supervisor's program. If a student did express interest in receiving help for himself or herself and the partner, the therapy used in referral would, preferably, be one that employed and thus modeled methods and attitudes consistent with the training program.

If a student encounters a problem with an authority figure, or some other personage or situation, the experiential therapist's objective would differ radically with the orientation of A. His goal would not be to work towards understanding alone, for with Z, he does not believe that represents change. He would, as in the case example, attempt to create a simulation that replicates the therapy situation. Displacement may be hypothesized, but the enactment can begin with an intent to help the student solve the problem immediately at hand. If, however, that simulation in fact discloses the operation of diaplacement, the experiential supervisor would regard it as part of his function to help the student cope with that problem. He would not tell the trainee nor imply that this is a problem he should not have or that it really is not what he thinks, but something else. That approach, he believes, would only exacerbate the trainee's dilemma by interposing a new authority figure, the supervisor. However, should such displacement take place with the supervisor, it would be used experientially as an enactment that could transfer back to the therapy situation.

The experiential supervisor thinks analogically with his student. He can begin with the presenting concern of the trainee, focusing on the surface structure. When Bob says, "That's scary. I don't want to mess her up," the supervisor starts with that concern and recreates an interaction field in which to work on it. But as soon as he begins to rehearse the anticipated therapy encounter, Bob spontaneously goes to another interaction field, and displacement occurs. The supervisor had been prepared to work with the student in solving the problem as initially presented, but he also was willing to go with him into the other field of interaction once its influence had surfaced.

Unlike Orientation A, in which the student's presenting concern is dismissed in order to get on to his general life, the experiential supervisor began with the therapy situation as presented. Unlike Z, which insists on keeping the focus of supervision on the presenting symptom, the experiential supervisor was able to move with the student to the deeper structure. It is not that the student and supervisor are moving to a new problem, but instead, to another level in the original problem. Bob's unfinished remorse with his brother was simply the depth dimension of an analogue that manifested itself at the surface structure, in his fear of becoming active and directive with his client. We were not, in the simulation, talking about a new problem, but a new dimension of the presenting one.

The supervision of the displacement, as the case example demonstrates, is far more than merely interpretive, as Haley defines the goal of Orientation A. Helping the student to see, pointing out, explaining, helping him to gain insight, and other such phrases fall far short of the interventions in experiential supervision. Directing the student to enact, to say directly, to rehearse, to practice new behaviors, to express disquieting feelings, are but some of the actions performed by the supervisor.

In Orientation Z, which insists on the primacy of problem solving over against personal growth, Haley is driving home the absolute importance of doing therapy under supervision while being actively observed. Growth experiences, lectures, readings, and so forth do not necessarily transfer into the practice of therapeutic effectiveness. And that performance, he insists, entails competency in planning strategies and giving specific directives that solve the problems presented by the client.

The experiential supervisor agrees with Orientation Z's belief that the acid test of learning takes place in the therapy situation itself. Communications training can enrich skills, experiential groups can clarify deep structures, and family voyages can facilitate individuation, but these learnings are of no avail, *so far as therapy is concerned,* unless they produce results. Bob's completion of unfinished business with his brother may be a highly beneficial growth experience for himself, but its fruitfulness for therapy comes in his capacity to direct his client through a potentially painful experience.

The experiential supervisor differs with Orientation Z in its implied view that personal growth experiences cannot and do not transfer into therapy. Bob's case is a prime example of the way a trainee's range of behavior is severely restricted by incomplete differentiation of self. So long as he viewed the anticipated therapy session as an over-under interaction, that framework was provoking fear and anxiety. One can argue, against Z, that while Bob experienced the situation as one in which he could do harm and come to remorse, the supervisor's giving directions would have compounded his stress. Had he not begun first with the simulation, and thus unearthed his student's framework on the situation, the supervisor could not have known that it was the fear of acting that caused Bob's bind.

The experiential supervisor agrees with the value Orientation Z places on live supervision in the team setting. Exposed not only to their own cases but to their peers', being able to observe and plan in a group setting in the supervisor's company, trainees' learning fields are greatly expanded. Moreover, the team approach allows for direct and immediate consultation and intervention while the interview is in progress. Student needs are met in this environment, but so are clients' as well. There is no lag in client care while, during the ensuing week, trainee and supervisor go over videotapes or process notes planning for the next session.

Live supervision provides access to data not available in many others modes. In the case of the female student confronted by the feuding couple, direct viewing behind one-way glass disclosed the visible strain in her face. In a self-reported verbatim the student working with Big Tex most likely would have excluded any mention of his own underlying intent, since he was unaware of it himself. Live observation allowed peers and supervisor to hear his repetitious interaction pattern.

In live observation the supervisor virtually participates in the therapy session with his or her student. Access is available not only to verbal information but to nonverbal auditory and visual channels. The supervisor is, therefore, better prepared to create a reenactment or simulation or rehearsal of the therapeutic system. Other trainees who are part of the team and who also have observed are better equipped to fulfill such functions as standing-in or playing roles. As the therapy field is replicated, the supervisor is ready to direct and facilitate its development.

Spontaneous Versus Planned Change

A second set of polar extremes in Haley's two orientations has to do with spontaneous versus planned change. In Orientation A, what takes place between student and supervisor is spontaneous and unplanned. The supervisor waits to see what concerns the trainee brings to each supervisory interview. As advisor and consultant, the supervisor is not responsible for the outcome of the case. If he has helped the student to understand himself and the case dynamics, the supervisor has done his job.

A's mode of supervision is consistent with the therapy approach in which it is grounded. What happens in a therapy session is unpredictable and spontaneous. It is unplanned. Being a consultant and advisor, the therapist helps clients understand and, armed with that self-understanding, to effect their own change. The therapist is a reactor, but not an enforcer of change.

Z's mode of supervision is to plan with his student what is to happen in therapy. He shares responsibility for case failure or success, and observing directly while therapy is transpiring, he will intervene immediately. Specific directives and actions are provided to help the trainee solve the problem at hand.

Z's supervision is consistent with his orientation to therapy, which is the strategic planning of each session. He is responsible for initiating and enforcing action and change. If not, he is not being responsible in the case.

The experiential supervisor agrees, in one sense, with A's reactive attitude. He realizes that events and phenomena are not always what they seem—that sometimes a trainee's presenting concern, framing of a situation, description of a dynamic, or initial response is not the whole story in the therapy session or case under scrutiny.

Had I rushed in with Bob, for example, to explain the principles and rules of gestalt and with specific directions about the conduct of a fantasized dialogue, I would have run roughshod over much of his experience. I might have said, "Bob, the basic rule is to keep everything occurring in the present. The way to do this is. . . .'" Bob might very well have taken those instructions, carried them out, and felt pleased and productive in doing so. And that success might have reached into and had impact on his unresolved anxieties with Rich, his brother.

But by operating with an attitude of sustained tentativeness, as in therapy itself, the supervisor can remain truly empirical, respecting the dimension of depth that exists in the student, in the client, in the interview process. He can expect serendipity, a paradoxical reframing, the onrush of novel and unexpected emotionality, or the onset of new behaviors.

The somewhat lengthy examination of a case in the literature will demonstrate the benefit of a reactive, spontaneous attitude in therapy and supervision. Sluzki (1978), who aligns himself with a strategic and systems orientation to marital therapy, rules out attention to intentions and motivations in effecting change. It is not that these and other interactional processes are not real and important in human life, but that the systems-oriented therapist *selectively observes* (italics mine) events, filtering in those that are relevant to his model. Those events that are deemed important in this orientation are effects, the organization of interpersonal sequences. The effect of behavior on behavior, not inferences about the intrapsychic dynamics underneath those effects, is the focus of observation and intervention.

Sluzki's orientation is deliberately digital, that is, a prejudging of relevant data for the sake of simplification and prediction. He carefully avoids any construction of processes "inside the black box," as the cybernetician would say, attending only to observable output and input signals.

The case in question began under the facade of individual therapy for a thirty-year-old woman completely crippled by a myriad of severe emotional and somatic symptoms, oppressive headaches, daily vomiting, intense anxiety, and severe depression. The wife of a diplomat, the woman's symptoms *were triggered* (italics mine throughout the case report) by a move to San Francisco from their country due to his work. The husband was engaged in the second therapy session, after one interview with the wife precipitated a stormy depression, accompanied by daily vomiting, headaches, and abdominal pain. Sluzki implemented the systems treatment principle of specifying the step or event in a sequence of events that led to the emergence of symptoms. The therapist proposed that there was some behavior in the nonsymptomatic spouse, the husband, that preceded and contributed to an explanation of the wife's symptoms. The suggestion was met by incredulity in both partners. After a flare up of symptoms following a period of quiescence, the therapist was able to detect and to show the couple that when the husband began to experience anxiety in connection with his complex job, the wife would respond to that cue with a flare of symptoms. The husband then began to care for the wife, and his anxiety would vanish, freeing him for effective performance.

The trade-off, thus, was that her symptoms allowed him to be *free of anxiety*, mainly around death and departures, which otherwise overwhelmed him. The husband's performance became quite shaky once, reports Sluzki, due to anxiety when the wife was on vacation and new requirements occurred in his job. His protective behavior, in turn, allowed the wife to remain *childlike* while remaining in control of most of the decisions in the relationship.

Then Sluzki describes an interaction sequence based on this homeostatic pattern. During a session in which the prospect of yet another move and change in job responsibilities was under discussion, the wife complained of headaches, less intense than before, but still present. The therapist acknowledged the wife's contribution to her husband in reporting these symptoms, praised her sacrifice, and praised him for allowing her to be so useful. It was prescribed for the husband, almost gamelike, that during the following week he should tell his wife immediately of his own anxieties and worries rather than appeasing her.

In the following session, they reported that he was quite anxious and that she didn't have any symptoms. He reported, and was told to tell his wife, that she so flooded him with her problems and symptoms that he hardly had a chance to express his worries. She responded that she was fully aware of his worries about his future job, to which he replied that his concern really had to do with completing his present duties. She brushed him off, writes Sluzki, saying in effect that he didn't have any problems at the office. The therapist commented that her definition of helping, right then, was to appease, while his of being helped was to be listened to. She stated, teary-eyed, that she felt frustrated because he did not allow her to open up to him, which *startled* him. He told her, astonished, that that her perception went completely against his sense of things, that *he considered himself very sensitive in relation to her and allowed her to speak to him about anything whenever she felt anxious in order to facilitate her relief.* She told him, tenderly, says Sluzki, that he was attentive when she was loaded with symptoms, but not in connection with other concerns. For her, he was almost *like a father, shushing her, minimizing her, treating her like a child.*

Sluzki stressed to both of them that her appeasing and his shushing had been useful, but that both were saying it was no longer satisfying. They agreed and concurred that they would defend each one's right to be anxious. The whole symptomatic pattern broke within three months, concludes Sluzki, and was replaced by one that was more mutual and that did not require symptoms.

For this experiential therapist and supervisor, this case, as presented, highlights one part of the digital, problem-solving, strategic orientation—its selective inattention to information. The consistent application of his own treatment principle—to search out the step of events that precedes what Sluzki (1978, p. 378) describes as the first step in a sequence—would require him to identify the husband's anxiety over death and separation as such a step. The wife's first symptoms *were triggered* by a recent move, a second set by the discussion of a possible upcoming move, and the husband's anxiety mounted on one occasion during the wife's absence on vacation.

Once that anxiety increases (and it is Sluzki, not the experientialist, who puts the emotion inside the black box, contrary to his own stated orientation) homeostatic mechanisms of the secondary order, to use von Bertalanffy's term, set in. The wife produces symptoms which deflect him from that anxiety, and even when he comes close to expressing his worries, she appeases rather than letting him undergo the full intensity of his emotion. For the experientialist, this is fusion of the first order, she inhibiting his full emotional intensity by a pseudo-appeasement. Likewise, by becoming preoccupied with her symptoms, he avoids the full impact of his anxiety—until, we may speculate, the next round of moves and separations.

To the wife, who protests her *childlike* state and her husband's fatherlike shushings, the experientialist, in a paradoxical reframing, might suggest that she be careful in saying that she wants a different kind of intimacy. She could get it. Should her husband truly express his emotionality associated with death and separation, conjectures the experientialist, she could well be faced with a husband who is vulnerable, and not father-like, which could heighten her anxiety at relating on an equalitarian, non parent-child basis.

In short, the experientialist asks what the most approximate definition of the problem is. If the strategic approach can move from the wife's presenting symptoms to the homeostatic mechanism in which those symptoms have a useful purpose, why not also to the husband's anxiety concerning death, departure, and separation? These latter dimensions could take the therapeutic process into more primary interaction patterns, following von Bertalanffy's concept. The data lend themselves to the hypothesis of some order of unfinished business on the husband's part, from whose emotional intensity the wife's symptoms serve as a shield. That hypothesis may not be borne out, but not to attend to the anxiety which appears to be a precursor to the homeostatic loop seems highly selective and circumscribed. Moreover, surely the reduction of the husband's painful anxiety is at least as important as allieviating the wife's painful symptoms. That reduction, in fact, could well be the only lasting prevention of yet another eruption of the wife's symptomatology during some later separation anxiety in the husband.

While the experiential supervisor and therapist flows with the spontaneous and unpredictable, his assumption of leadership in the therapeutic process is active and vigorous. So willing to take charge is the experientialist, in fact, that his response to an anxious concern is immediate. The creation of the interaction field is begun, the therapist or supervisor giving numerous and specific directives: sculpt; say it directly; exaggerate that position; it's painful, but say it; what are you going to do about that? (With Bob, for instance, my response to his feeling of fear was instantaneous. We did not talk *about* it, but began immediately to enact it.) Attending to phenomena as they poured forth, the supervisor formulated patterns and interceded with specific directives. Reacting to events, on the one hand, and making them happen, on the other, the supervisor was both respondant and initiator in the enactment.

The expectation of brief, intensive therapy is constantly present for the experientialist. Deep and long-standing patterns can be evoked, addressed, and clarified in the first session. The therapist's approach, in effect, says to the couple, "Let's reconstruct this situation and take a look at it." And as that replication transpires deep levels of interaction and antecedent conditions can be elicited and confronted rapidly.

The experiental supervisor stands with Orientation Z in sharing responsibility with the student for strategic planning of sessions and for the overall course of therapy. Trainee and supervisor work together in tracing and sorting information, forming patterns, setting goals, and designing interventions. Bob's simulation followed on the heels of planning for the forthcoming therapy interview that same evening. The supervisor, hearing his student's expressed fear and anxiety, responded immediately by initiating a simulation to explore and rehearse the anticipated situation. When the trainee spontaneously moved to another, antecedent field that was bearing on the impending therapy session, the supervisor went with and guided his student through that other level of concern. Having clarified and completed that unfinished business, the anxiety level reduced, the supervisor immediately came back to the therapy session and directed his student in a rehearsal of it. The proof of that strategy came in Bob's active direction that evening of the mutually planned therapeutic design.

Understanding Versus Action

The final set of polarities in Orientations A and Z has been implicit in the two preceding, but it still merits explicit consideration. One Orientation, A, regards understanding as the basis of change, while the other, Z, views action as its cause.

A assumes that people, in becoming more aware and understanding themselves cognitively and experientially, will change. This approach seeks, therefore, to lift repression by making the unconscious conscious, to emphasize the expression of real emotionality, to interpret communication, and to facilitate understanding of interaction patterns. Stressing self-awareness and individual experience, supervisor A may bring clients together in simulated families, or real families, in the conviction that learning and understanding will produce change.

Supervision, in A's orientation, consists of talk and discussion of the trainee's conduct in the case. If the student can form an understanding of his involvement with his clients, he will become a competent therapist. Self-knowledge being the goal of training, students are brought together in encounter groups, are referred for personal therapy, are expected to participate in simulated family exercises, and/or assigned the task of contacting relatives to help understand their involvements in the extended kin network.

Z, by contrast, believes that the therapist must plan strategies and devise directives requiring new behavior. These behavioral programs may be planned for individuals or for the family together, but in either case they are designed for and within the natural group. Problems cannot be solved by talking about them; therefore, they have to be brought into the therapy session itself and action taken there.

In supervising, Z offers active, specific directives for solving the problems of therapy. Group activities are for planning strategy and stages of therapy.

Z, in fact, feels so strongly about the inappropriateness and worthlessness of such experiences as simulated families, personal therapy, and other related activities that he consents to a student bill of rights which says that

> no teacher may inquire into the personal life of a therapy student, no matter how benevolently, unless: (1) he can justify how this information is relevant to the immediate therapy task in a case, and (2) he can state specifically how this inquiry will change the therapist's behavior in the way desired. [Haley 1976]

It is in between the extremities of understanding and behavior that issues have to be compressed, into a continuum which, to be sure, does not appear so crisp and sharp, but which may be a more faithful conception of reality. There are gradations of understanding.

Take Bob, the student therapist, for instance. Bob read about the fantasized dialogue procedure and, therefore, had some abstract knowledge concerning it. That knowledge, as Orientation Z would hold, was worthless until applied, that is, practiced in face-to-face therapy. Once could hold, in fact, that Bob's abstract knowledge, knowing the rudiments of what to do but never having done it, was precipitating his anxiety. A second grade of understanding would be at the level of recognition. Bob had seen and heard the fantasized dialogue modeled by the supervisor and peers. Using abstract theory that students had read, the supervisor had broken open the procedures into observable cues and stages that could be imitated. This ability to perceive the elements and sequences in the procedure constituted a further stage of learning. Practicing the procedures in a simulation would bring the trainee even closer to the intervention and thus form a new grade of knowledge.

Once the student begins to practice the behaviors, to rehearse the giving of directions, he shifts from understanding based on comprehension and recognition to one grounded in doing. He is now emitting audible and visible actions that constitute behavior. He suddenly frames the situation as an over-under interaction. That interpretation or cognition, for the experiential supervisor, is likewise behavior, for it reconstructs the situation. The student's behavior now takes place in an interaction field of his own making, and that formation of a new mental habitat for himself is, likewise, behavior. In fact, the construction of a mental framework is a powerful act of behavior, because now the student, the prospective client, and the supervisor exist in that world of Bob's making.

Into Bob's reconstruction of the situation has gone displacement, the projection of another field of interaction onto the present one. And that projection, too, for the experiential supervisor, is behavior. It is an organized mental state which is objectively accessible with proper methods of investigation. Having thus interpreted the therapy situation the way he did, evoked in the student was a cluster of emotions, particularly fear and anxiety. And that emotionality, too, is behavior, experienced in feeling states or in kinesthetic sensations in the organism. The student wants to avoid that situation as he has it framed, and that intention is likewise behavior. Uttering such words as, "That's scary," and representing his underlying emotionality via a hushed tone of voice and a flushed facial expression are, likewise, behavior.

When Bob confronts his brother in the enactment, that, too, is behavior. The deep structure, at that moment, is not back there, but is immediately present. It is analogically represented through the channels of his tears, his visible facial and bodily strain, his agitated tone of voice. *His symbolic reenactment of the past in the present is as much an organized and repetitive interaction sequence as the homeostatic mechanisms of the surface structure.* It is, if the supervisor will remain empirically open to it, as observable and accessible as other orders of behavior.

As to the student bill of rights proposed by Z, the experiential supervisor has the following response. He would strongly encourage trainees to undergo communications training, experiential groups, and family voyages, not because they necessarily transfer over to therapy, but because they can add skills and facilitate objectivity in the student. But the experiential supervisor would not inquire into the student's personhood unless and until his or her subjectivity intrudes itself inappropriately into the therapeutic process. Then, the experiential supervisor would intervene, viewing such displacement as one of the optimum moments for the trainee's personal and professional growth. The student, at such a time, is truly disclosed in a concrete field of interaction, where past and present, the overt and the covert, are intertwined. *A decisive breakthrough in professional performance can affect personal growth, and, a decisive transition in personal growth can effect giant leaps forward in professional competence.* At such a time the supervisor would be irresponsible not to respond to the student's personhood. Failure to do so because of his own selective and restricted understanding of behavior would be a highly subjective and biased orientation.

The bill of rights should be amended to include the following:

> Moreover, no teacher may refuse to inquire into the personal life of a therapy student when that experience has intruded into and is interfering with his performance as a therapist.

The Continuing Task

It is a mistake to assume that the therapist's tendencies towards displacement are necessarily resolved once and for all with the completion of formal training and supervision. Each of the countless therapeutic involvements undertaken becomes a new and unique multipersonal system. In each one the possibilities are there for the therapist himself or herself covertly to make a subjective assignment onto one or both clients. Or again, unknowingly, the therapist can comply with an assignment made by one or both clients, becoming an object who subsequently distorts and obstructs therapeutic progress. For the therapist a given couple's situation can become a symbolic reenactment of some past and yet unfinished interaction field from his or her own history. Old interaction patterns then come into play, inappropriately rendering the therapist inflexible, relatively closed, and rigid in his or her therapeutic actions.

In the therapeutic system, as in all human relationships, the therapist is called upon to move in and out of a number of relationship phases and to keep the boundaries clear in each of these interactions. Thus, the delicate balance must be maintained at all times between becoming involved without becoming enmeshed, acting autonomously without becoming disengaged, moving incessantly toward termination without pushing too fast nor holding on too long, fostering individuation without producing emotional cutoffs, facilitating rejoining without provoking a rebinding of clients into dysfunctional patterns. While he or she is negotiating the ebb and flow of these stages the possibility is everpresent for fusion. In whatever form it takes, such displacement causes the therapist to function with heightened anxiety, to become emotionally overwhelmed, and thus to operate with diminished objectivity.

The cycle of becoming involved includes such actions as listening, being empathetic, joining, accommodating, risking vulnerability, and even using oneself therapeutically in the client's subject-object assignments. Running alongside and throughout this phase is the risk of overinvolvement. Then the therapist becomes too nurturing, too willing to give in during the battle for structure and leadership of the system, too in need of affiliating and belonging, too overresponsible for the work that is done, too in need of the displacements that are made upon himself or herself.

As Boszormenyi-Nagy (1965), Liberman (1972), Minuchin (1974), and virtually every other author has stressed, failure of the therapist to become involved by forming and maintaining a warm and trusting relationship with clients will result, probably, in his or her not having the chance to assume more active and direct leadership operations. The game is lost before it really begins. But if the therapist needs too much to join, almost symbiotically, too much to belong and be thought well of, too much to rescue, too much to succeed, too much to get results, the door is open for the manipulations, the fusions, and the impasses of displacement.

As is so often the case, the more tacit and subsidiary such displacements are, the more counter-productive they can become. Goulding (1972), for example, cites the pitfalls of the therapist's use of the counter-injunction and the witch message, that is, placing himself or herself in the position of a surrogate and nurturing parent with the client(s). Viewing the client as a victim of his or her parents' conditions of worth, or injunctions, the therapist moves to become the "good" parental figure. Clients are encouraged to deny their real parents, to turn off the "witch messages" given in the family of origin, and to operate instead on the new conditions or counter-injunctions now provided by the therapist.

Recognizing that such methods can work, Goulding nevertheless has found that in the long run clients change by recognizing and experiencing their earlier life decisions made in response to the parents' injunctions and by existentially redeciding them in the therapeutic environment. Otherwise, the client does not really say goodbye to the past, holds others responsible for his or her situation, clutches to long-standing resentments, and continues to live in self-defeating scripts or games.

If the therapist does not interpose himself or herself as the substitute parent, however, the client can continue the therapeutic process of coming to terms with the family of origin. Recognizing that the parents were real people whose actions can be understood in the light of their situation, the client can perhaps forgive them, perhaps rejoin them. They were perhaps hurt and disappointed themselves and passed some of their pain on to their children.

While there are those therapists who deliberately utilize the counter-injunction and know that they are doing so and why, the danger comes in projecting oneself into that role and not truly realizing it or knowing why. To mystify the client's parents as witches or monsters may well reflect the therapist's own unfinished past, lingering resentments, and lack of forgiveness and rejoining. The therapist then aborts the continuing progress of his or her clients towards a resolution of the past and its pain and disappointments, as well as a rejoining with the parents on some new basis of belonging and mutual understanding. The therapist may then be the active agent of the emotional cutoff observed by Bowen (1978).

The autonomous phase of interpersonal interaction requires the therapist to engage in such actions as assuming leadership, battling for structure, directing, creating, and in general taking those steps necessary to alter, restructure, redirect, and change the maladaptive marital relationship. The risk of disengagement comes in becoming too active, too insensitive, too intentional or cocksure of one's self, too precipitous, too hasty, too selective in one's attention and interpretations. A too rigid boundary cuts the therapist off from receptivity to the clients' emotionality, frame of reference, metacommunications, and emerging stream of experience. The tentativeness that allows for the unexpected, the novel, and the sudden reframing can be suppressed or lost. Therapy as an evolving and cascading process can be nipped prematurely, resulting in perhaps a superficial or one-sided form of change.

Yet another relationship phase that the therapist constantly encounters during his or her work with couples is that of individuation. Partners differentiate from each other and from their respective families of origin. The therapist is continuously acting to ensure that partners speak only for themselves and that they attend and listen to the other accurately. Individuality and separateness are preserved and fostered in the midst of mutuality and togetherness.

In therapeutic sessions, therefore, the therapist is ever and again telling clients to address each other directly, is blocking their attempts to speak for or to coerce the other, is making explicit what is implicit and often covert, is inhibiting projections, is facilitating awareness, or is prescribing action. In the creation and direction of enactments, rehearsals, and fantasized dialogues the therapist comes into the presence of high and intense levels of emotionality, ambiguity, paradox, and impasse.

The potential for fusion and displacement is intensified during such moments. The therapist may hesitate, pull back, avoid, become overwhelmed, or otherwise become stymied in the presence of such face-to-face encounters. Standing by and remaining firmly in control of evolving events can, if displacement occurs, be severely restricted. The therapist's own boundaries become slurred, and diffusion sets in.

Bowen's (1978) findings regarding the importance of the therapist's own continuing differentiation of self can be explained by the following hypothesis: that the more one researches one's family and comes into direct and immediate encounter with a variety of significant others, the more one is equipped to face disquieting emotionality and ambiguity in clients. One can stand by and participate in the struggles of clients because one has already confronted the full impact of such face to face encounter.

Finally, again as in all human relationships, the therapeutic system has to be dissolved. As Paul (1967) aptly notes, the goal of therapy is termination. But once more, displacement on the part of the therapist can skew and delay this objective.

Woven into the very fabric of couple therapy are many instances of relationship dissolution. Such therapy, in fact, often begins with an outright or implicit prospect of relationship rupture. In this stage, as in most instances of grief, marital partners will confront the therapist with varying degrees of anger, guilt, idealization, sadness, blame, helplessness, and failure. Besides keeping himself or herself suitably differentiated from such deep emotionality, the therapist must walk the narrow line between siding with separation versus siding with togetherness.

In the implementation of enactments and rehearsals, moreover, the therapist will be exposed to many instances of unresolved relationships. Individual partners may need to say goodbye to some beloved relative, and while doing so, can bathe the therapist in strong levels of pain, disappointment, and loss. There can be, for some clients, the intense hurt of leaving some script, some invisible loyalty, some role in the family of origin that seems to relegate someone else to a life of misery and meaninglessness. The parentified or triangulated child, for example, often undergoes extreme anguish in deciding to leave that position with its apparent, as experienced or fantasized by the client, awful consequences for the parents and their relationship, or lack of it.

That therapist who cannot, for whatever reason, enable his or her clients to complete these dissolution stages tends only to prolong their displacements, and thus the therapy process itself. Therapy can become one more effort to delay the act of dissolution, to replace or hold on to the lost relationship or some aspect of it, or to use the therapist as an object for ventilating the resentments and pain of some other extrinsic but unfinished relationship.

Resources

Acknowledging the therapist's never-ceasing task of moving in and out of so many relationship phases in a clear and adaptive way, numerous authors have offered proposals for coping with the problem. Napier with Whitaker (1978) has demonstrated the viability of the cotherapist relationship and the joint assistance that each therapist can give the other. Boszormenyi-Nagy (1965) has outlined the ingredients of the cotherapist union within a team context. Goulding (1972), much of whose time and energy has gone into the continuing education of group and family therapists, has rarely found a professional who is still not operating out of some script or remnants of it. Thus, the therapist who continually feels frustrated because his clients do not seem to progress, for example, is probably doing something, or avoiding doing something, that would enable them to move. Or again, the therapist who sets certain goals for therapy and then will not (not *cannot*, as Goulding notes) live up to them is using methods that permit the client(s) to maintain control of the system and frustrate the professional. Goulding, then, offers week-long or month-long workshops that provide an environment in which therapists can replicate and redecide their scripts.

There is a tremendous need within the profession of marriage and family therapy for a resource to meet these recurring teachable moments of personal and professional growth. Such a vehicle would hopefully offer something more than occasional catch-as-catch-can consultation or, as occurs in professional meetings, the presentation of new techniques, outcome results, or demonstrations of magic by the super-therapist. Some of what is required is already happening.

To draw upon a personal anecdote, a few years ago the state marriage and family therapy association of which I was a member decided to offer programs that would directly meet some of the personal and professional needs brought by members to our quarterly and annual meetings. Thus, if the program emphasis was sexual therapy, a training design was carried out that converged on the participants' own sexual attitude restructuring. If the board members and other leaders of the association wanted to focus on their own relationships as a group, a social psychiatrist was brought in to conduct an interpersonal and organizational laboratory for us. This service orientation no doubt accounted for some of the fairly rapid growth of the state group.

But it is on one such workshop that I particularly want to focus. In private practice at the time, I had been for several months mildly depressed and was becoming more so. I was seeing more clients than I really wanted, my economic situation could not have been better, and I was associated with a colleague with whom I truly enjoyed working and knowing as a friend.

But that was precisely the problem. I was doing too much clinical therapy and not enough other things that I also enjoyed. I wanted to teach, to write, to supervise, but with all the clinical involvements, there was not (I was not giving myself) time. There were also occasional clients' life-threatening crises that occurred in the early hours of the morning and which added to my feeling of being overinvolved.

When the next quarterly meeting of our state group came around, then, I made sure I was there. And I went fully determined to work on the depressed experience that I carried with me, to give myself a chance to move out of the isolation and loneliness I was feeling.

I went to a workshop on gestalt therapy. When the leader asked for volunteers who wanted to work, I stepped out, anxious but resolved. When it came my turn to work, I realized instantly that the very act of entering the group of volunteers had been the long-standing decision I had needed to make. I framed the group, some of them friends and others strangers, as my brothers and sisters and the leader as my father. When I addressed them, I told them that I was tired of being alone and wanted to let them know that I needed and wanted them. When the leader afterwards asked me what more I wanted from him, I told him that I wanted to be held and to thank him for taking care of me. As I looked beyond the immediate scene to my friends in the audience and saw their tears, I felt the encouragment and support that the larger group can provide.

The historical context was this. My father left my mother and me when I was two, and I had no further contact with him. It was not until thirty-five years later that, through the gentle nudgings of my friend, Norman Paul, I undertook to retrace my father's history and to visit his grave. But that broaches a whole new story.

Without a father, I became my own parent, precociously and overresponsibly caring for myself and others. It was as if, I realized years later, I decided to show him how he ought to have done it (genealogical research taught me to ask what had happened in his life, with what had he coped). Along with my extreme overresponsibility were also feelings of resentment and envy of others that I had been put in this place.

Thus, in my work with clients the same tendencies that probably made me a committed therapist also made me a resentful and depressed one. Letting myself experience the care I had so long wanted but denied broke the depression and permitted me to make some redecisions.

I cut back on my hours to a limit with which I was comfortable, let myself get back into the writing, teaching, and supervision that I had missed, and in general brought my life back into more manageable proportion.

The reader may by now have recognized that the dynamics I have just been describing constitute some of the deeper levels of the dream simulated in chapter four. Needless to say, with my son, as revealed in the dream, I was both overresponsible and resentful, to say nothing of being envious of him for having a father.

As with training and supervision, therefore, there needs to be a place where the teachable moments that occur in our therapeutic systems can be explored in depth. In professional workshop settings we can replicate those therapeutic relationships that have us stuck, experience our feelings, assumptions, and patterns in them, and redecide some new steps. At the same time, this forum can provide a highly visible and concrete medium in which to examine new methods and procedures. The leader can model his or her magic for us.

To be sure, such work is risky and discloses our vulnerability. Like all teachable moments, however, it is also fraught with opportunity. At a minimum, we will place ourselves where we so often ask our clients to put themselves. Like our clients, we may fear to tread new paths, lest they become one-way and we get lost. Yet to remain conservative, afraid to risk and to change, may mean that both personal and professional life can pass us by. Balancing precariously between letting go and hanging on is hard and awkward. But at least it is vital. And that is what makes the field of marital and family therapy exciting and worthwhile.

Glossary of Interventions

The following is a list of observable procedures used by the therapist in implementing experiential intervention designs. A definition of each procedure is provided along with an example taken from case materials appearing throughout the volume.

Addressing through metaphor. The therapist directs a message to one or more clients by using a figure of speech in which a term or phrase is applied to something to which it is not literally applicable, in order to suggest an analogy or correspondence. The metaphor is especially effective if it has arisen in the course of therapy.

Example. A wife is expressing an anxious sense of responsibility for her husband during an estrangement from him. She is concerned that he may not really know what he is doing or why he is doing it. During therapy she realizes that she is replicating and symbolically reenacting her mother's attitude toward her father. Simulating her mother's example during a fantasized dialogue, she role plays her parent hovering over her husband, telling him how to take care of things around the farm, like the tractor. Abruptly, she leaves the simulation and says to her mother, "Let him fix his own tractor!" She discovers in these experiences her own overinvolved concern with her son.

As a way of consolidating these therapeutic exchanges, the therapist addresses her through metaphor. "You can let him fix his own tractor," he says, referring to both the husband and the son. He applies the phrase to clarify the boundaries, limit her enmeshment with both, affirm their individuality and separateness, and comment on the intergenerational parallels of interaction.

Asking process questions. The therapist asks a client for information on a specific element of his internal experience during an interaction event. Keeping the conceptual scheme of the awareness framework in mind while conducting an ongoing analysis of the client's responses during the interaction unit, the therapist asks questions to elicit missing dimensions of experience. Thus, the therapist inquires what the client is hearing, seeing, thinking, feeling, wanting, or doing.

Example. With Mark during the relationship checkup, the therapist observes that the client consistently interprets his fiancee's subjectivity while never openly sharing his own feelings and intentions. The therapist asks Mark three times what he feels when his partner is hinting and being oblique. Finally, after reflection, Mark says that he feels "like I'm going to be attacked or something." The therapist infers on the basis of this clinical datum that Mark feels threatened and then proceeds to unearth more interpersonal information that discloses the partner's passive aggressive pattern.

Assigning homework. The therapist provides one or both partners with specific suggestions for performance outside and between therapy contacts. Tasks to be carried out extend and elaborate changes, discoveries, and rehearsals that have begun during therapy sessions. They range from the continued shaping of new communication skills that have been modeled and practiced, to face-to-face conversations with significant personages who have been encountered in an enactment or fantasized rehearsal.

Example. Having directed Mark through a simulated rehearsal of an anticipated encounter with his maternal parent, the therapist suggests that the client now talk over some of his discoveries and hunches with her, to test them out. Having evoked new feelings of empathy towards his mother and having generated some new hypotheses that reframe his image of her, he is encouraged to check them out with her. "You might ask her about that," suggests the therapist. This homework task has the potential of clarifying and concretizing the intergenerational transmission process, of furthering Mark's differentiation from the mother and the family of origin, and of facilitating his rejoining his parent on a new basis.

Attending and feeding back. The therapist pays strict attention to visual cues given by one or both partners, and then feeds these perceptions back by carefully conveying an impression designed to reveal their appearance. The client, having had these visual outputs thus described, can contact and interpret the facets of his or her experience that are represented by them.

Example. Kathy has been talking about her tendency to hint and be indirect in making her wishes known to her fiance. The therapist notices her knowing smile and reflects his perception by saying, "You made an expression at that point." She responds by interpreting her awareness evoked by the feedback, "Yeah, I think I should have just come right on out with what I wanted."

Audiotape playback. The therapist plays back for the client some portion of his or her previously recorded material. This playback enables the client to hear not only his or her words but also such auditory cues as tone, volume, or rate of speech. Such self-encounter facilitates the client's empathy with his or her experience represented by these auditory channels, as well as hearing the self as heard by the partner.

Example. Although audiotape playback was not actually used by the therapist in directing Bev's enactment within her family of origin, it could easily and appropriately have been employed. Even after experiencing her parentified position in her childhood family and deciding to opt out of that role, she continues to tell her father and brothers how to handle facets of their lives. Audiotape playback of her simulated directions to each family member could provide her with feedback on her overinvolved, parentified tendencies. She could hear herself continuing to play mother and wife surrogate.

Awareness continuum. The therapist directs the client to amplify or complete some portion of his or her experience that has been represented by some audiotry or visual channel, to become more aware of it, and to assume responsibility for it. The aim is to facilitate the client's contact and awareness of some message being expressed by such observable cues as a certain body posture, a movement, a gesture, tears, or a frown. Sometimes the directive instructs the client to complete, perhaps even to exaggerate the sensory output. At other times, the client is instructed to become the sensation, that is, to identify with it and to speak for it.

Example. A therapy trainee, Bob, has expressed apprehension about directing experiential grief work with his client in a forthcoming session. He does not, as he puts it, "want to muck her up." Directed by his supervisor to carry out a fantasized dialogue with his client, Bob mentally reconstructs the situation and experiences himself once again face-to-face with his twin brother, with whom he has some unfinished business. Tears come to his eyes. The supervisor instructs Bob to become his tears, to speak for them. "What are they saying?" he asks. The student then pours out the pent-up emotionality contained in and represented by his tears. In doing so, he begins to clarify the fusion that has occurred between his brother and his client.

Be there. The therapist, sensing a client's inclination or need to withdraw from activities and concerns in the immediate foreground of attention, directs him or her to be at a place or state that is more comfortable or relevant right at that moment. Specific instructions include such statements as, "Be there in your imagination," or "Be where you want to be." The directive sanctions the pulling back, respects it, and can enable the client to make contact with states or feelings that lie in the background of experience.

Example. Peg has reported disappointment and frustration over what she perceives to be a breakdown in a homework task that had been given to her and her husband the previous week. Her mood moves to one of pervasive discouragement and helplessness, and she declares, "We don't really get to the core." Glancing at the clock, she expresses in her next few exchanges with the therapist an inclination to withdraw from the topics and concerns in the immediate foreground and to be someplace else. She looks down and sighs. The therapist instructs her, "Be there, Peg. There's plenty of time. Where do you want to be?" Pausing, reflecting, she goes in her imagination to the hospital nursery at the time of her son's premature birth. Having gone to that time and place, the therapeutic process now begins an exploration of this new field of interaction.

Be the symbol, image, or metaphor. The therapist directs one of the partners to identify with some symbol, metaphor, or image that has surfaced during the course of therapy and to speak for it or role play it in the first person and in present time. Assuming that the image is analogically connected with several dimensions of the client's experience, such enactment enables him or her to explore and to encounter these levels and their meaning in the present interaction event. Both overt and covert associations can be evoked through this procedure.

Example. A young woman has expressed considerable impatience with her parents over what she perceives to be the blandness and emptiness of their marriage. Wanting to do something about it, she is particularly concerned with her father's disengagement, referring to him as "a hermit." In order to explore the meaning of that image for her, she is instructed to "be the hermit." She goes to a corner of the consultation room and kneels there in what later proves to be a supplicant posture. Others in the group double for her father, teasing out of her image a recognition of his plea for understanding and empathy. Role playing the image permits her to draw together her many perceptions, thoughts, feelings, and wishes in connection with her parent.

Blocking dysfunctional communication. The therapist acts to obstruct one partner's transgressing the other's boundary. When one mate attempts to speak for the other or to coerce the other's thoughts, the therapist can indirectly impede the trespass by being selectively inattentive to the intruder, or by continuing to look at the second and inviting the declaration of his or her own experience. By holding up his hand to the transgressor, the therapist can directly block the overstepping of the partner's boundary and preserve an appropriate separateness and individuality.

Example. In the early stages of the checkup interview with Mark and Kathy, the therapist noted Mark's pronounced tendency to interpret his fiancee's intentions, saying things like, "She didn't know whether I'd go for it or not." By continuing to look at Kathy and being selectively inattentive to Mark's remark, the therapist invites her to speak for herself. Asking her for more information regarding her intentions (a process question), the therapist marked her boundaries even further.

Changing "can't" to "won't." The therapist instructs a partner to convert a statement, "I can't," to "I won't." This procedure probes the client's reluctance or unwillingness to complete some action or to redecide some attitude in the field of interaction. The probe requires the partner to assume responsibility for the reluctance and the impasse implied in it.

Example. During her enactment of her family of origin, Bev has encountered her parentified child position and her propensity, even now, to assume responsibility for her father's and brothers' well-being. At one point, addressing them directly in a simulated conversation, she tells them, "I just can't keep on doing this!" The therapist asks her, "Can you say, 'I won't do this'?" This probe confronts her with her impasse, her invisible loyalties, her guilt, and her resentment. It also lifts up to her the finality of redeciding, with the new attitude and boundaries that implies. She also is confronted with the fact that holding on to her parentified position is her decision, made to avoid the emotional consequences of changing.

Clarifying. This procedure is designed to elicit more information from a partner, but is more general in scope than a specific process question. The therapist may say something like, "I'm not following you there. Can you say more?" This intervention also permits the therapist to check out some interpretation or judgment he has made but which needs the client's corroboration.

Example. In a simulated conversation with his mother on the subject of religion, Mark has encountered the possibility of an intergeneration transmission process from her to him. His movement toward individuation, he realizes, may well be causing her to recall long-dormant ambiguities concerning separateness and differentiation. He realizes it is possible that invisible loyalties in her experience are being reactivated by his relationship transition with her. He says, "I never thought of her this way." The therapist, sensing a possible reframing of the parent taking place in Mark's mind, says, "How are you seeing her now?" This clarification enables the client to develop his new image of the mother.

Coaching. In this set of procedures the therapist serves as a consultant to one or both partners while the latter engage in family voyages or researches in the extended family network. While the client is engaged in face-to-face encounters with family members, the therapist is available to monitor the extended field of interaction and to give advice and make suggestions. Coaching can make use of reenactments, recordings, and rehearsals in order to gain a total picture of the elements present and operative in the voyages.

Example. A therapy trainee is experiencing considerable anxiety and intimidation in the presence of an aloof and disengaged father in a client family. In supervision the student becomes aware of a displacement that relates to his own incomplete and unresolved relationship with his own father. In subsequent weeks he conducts a family voyage and begins to research his father's immigration to this country, as well as some of the emotional cutoff that accounts for the parent's somewhat disengaged interaction pattern. The student moves closer to his father and breaks down the barrier, in part through the analogue of joining with his parent in the food preparation and management of his restaurant business. The supervisor also gains the secondary benefit of several excellent foreign dinners.

Confronting the framework. The therapist, who has tracked and understood a partner's perspective on some subject or event, takes this information and reorients it or reorganizes it in a way that counters the previous framework. Having first experienced the therapist's empathy and acceptance of the original viewpoint, the client can integrate the reframing into his or her perspective, modifying it. The therapist's intervention is, in effect, "Yes, I hear you, but. . . ."

Example. A therapy trainee is reenacting a previous session in which he feverishly attempted to explain a client's behavior to him, to move him to a point of insight about it. The supervisor is role playing the client and, through his demeanor, both accepts the trainee's explanations and impels him to try harder. Urged on by the supervisor's feigned confusion, the trainee tries even more to drive home his point. Abruptly, the supervisor turns to the other students present in the enactment and says, "I've got him really working hard, haven't I?" "Oh, to hell with you!" shouts the trainee, confronted by this new perspective on his actions. The client, not he, has been in control of the session.

Directing communication. The therapist guides and regulates one or both partners through specific elements and sequences of communication. Self-disclosure directives can be given, such as, "Tell him (or her) what you see—hear—think—feel—want—or do." This set of procedures also includes the management of listening behaviors like clarifying, paraphrasing, and feeding back the other's messages. Used in combination with process questions, in which one partner's responses to the other's messages are solicited, these interventions can enable the therapist to bring order and modulation to the couple's communication exchanges.

This same group of interventions can also be employed in directing a partner's fantasized or simulated communication with symbols, metaphors, and sculpture stand-ins.

Example. In the opening phase of the relationship checkup with Kathy and Mark, the therapist directed the communication flow by giving specific instructions. "Tell her what you saw and heard her doing," he says to Mark. "Tell him what you felt when you saw him hesitating," he instructs Kathy. "How did that make you feel?" he asks Mark. "Could you tell her. . . ." (motioning him to speak directly to his fiancee), the therapist continues his regulation of their communication exchanges.

Or again, in the fantasized dialogue between Mark and his mother, the "parent," being role played by Mark himself, says, "Well, there's his point of view." The therapist, wanting to facilitate integration between the parent tape in Mark's mind and his own separate selfhood, asks the "mother," "Could you tell Mark what his point of view is?" This instruction asks the "parent" to paraphrase and feed back the son's point of view.

Documenting. The therapist directs one partner to tell the other what he or she has heard or seen that has led to certain interpretations and conclusions. The procedure serves to ground a partner's impressions and images of the other in a firm bedrock of sensory information. It also provides the partner with data about himself or herself that is resulting in certain thoughts and meanings in the other's mind. Where sensory cues are not available, that is, cannot be documented, the intervention functions to elicit a partner's mind reading or opinionated tendencies.

Example. In the simulated enactment between Mark and his mother, "she" states at one point that her son is "going his own way, another way." The therapist asks her, "What is he doing?" This question asks "her" to provide information about what she is hearing and seeing Mark do. The query, in effect, directs him to view his behavior as he thinks his mother views it. "Well," Mark says, role playing his parent, "he gets huffy when I try to talk to him about it." The intervention documents, from the mother's perspective, why she thinks that he is going his own way, that is, differentiating.

Doubling. This intervention can be used in a variety of ways. In one form, the therapist temporarily becomes a counterpart for one of the partners in the imitation and practice of some communication skill. The therapist momentarily substitutes for the client and lends him or her communication resources for the actualization of the new skill. In another variation, usually during an enactment, the therapist is required to interpret some portion of a partner's experience that is immediately present and to stand in temporarily as a second self. Having inferred that some feeling or attitude, for instance, is operative in the interaction field but has not been voiced or visibly demonstrated, the therapist attempts to replicate it audibly, through words, tone, or speech rate, or visibly, through body posture, facial expression, or movement. The aim is to provide the client with a concrete portrayal of the experience so that it can be contacted, and responsibility taken for it. In yet another form, the therapist instructs members of an experiential group in the execution of this function during an enactment. In order to guard against too much imposition of their own scripts while doubling, participants are directed to keep their contributions brief and pointed.

Example. The therapist is working toward the goal of augmenting Kathy's listening skills, so that she can better provide the interpersonal conditions in which her partner can feel greater freedom to express his feelings and wants. The therapist doubles with Kathy in practicing the skill of reflective listening. Moving alongside her and looking at Mark, he says, "So you feel anxious and hesitant when I hint around and don't come out with it."

Or again, Bev, during an enactment of her childhood family, is engaged in a fantasized dialogue with her deceased mother. She is experiencing a host of thoughts and emotions: that her mother is unfair in enjoining her to help out so much in the home, that she wants to decide out of her parentified role and feels guilty for wanting that, that she feels considerable resentment at being maintained in this position. A group member walks to a place beside the mother stand-in and says to Bev, "But can't you see how overwhelmed I feel, too?" Bev accepts this offering, tears come to her eyes, and she now has evidence to account for the mother's injunction, "Help me out." A basis is established for understanding, perhaps forgiving and rejoining, the mother.

Educating. The therapist, out of his own knowledge of interpersonal and family process, imparts information that bears on some particular concern or issue that exists for either or both partners. The therapist informs or furnishes additional information that relates to some circumstance or event that has arisen during the course of the therapeutic process.

Example. During the checkup Mark has indicated that he hesitates in responding to his fiancee's hints, partly in order to "make her spit it out." The therapist, recognizing a degree of appropriateness in that action, attempts to elaborate on it and to impart knowledge on the negotiation process. He says, "That makes a lot of sense to me, not to agree to something until you're sure what it is you're agreeing to." In effect, the therapist acquaints the couple with the fact that agreements made without clear communication can be weak and counterproductive.

Exaggerate. The therapist directs the client to magnify some nonverbal output that has been initially abortive, undeveloped, incomplete, or casually slurred over. Since such postures, expressions, and movements can represent significant channels of communication, the therapist focuses on them to bring them more fully into awareness. Disproportionate representation of the tapping finger, clenched fist, or waving arm can tease out an inner meaning that complements or contrasts with the client's more overt presentation of himself or herself. Incongruent, mixed, and conflicting levels of experience can often be evoked through this intervention.

Example. A therapy student, Bob, has been rehearsing a forthcoming session when spontaneously, abruptly, he goes into another field of interaction, his relationship with his brother. In their interaction Bob occupies the favored, superior position. The supervisor directs Bob to stand on a chair and to look down and talk with his brother, symbolized by an empty seat opposite his. Having thus to magnify the over-under interaction pattern with his brother, Bob spontaneously jumps down from his lofty perch and kneels in front of the empty chair that stands for his brother. Tears are pouring down his face and he expresses his strong affection for his brother, asking the latter's forgiveness. In a reversal of roles, he has moved from the superior position to its polar opposite. As the enactment progresses the relationship becomes more equal.

Expanding the framework. The therapist, who has been following and understanding a client's frame of reference, adds his own thoughts to the perspective so as to enlarge it. Having first accepted, empathized with, and reflected back the client's viewpoint, the therapist edits the message to inject his own elaboration and extension of it.

Example. During the enactment of his anticipated conversation with his mother, Mark has been role playing his parent. "She" has shared with the therapist the things she has seen and heard that lead her to believe that her son is changing, going his own way now. Though she has never actually expressed it, there is a tone of disbelief in her voice, suggesting that Mark on his own would not do this. The therapist picks up on that implicit thought and says to her, "You really haven't said this, but I get a sense that you don't think Mark would do this on his own. Somebody has to be leading him." The therapist calls out and elaborates a portion of her experience that has been there, but not fully expressed, perhaps not yet fully evoked into awareness.

Facilitating current encounter. In this intervention, which can take a variety of shapes, the therapist promotes communication that is direct and present-centered. Partners are instructed or motioned to talk to and with each other. They are directed to use first person "I" language to encourage involvement, contact, and responsibility. Talking about subjects, gossiping, and other abstract and avoidance behaviors are quickly drawn back into the current interaction. When one or both partners reverts to some past field, the therapist promptly instructs them to talk in the present, thus integrating this historical material into the immediacy of the moment. The objective is the client's confrontation with the anxiety, increased emotionality, and fusions of direct encounter.

Example. A young wife has emotionally withdrawn from the therapy process during a session and, being given the sanction to be where she wants to be, reverts to another time and place. She starts to recall an incident of going to the hospital nursery for the first time, to visit her son born prematurely. The therapist interrupts her narrative to say, "Peg, I'd like you to relive it. Go through it in the first person, as if it were happening right now." She does not understand at first, and the therapist gives her a cue, "I'm walking into the nursery. . . ." From that point on, her reenactment becomes more pregnant, filled with immediate emotionality and direct encounter.

Fantasized dialogue. The therapist directs a client to conduct a simulated conversation between two parts, divisions, or mixed tendencies in himself or herself. Moving back and forth between two spaces, chairs, or stand-ins that represent the two sides of the split, the client first speaks for one and addresses the other, then imagines the response and speaks for the other, then moves back to reply once more, and so on. The aim is to clarify and integrate the two opposing polarities and thus to pass through an impasse or stuck position.

Example. A young husband is experiencing considerable stress in reconciling the many claims on his time and energy. Using four portable chairs as symbolic stand-ins for the four dimensions of pull, he arranges them in what he initially considers their present relationship and distance from one another. Then he speaks for each one and addresses the others, all the while rearranging the stand-ins to fit his changing perception of them. As he copes with this inner split, an altogether unexpected discovery is made. Slowly, and at first imperceptibly, he has moved his field of attention away from his wife and toward the other foci. He has, unawares, replicated what his wife perceives as the current state of the marriage, one in which she feels left out and discounted.

Fantasy trip. The therapist instructs the client to project the future consequences of certain outcomes of interaction. The procedure is especially useful in having the client construct a mental image of future interaction patterns and experiential states that will ensue if certain actions are taken, or if they are not taken. The client is told to visualize the effects on himself or herself, as well as on others, of failure to transcend some impasse, to make some decision, or to take some course of action.

Example. Bev, during an enactment of her family of origin, has encountered her precocious and overresponsible role with her brothers and father. She is feeling overwhelmed, resentful, trapped, and loyal all at the same time, and she wants to change the situation. Yet part of her cannot change, because she would be faced with feelings of guilt for letting her relatives down and relegating them, as she views matters, to a state of helplessness. She is stuck and frenzied. The therapist could, at this point, ask her to take a fantasy trip, to project ahead the consequences of redeciding her position. "Where will you be five years from now if you stay where you are?" he asks, and then gives her time to develop that scenario in her imagination, perhaps even to enact it. "And where will you be if you change it?" he asks, again giving her time to explore that outcome.

Feeding a sentence. The therapist, having listened empathically to a client's stream of experience, infers the presence of some element or attitude that has not yet been fully expressed, and proposes a sentence that articulates it. The therapist does not simply interpret the element, but says it in the first person, as though it were the client's own message. There is an interpretive function in this procedure, but the client is invited to participate in the therapist's statement, to make contact with the element that has been evoked, and to assume responsibility for its further development. If it does not fit, the client can reject it.

Example. Mark, during his simulated conversation with his mother, has told her some of the reasons why he feels drawn to his fiancee's church and increasingly disinterested in his own. The therapist, wanting to summarize and consolidate the client's message, says, "Let me feed you a sentence to see whether this is what you've been saying. 'Mom, the worship service back home became old hat, boring. And I take responsibility for the fact that I felt bored.'" The aim of the intervention is to permit Mark to hear his own experience in its discreteness and to claim the emotionality inherent in it. This can facilitate the further differentiation of his feelings over against the mother. In this particular instance, the intervention also establishes that Mark's attraction to Kathy's church is his feeling, for which he, not his fiancee, is responsible.

Interpreting. Working in concert with the partners, the therapist brings out further meanings, elucidates, and reflects on certain dynamics *after* they have been encountered in the therapeutic process. The aim is to consolidate learning at the cognitive level, in part to make certain events and dynamics meaningful, in part to help the partners recognize them in any future occurrence.

Example. In her reenactment of her visit to the hospital nursery to see her premature son for the first time, Peg has evoked her fear of becoming emotionally involved and committed, lest she be hurt through his possible death. She spontaneously goes to another time and place, the death of her father from a heart attack when she was quite young. She knows the trauma of grief and loss, and she withholds herself from having to incur that experience again with someone she loves. Having finished the enactment, she and the therapist work together to elaborate the further meanings of her experience. "You know what it's like to lose somebody you're close to," says the therapist, interpreting the meaning of her lack of commitment. The intervention also elucidates the parallel between the two fields of interaction.

Listening reflectively. The therapist listens empathically, acceptingly, and with genuine regard to the client's experience, infers some element that has not been fully evoked into awareness, and then states it in his own words. If the therapist's articulation matches the client's experience (and he or she remains the locus of that evaluation), the inchoate, denied, distorted, or concealed element can be contacted and brought out of the deep structure. Responsibility for the element can then be taken in the interaction pattern. The intervention also demonstrates to the client, in ways that can be grasped, the therapist's intent to join him or her and to provide conditions of freedom, acceptance, understanding, and positive regard.

Example. The therapist has asked Mark three times what he feels when Kathy is being indirect and oblique, and each time the client fails to respond to the question, tending to distort or conceal his reply. With the third query, Mark pauses, reflects, and says, "Like I was going to get hit or something." His demeanor suggests to the therapist that Mark's experience at the moment is still rudimentary and ill-formed, but the inference is drawn that the client feels threatened. Having already determined that reflective listening would be a useful form of intervention with Mark, the therapist says, "Do you feel coerced at those times?" The reflection appears to express at least one facet of Mark's experience at that moment in his interaction with Kathy. It also demonstrates the intent of the therapist to provide a climate of empathy, acceptance, and understanding that invites the client's continued exploration of his experience.

Making the rounds. Hearing a client express some concern or theme that relates to the wider cast of characters in a field, the therapist directs him or her to address each of the others in the designated group. The directive can be varied to include movement, touching, and other visual actions. The aim is to explore the interaction theme implicit in the client's concern.

Example. A therapy student with considerable experience and professional standing expresses concern to the training group about their observing her during a forthcoming interview. Not knowing what the issue is but noting its emergence into the foreground of her mind, the supervisor instructs her to make the rounds and express her concern vis-a-vis each trainee and supervisor present. She makes a statement to each one, and the exercise goes fairly easily and comfortably for her until she addresses a particular female supervisor. Her concern having been located in terms of its referent, she is instructed by the supervisor to address the female trainer directly. This direct address elicits an interaction theme of anxiety regarding criticism. In the subsequent exploration of this fear, she reverts to an earlier relationship with her mother. Displacement from that field, and the theme of criticism inherent in it, have been brought out by making the rounds.

Manipulating space. In this intervention the therapist directs the client to manipulate objects, stand-ins, and seating arrangements to delineate the interaction field and the interrelationships of foci within it. The client's evolving manipulations can disclose such dynamics as diffuse and disengaged relationships, triangles, coalitions, and subsystems, and thus serve to mark, clarify, and restructure boundaries.

Example. In the simulated conversation between Mark and his mother, the therapist wants to clarify and potentially realign the intrapsychic boundaries within the client's current interpersonal impasse. The therapist instructs him to sit in one chair to role play his mother, that is, the mother imprint in his mind. Then he is directed to move to another chair to be himself responding to the parent's stimuli. The split between parent and child gestalts in his experience is thus clarified. More importantly, the two images are counterpointed over against each another. The intervention not only facilitates integration of two conflicted sets of emotions inside Mark, but also clarifies and restructures dynamics in which his fiancee has been triangulated into the parent-son bind. A comment by the therapist like, "Let's put Kathy over here out of this thing," accompanied by placing a chair outside the mother-son focus would serve to delineate and restructure the maladaptive triangle which Mark brought to the therapy session.

Mimesis. The therapist joins with one or both partners by implicity imitating some experiential element or by explicitly making a statement that demonstrates his siding with and accommodating to that element. Thus, in using an intervention like reflective listening or feeding a sentence, the therapist replicates the client's tone or rate of speech. Or again, in using the procedure of doubling, the therapist replicates some visual cue from the client, some body posture or facial expression. Thus, the therapist both joins with the client and imitates his or her immediate experience to provide an exact replica for hearing and viewing.

Example. Mark is addressing his mother in a simulated conversation with her on the subject of religion. As the therapist listens to the client role play the mother, he hears a heavy, slow, and labored tone that he infers is associated with feelings of obligation, loyalty, and guilt in Mark's mind. Moreover, as Mark talks about his feelings of boredom in his childhood church, his tone once more becomes sluggish, lifeless, and deep. When the therapist feeds the client a sentence or when he doubles for him in talking with the mother, he, too, adopts this slow and laborious tone and manner of speaking. The aim is to replicate the emotionality that is associated with Mark's words, and thus to make the therapist's interventions a complete accommodation to the client's current state.

Similarly, Kathy is focusing on her difficulty in expressing her wants and wishes with her fiance. The therapist joins with her by saying, "I know what you mean. It's hard for me to come right out with what I want in some relationships." The aim is to demonstrate a common human experience.

Modeling. The therapist enacts certain behaviors that serve as cues for client's imitation or identification. Such actions can be explicit, as when the therapist doubles or otherwise demonstrates the use of some communication skill. The intervention can also be implicit and analogical, in which case the therapist uses himself in the therapeutic system to exemplify certain interpersonal actions. The aim is to address the client through the metaphor of this action and thus to provide a new pattern that can be imitated.

Example. A female client's concern is her husband's sexual pushing and her resulting anxiety about complying or resisting. The therapist wants to explore this interaction theme and begins an experiential enactment to let it unfold. But when he gives the client certain directives, she immediately looks and sounds stressed, not wanting to comply with the instructions and not wanting to resist, lest, as she reports later, the therapist be upset with her. The therapist backs down, saying, "Well, I don't want you to go some-place that you're uncomfortable." In so doing, he models for the husband the act of accommodating to the wife's anxiety and waiting for her to sort out the response she genuinely wants to make. Later, the husband says that this example showed him another way to behave in the situation.

Probing the sculpture. The therapist directs members of an experiential group through steps which break open a participant's sculptured interaction field. Instructions include walking among and about the objects and stand-ins that comprise the sculpture, sharing their perceptions of what they see without interpreting any possible dynamics, and then speculating about the delineations that may be deciphered from the spatial arrangements. The aim is to treat the member's sculpture as an objective projection of an interaction field and to use the perceptions and thoughts of others to tease out the systems, boundaries, and dynamics present in it.

Example. After Bev has finished sculpting her family of origin, using members of the group as stand-ins for her relatives, the therapist directs other participants to move about in the visual and spatial model and to examine thoroughly what they see. When asked by the therapist to share their perceptions, some do, but others proceed directly to interpreting what they see. These premature interpretations are blocked by the therapist in order first to make use of all the sensory resources present in the group. Then speculations are elicited, and a number of interpretations place Bev at the center of her family in a parentified role, responsible for her father, her brothers, and her sister, just as, it turns out later, her deceased mother had once been. In her sculpture Bev stands in front of the mother image, facing the rest of the family. This placement depicts the fact that she has taken on the mother's overresponsible function in the family.

Recounting in the first person. The therapist instructs a client to relate the facts and particulars of some past event or dream in the first person, as though it were happening in the present. Talking *about* details and actions is blocked by the therapist, who tells the client to use "I" language. Instead of the client's saying, for example, "My voice is trembly," the therapist directs him or her to say, "I am trembly." The aim of this simple and somewhat mechanical procedure is to promote involvement, immediacy, and responsibility. Also, such participatory language places the client in the role of an active agent in the interaction which is being narrated.

Example. A client is relating the details of a dream, and the therapist instructs him to recount it in the first person, as if it were happening now. The client responds with, "I am walking with my son down a gray hall in the basement of a building. . . . " The retelling centers on the theme of the client wanting to rescue his son, and each time he comes upon a side passage that might afford a way out, he is confronted by a blank wall with a barred window at the end. Hearing the client say, "It makes me feel panicky," the therapist interrupts and redirects the narration. The sentence, "I feel panicky," places the client in contact with himself as an active agent in the event. The intervention serves to keep the emotionality of the dream an efficacious force in the narration.

Reframing. This intervention, which stands on a continuum with such procedures as confronting or expanding the framework, is more radical and existential than the other two. The therapist works with the partner(s) in fitting together and uniting elements of their interaction pattern in a new and decisive way. The new conception fits the previously disclosed facts and particulars of the pattern, but it reconstructs them in a form that more adequately encompasses the discoveries, new perspectives, and interactional breakthroughs that have taken place during therapy. The aim of the intervention is to match and consolidate the new emotionality, actions, and decisions that the partners have integrated into their relationship.

Example. After Mark has finished his simulated conversation with his mother, the therapist solicits his fiancee's response. She has been present, and has been immersed in the emotionality of the interaction bind that characterizes her fiance's current relationship transition with his mother. The enactment clarifies for her the origins of Mark's wariness and tentativeness, and the conflicted emotions that he feels in such close interaction. She has seen that his behavior with her represents a displacement from this other relationship and its unfinished business. Such empathy furthers her understanding and acceptance of Mark's interaction pattern and delivers her from blaming herself unduly for his behavior with her. Also, she is set free from being held responsible by her fiance, or his mother, for his movement toward autonomy and differentiation.

Mark, too, has come to view his mother in a new and more accepting light. In fact, he now empathizes with her and the family transmission patterns that might possibly have descended on her. He realizes that he may be standing in the same situation.

The reframing is indicated by the knowing smile which Mark sends to his partner, acknowledging his reconstruction of the situation. His new perspective matches the therapist's interpretation of the clarifications and realignments that have occurred.

Repetition. The therapist directs a partner to repeat some statement that appears to be important, but which has been expressed in a tentative, incomplete, or undeveloped manner. Like exaggeration, which futhers contact with visual acts of expression, repetition facilitates encounter with glossed-over verbal contents or auditory channels. The therapist says, for instance, "Repeat that sentence," or "Say it again." The utterance can be repeated several times until the underlying tone, speech rate, or volume level are more fully catalyzed into the current interaction.

Example. In the simulated conversation with her father during the enactment of her family of origin, Bev has told the parent that she cannot continue to be his "wife," taking care of him and making his life meaningful. To probe the decisiveness of her intent, the therapist asks her to convert the "can't" to a "won't." She accepts the "won't" and the firmness implicit in it, but when told to repeat it to her father, her tone is still pleading, appealing for permission. Told once more to tell the father, "I won't," Bev confronts the decisveness and finality of her resolve. The repetition compresses all the emotionality of saying good-bye, of guilt, and desertion into the intensity of the moment and places before her the existential quality of her redecision.

Reversal. The therapist directs a client during the enactment of some event to alter his or her actions or tendencies to the opposite of their immediate or usual character. For instance, if the customary outcome of the client's interaction is compliant and unassertive behavior, he or she is instructed to become resistant and uncooperative. This procedure enables the client to make contact with latent or underlying tendencies and to rehearse their expression. While increasing the client's anxiety, the intervention provides an opportunity for him or her to explore dormant or underdeveloped patterns of relating. Typical or habitual interaction themes and outcomes are thus inverted, reversed, and simulated.

Example. While enacting a forthcoming therapy session with his client, Bob has spontaneously reverted to another interaction field, to his relationship with his twin brother. In the replication of their relationship, Bob immediately assumes the dominant position, the achiever who has customarily won the parents' adulation and esteem. Having followed the therapist's directive to stand in a chair and to look down at his brother, Bob then jumps down and adopts a kneeling posture, looking up at his twin. Noting the voluntary reversal of Bob's usual attitude, the therapist directs the trainee to address his brother from that position. The student expresses his guilt and his implicit plea for forgiveness, thus inverting the customary interaction pattern. He makes contact with his own underlying feelings of guilt in relation to his twin.

Sculpting. The therapist directs the client to represent an interaction field by placing stand-ins, physical objects, or symbolic images in visible arrangements. Carrying out this directive, the client objectifies intrapsychic space into external, perceptible, and manipulable configurations. The sculpture functions like a thematic apperception instrument. It can serve to elicit both overt and covert levels in the client's perspective on the field. Positioning or molding the stand-ins, objects, and symbols, the client portrays the cast of characters in the field, his or her image of each as depicted in visual cues like facial expressions and body postures, the closeness or distance between elements, and the groupings among them. Subsequent probing of the sculpture can evoke the client's mental delineation of the field, diffuse or disengaged boundaries within it, coalitions or triangles that may be present, and the press and responses of characters on one another. In the enactment following, the sculpture can be developed and explored further through the application of additional experiential interventions. As it evolves, the design can be used both for information gathering and for direct and immediate restructuring of interaction patterns.

Example. Bev has returned from a recent visit with her family of origin and has expressed considerable distress and unfinished business regarding it. Wanting to replicate the event rather than merely talking about it, the therapist instructs her to select members of the experiential group and to position them as stand-ins for the members of her family whom she believes properly belong in the sculpture. She is also directed to execute her design silently, to mold and arrange the stand-ins in a fashion that expresses her image of each through visual cues. She violates this instruction inadvertently, uttering words like "sloppy" when shaping one stand-in's body posture, thus adding verbal cues concerning this personage in the group. She places three male figures side by side, another at an angle some distance from the field, a female character sitting in a chair to one side of the total group, and another standing up facing all the others, her hands outstretched and open. The female figure to one side is bent over, her head in her hands, and looking down. One male figure holds some object in his hand. The stage is now set for the sculpture to be probed. The therapist instructs other members of the group to walk around and within the field and to share their perceptions.

Shaping. The therapist provides one or both partners with structured homework tasks that serve to consolidate and strengthen communication skills that have been modeled, doubled, and practiced during therapy sessions. Having a clear grasp of the skill and having already rehearsed it, the client is instructed to be aware of times during the week when he or she observes its appropriateness, when a certain experiential element is sorted out, and when the skill is actually implemented. The task includes careful record keeping, such as a written verbatim and commentary on exchanges with the partner, the context, the portion of awareness that is relevant, and the message that is actually sent. Records are reviewed in subsequent therapy sessions and modifications introduced as needed, including further modeling, doubling, and practice.

Example. Kathy has become aware of her tendency to be indirect and oblique in expressing her wants to Mark, and the therapist has modeled and doubled with her in the communication of her intentions. Having practiced this new skill, Kathy is instructed by the therapist to be aware during the following week when she shares her wants and wishes with her fiance. She is directed to keep a careful record of at least two of these occasions, writing down what Mark says, what she says, and her comments on the intention she wants to express. She is further directed to bring these written verbatims and commentaries to the next session. Success in executing the skill and improved communication with the partner become their own reward.

Simulated conversation. The therapist directs the client to address a significant person in an interaction field as though the other were actually present. He or she may also be instructed to place an empty chair opposite as a stand-in for the other. The stand-in can be further developed by requiring the client to close his or her eyes and to imagine auditory and visual properties that characterize the other. The client makes a statement, then role plays the other, adopting as many of the other's communication channels as possible, and then replies with a second message of his or her own. The aim is to have the client directly encounter the significant other and to enter into all the anxiety, disquieting emotionality, and fusion that can and do occur. The intervention facilitates interaction that has been avoided or that has been anticipated. It simulates the client's being fully present.

Example. Mark has expressed concern about his mother's queries regarding his changing religious practices. He is beginning to feel intruded upon and resentful. The therapist, wanting to ground therapeutic process in the actual situation that is causing stress, instructs Mark to conduct a simulated conversation with the parent, that is, to rehearse the anticipated and dreaded event. Mark first role plays the mother, drawing upon his memories of her characteristic behaviors, and even while doing so, emits a depressed and sluggish tone which reflects his response to the mother stimulus. Then he speaks for himself and replies to the mother, clarifying his intentions and feelings over against her. The interactional impasse is thus confronted directly, and the unresolved feelings associated with Mark's changing relationship phase with his mother are evoked into action.

Soliciting the partner's response. After one partner has completed the enactment of an interaction event, or a portion of one, the therapist solicits the other partner's response. Frequently, that response is made spontaneously or involuntarily through such channels as tears, a frown, a smile, or other nonverbal manifestation. The therapist can ask, "What are your tears saying?" The second partner then shares the feelings, thoughts, and perceptions that have been stirred into motion through that enactment. Sometimes, the therapist's entreaties are more ambiguous and consist of a question like, "Where are you with that?" leaving the partner to respond from whatever vantage point he or she elects. The aim is to elicit the cross-encounter, the tuning in, and the empathic resonance that has been evoked. The second partner is able to share the clarifications, the understandings, and the realigned emotionalities that have taken place during and as a consequence of the other's work. The intervention provides a chance to explore and clarify boundaries, fusions, displacements, and parallels that have taken place and to restructure the couple's pattern of relating. A wife might say, for instance, "I had always intuited that he (her husband) was a gentle and kind person, but now that I see and hear some of his feelings toward his mother, I understand more why he kept things to himself."

Example: Kathy has been present and vicariously involved in Mark's enactment of a conversation with his mother. When the enactment is finished, the therapist turns to her and asks her response to what she had seen and heard. She replies by identifying the new and deeper understanding of Mark that has arisen during the enactment. She has encountered firsthand the origins of his behavior with her, his tendency to be hesitant and wary, his resentment over being coerced or intruded upon. More importantly, she has been immersed in the mixed emotionality and the impasse that such situations provoke in her fiance. The displacements and fusions that have been occuring are clarified, and Kathy encounters her partner at a depth which she has not known before. Her therapy objective, to get to know her fiance better, has been realized at both a surface and deeper level of understanding.

Staying with it. The therapist instructs the client to stay with and complete an action or feeling that he or she very much wants to avoid or deflect. The action to be finished is usually quite uncomfortable and anxiety-provoking, and the client wants to turn away from it and move on to something else. The therapist directs him or her to continue with the disquieting action, saying something like, "Tell him (or her) or where you are," or "Finish it." A crucial intervention, this procedure requires the client to complete some interaction that has long been avoided and unresolved and which has led to impasses and interpersonal fusion. The other person has to be faced directly and told clearly and forthrightly what one is experiencing.

Example. Peg is reenacting her first visit to the hospital nursery to see her son, born prematurely. The nurse has offered to let her hold the infant, which she has accepted. Seated and holding him, she begins a simulated conversation. She begins to cry and tells the child that she feels nothing for him, except guilt for not feeling. She goes on to say that the reason she cannot let herself feel anything is—and she hesitates. The therapist directs her to finish her message. She sobs even more profusely and tells her son, " . . . because I'm afraid you'll die." Saying this, Peg is overwhelmed with the pain of loss and grief, and the enactment then evolves to an earlier instance of death in her history.

Taking responsibility. The therapist, perceiving a partner display potential decisiveness or resoluteness about some aspect of experience, instructs him or her to say the phrase, "I take responsibility for (the feeling, the intention, the thought, and so forth)." The aim of this intervention is to bring a quality of conclusiveness and finality to the experiential element and to have the partner claim it and be accountable for it. The procedure can serve as an instrument for differentiation and self-definition, that is, marking the individual's boundary.

Example. Mark, enacting a simulated conversation with his mother, has shared some of his perceptions and feelings regarding the worship services in his boyhood church. He tells her how much more he enjoys the services in his fiancee's church, and how much more involved he feels there. He has used the word "bored" in describing the services of the childhood congregation. The therapist directs him to tell the mother, "I take responsibility for feeling bored." The intervention places the locus of the emotion in Mark, thus marking his boundary and differentiating him from his fiancee's influence. Previously, he had tended to hold Kathy responsible for leading him toward her church, and thus for the stimulation he found there.

Tracking. The therapist follows the couple's narrative regarding some event or situation in order to learn their perspective on it. The aim is to elicit more information about the focus of concern as they view it. The procedure consists of many features, including paraphrasing, a statement showing interest, the brief request for expanded content, the minor clarification of a point, and other attentive behaviors through which the therapist follows the couple's account. This intervention differs from others, such as process questions, clarifying, and reflective listening, where the therapist is conducting an ongoing content analysis and elicits specific bits of information. Through tracking, the therapist can join with the couple and their view of an event.

Example. Mark and Kathy have requested an appointment specifically for therapy, unlike their previous checkup interview. Not knowing what the presenting concern is, the therapist tracks their narrative, especially Mark's. Mark is feeling quite stressed, torn between his mother and his fiancee. He frames his distress in terms of changing religious sensibilities. He refers to visits to his family of origin, and to his mother's questions and probes that clothe, as he senses it, her displeasure. The therapist follows the account, asks an occasional question to clarify, and encourages Mark to expand on a point here and there, until a fairly clear picture of the issue emerges. Then, when the therapist moves to set up an enactment of the anticipated conversation between Mark and his mother, the client will have some basis for believing that his presentation of the problem has been understood and will be contained in the therapeutic strategy.

Using self. The therapist, sensing himself the object of a client's displacement in the interaction field, tacitly and unobtrusively role plays the assigned position as a vehicle for change. Since the client's assignment is taking place at a covert level, the therapist uses himself as an analogue, a temporary stand-in, for the personage in relation to whom the subjective state originally occurred. Thus, the intervention takes place at and addresses a subsidiary level of awareness, but nevertheless coalesces into motion and discloses the client's experience connected with the particular subject-object relationship. The therapist's actions in the role can evoke reciprocal feelings and behaviors in the client, and thus reveal the fixated relationship phases, the impasses, and the fusions that are occurring. A momentary procedure, such role playing often elicits the client's spontaneous reversion to the original interaction situation. Once contacted, this antecedent field of experience can be enacted directly.

Example. A female client involved in sexual therapy makes the statement that a wife should respond to her husband's needs. She asserts this view as if it were self-evident. Asked by the therapist from whom she learned this, she replies that she doesn't know. The therapist, wanting to conduct a fantasized dialogue between the client and some other personage who transmitted this injunction, directs her to get up and to role play someone giving her this message. But the client balks, looks down, and appears stressed. She says, "I don't like to play those kind of games." Yet she apologizes and becomes reticent, and hopes she has not hurt the therapist's feelings. The therapist infers at this point that he is the recipient of a displacement, that some subjective state in connection with some other personage is being transferred onto him. He backs down from his previous directive, believing it important to do so in this particular set of exchanges. The client sits down but continues to express guilt at letting the therapist down, though she appears equally firm in her resolve not to go on with the earlier directive. Using this set of covert exchanges, the therapist derives a picture of her being coerced on the one hand and wanting to resist on the other. She does not revert to the original relationship precipitating her impasse, but in later therapy sessions the subject of incestuous demands from her father comes to the surface. The therapist telling her to do something she did not want to do was sufficiently like the antecedent experience to provoke a transference assignment.

Videotape playback. The therapist plays back for the client some portion of his or her previously recorded material. Such playback enables the client to retrace both the content of his or her words and nonverbal channels of experience. Auditory cues, such as tone, volume, and speech rate, and visual cues, such as facial expressions, body posture, and gestures, can be encountered. Such self-encounter provides the client with a vivid demonstration of his or her observable self, often for the first time. The partner can see and hear himself or herself from the mate's perspective.

Example. A female therapy trainee sits opposite a highly conflicted and estranged couple who are hurling invectives at each other. Though some action to regain control of the session is in order, she is virtually immobilized. Her face is visibly stressed. Later, in the self-encounter made available to her through videotape playback, she recalls her feelings of pain in hearing the couple's abuse of each other and reverts to the time of her own parents' impending divorce. Caught in the middle of that earlier conflict and feeling responsible to reconcile them, she had, as a child, failed. The videotape confronted her once more with herself during this time of overresponsibility, conflict, and pain.

Annotated Bibliography

Bandler, R. and Grinder, J. *The Structure of Magic: A Book About Language and Therapy, I.* Palo Alto: Science & Behavior Books, 1975.

> The authors elucidate a general theory of linguistics in therapy. Viewing language as the system through which an individual represents his or her perception of reality, they demonstrate the incongruities that can occur between the surface and deep structures of verbal content, resulting in deletions, distortions, and generalizations of experience. The therapeutic process is examined as the step-by-step transformation of grammar and syntax, thus integrating the two structures, and altering the person's frame of reference.

Bandler, R. and Grinder, J. *The Structure of Magic: A Book About Communication and Change, II.* Palo Alto: Science & Behavior Books, 1976.

> The authors extend their model of communication to a consideration of the nonverbal auditory, visual, and kinesthetic channels through which an individual can represent his or her experience. The therapeutic use of these para-messages in making contact, adding to, and enriching the client's representational repertoire is examined.

Bertalanffy, L. von. *General System Theory: Foundations, Development, Applications.* New York: George Braziller, 1968.

> The author, a pioneer in the organismic view in the biological sciences and in the construction of a general theory spanning many fields of inquiry, here briefly defines

the basic system model. Such concepts as the open versus the closed system, steady state, feedback loop, equifinality, primary versus secondary interaction, and hierarchical organization are fundamental to contemporary marital and family therapy.

Bockus, F. A Systems Approach to Marital Process. *Journal of Marriage and Family Counseling*, 1975, 3, 251-258.

An event of couple interaction is conceived as an open system composed of many elements and stages. Couple communication is viewed as a feedback loop based on the congruent transmission and effective reception of personal and interpersonal information. Couple negotiation is examined as a system in development with connections between component subsystems mapped along with progressions from one stage to the next. Implications for interaction analysis in therapy and research are discussed.

Boszormenyi-Nagy, I. Intensive Family Therapy As Process. In: I. Boszormenyi-Nagy and J. L. Framo (Eds.), *Intensive Family Therapy*. New York: Harper & Row, 1965.

An excellent overview of the psychodynamic orientation to marital and family therapy. The author explicates such processes as the relationship modes of being the subject or being the object, relationship phases such as overinvolvement or unrelatedness, symbolic reenactment, and displacement and shows how they result in multipersonal systems that span family generations and in repetitive interaction sequences that restrict spontaneity and growth. Parallels with the scripts of transactional analysis are suggested.

Boszormenyi-Nagy, I. and Spark, G. *Invisible Loyalties*. New York: Harper & Row, 1973.

An intergenerational approach to family therapy. The volume explores the hierarchical network of obligations that characterize family relationships. Within this matrix of identity the authors discuss the dynamics of debt and credit, horizontal and vertical bookkeeping, belonging and separating, and other processes through which family members continuously balance their mutual rights, expectations, and injustices.

Bowen, M. *Family Theory in Clinical Practice.* New York: Jason Aronson, 1978.

> The collected works of one of the seminal thinkers in family therapy. Reflecting the historical development of the Bowen Theory, the volume provides an in-depth look at such concepts as differentiation of self, triangles, fusion, the family projection process, multi-generational transmission process, and other key motifs. The therapy of coaching and the person-to-person family voyage are examined in their personal and professional evolution.

Brodey, W. M. A Cybernetic Approach to Family Therapy. In: G. H. Zuk and I. Boszormenyi-Nagy (Eds.), *Family Therapy and Disturbed Families.* Palo Alto: Science & Behavior Books, 1967.

> The active augmentation of learning skills is the author's projected future for family therapy. Therapy will entail the provision of a new language and set of coping skills in real time to assist families to maintain their stability while adapting with change. An adaptational and preventive vision.

Bronfenbrenner, U. *Two Worlds of Childhood.* New York: Russell Sage Foundation, 1970.

> Of particular importance to the marital therapist is the author's examination of the modeling process in parent-child relationships. The primacy of the parental model, the properties of the model, and the cues and sequences of the identification process are clearly delineated.

Caplan, G. Preface. *A Chance to Grow.* Boston: WGBH Educational Foundation, 1967.

> In his preface to this program of recorded and transcribed interviews with several families undergoing a major stage or change in life, the author provides a brief introduction to developmental crisis theory and dynamics. The characteristics of normal, transitional crisis are reviewed along with the

behaviors usually associated with effective coping and mastery of the task. Contains numerous implications for an adaptational orientation to marital therapy.

Constantine, L. L. Family Sculpture and Relationship Mapping Techniques. *Journal of Marriage and Family Counseling,* 1978, 2, 13-23.

A comprehensive overview of a body of techniques to assist a client in objectively portraying inner processes and events through spatial analogues. Heuristic guidelines for creating and processing these spatial metaphors are presented along with types of sculptures suited to simple, boundary, system, and special situations.

Fagan, J. The Tasks of the Therapist. In: J. Fagan and I. L. Shepherd (Eds.). *Gestalt Therapy Now: Theory, Techniques, Applications.* Palo Alto: Science & Behavior Books, 1970.

An overview of a number of therapeutic tasks, including patterning. Therapeutic functioning requires a comprehensive understanding of interacting events and systems in the clients, the specification of connecting points, the identification of points of optimum intervention in order to make rapid and lasting change, the determination of risks so as to minimize the disturbance of extraneous factors, and the conceptualizing of outcomes to replace previously dysfunctional actions.

Framo, J. L. Personal Reflections of A Family Therapist. *Journal of Marriage and Family Counseling,* 1975, 1, 15-28.

A personal account of the evolution of this therapist's perspective on such dynamics as the multipersonal system, object relations, and symbolic reconstruction and on such therapy issues and modalities as the multiple-couples group, work with the family of origin, and the therapist's own personhood and family situation in therapeutic functioning.

Goulding, M. M. and Goulding, R. L. *Changing Lives through Redecision Therapy.* New York: Brunner/Mazel, 1979.

A comprehensive and detailed look at redecision therapy, including the use of contracts, the definition of impasses and redecisions, the place of emotionality and saying good-bye in the process of change, and the changing of stroke patterns. Contains taped case material and vignettes to bring the therapeutic process alive.

Goulding, R. New Directions in Transactional Analysis: Creating An Environment for Redecision and Change. In: C. J. Sager and H. S. Kaplan (Eds.), *Progress in Group and Family Therapy*. New York: Brunner/Mazel, 1972.

> Writing from the perspective of transactional analysis, the author shows the workings of such dynamics as ego states, first act experiences, injunctions, decisions, and rackets in the formation and maintainence of a life script, but then demonstrates innovative methods for creating a therapeutic environment for redecision and change. Blends psychodrama, gestalt, systems, communication, sculpting, and other modalities in the replication of the client's script and change within it.

Guerin, P. and Fogarty, T. Study Your Own Family. In: A. Ferber, M. Mendelsohn, and A. Napier (Eds.), *The Book of Family Therapy*. Boston: Houghton Mifflin, 1973.

> A personal account of how one trainee, in the tradition of Murray Bowen, undertook to research his own family in his individuation work. Shows the use of such vehicles as the genogram, the face-to-face interview, the detriangulation process, and the active confrontation of fusion in the differentiation of self.

Gurman, A. S. Contemporary Marital Therapies: A critique and Comparative Analysis of Psychoanalytic, Behavioral and Systems Theory Approaches. In: T. J. Paolino and B. S. McCrady (Eds.), *Marriage and Marital Therapy*. New York: Brunner/Mazel, 1978.

> A detailed and critical examination of the advantages and disadvantages of three major approaches to marital therapy followed by a comparative analysis of the position of each system on such variables as the role of the past and unconscious, the nature and meaning of presenting problems, the

importance of mediating and ultimate goals, and the roles and functions of the therapist. Suggests some future lines of development for the field.

Haley, J. Toward A Theory of Pathological Systems. In: G. H. Zuk and I. Boszormenyi-Nagy (Eds.), *Family Therapy and Disturbed Families*. Palo Alto: Science & Behavior Books, 1967.

A classic and early conceptualization of the perverse triangle in human relationships, especially the family, in which the hierarchical boundaries between the generations are breached, a coalition between two persons at different levels is formed against a third, and in which the dysfunctional union is denied overtly but maintained covertly through conflictual metacommunicative levels of interaction.

Haley, J. *Uncommon Therapy: The Psychiatric Techniques of Milton H. Erickson*. New York: Norton, 1973.

After years of professional conversation with his colleague and mentor, the author compiles an overview of Erickson's uncommon style of therapy. Viewing symptoms as the arrest of development either in schedule or demand, Erickson provokes change through such illogical and unexpected techniques as encouraging and using resistance, providing a worse alternative, utilizing metaphor, and encouraging responses by inhibiting them. Replete with case examples of designs that worked.

Haley, J. *Problem Solving Therapy*. San Francisco: Jossey-Bass, 1976.

Converging on the clients' presenting problem as the object of change in therapy, the author demonstrates how that focus can be approached analogically and metaphorically, how behavioral directives can be given to modify the relational dysfunctions implicit in the symptoms, and how therapeutic goals can be pursued through stages in an overall design. Compares and contrasts ethical issues and assumptions in two broad orientations to therapy and training.

Henry, W. E. *The Analysis of Fantasy*. New York: John Wiley & Sons, 1956.

An extensive treatment of thematic apperception interpretation, this volume is useful to the marital therapist in
providing a conceptual model for tracing partners' evolving
frames of reference during an event of interaction. Viewing
couple interaction as a field of forces reciprocally acting on
one another, the therapist is afforded a cognitive scheme for
eliciting, sorting, and analyzing information. Also useful in
the creation and processing of an experiential enactment.

Jackson, D. and Lederer, W. J. *The Mirages of Marriage.* New York:
W. W. Norton, 1968.

Intended as bibliotherapy, addressed to the couple itself
rather than the therapist, this volume first examines the
many anachronisms and myths that make marriage un-
workable in contemporary life and offers numerous ty-
pologies of dysfunctional relationships. The authors then
discuss the concept of the *quid pro quo,* the interlocking
system of reciprocal actions and responses, much of it tacit,
that goes into the makeup of the relationship and provide
extensive guidelines and exercises for the couple to do to
improve their functionality.

Jacobson, N. S. A Review of the Research on the Effectiveness of
Marital Therapy. In: T. J. Paolino and B. S. McCrady (Eds.),
Marriage and Marital Therapy. New York: Brunner/Mazel, 1978.

A review primarily of outcome studies in marital therapy.
After specifying methodological criteria for inclusion in his
survey, the author examines outcome research and findings
basically in the communicative, relationship enhancement,
behavioral or social learning approaches and challenges
other less-structured, long-term therapies to demonstrate
their efficacy.

Kempler, W. *Principles of Gestalt Family Therapy.* Costa Mesa, California: Kempler Institute, 1973.

Explication and demonstration of the gestalt principles of
staying with the current, present interaction as the focus of
therapy. Such procedures as facilitating or blocking communication, making the rounds, saying it directly, no gossiping,
awareness continuum, and others are illustrated.

Laing, R. D. Mystification, Confusion and Conflict. In: I. Boszor-menyi-Nagy and J. L. Framo (Eds.), *Intensive Family Therapy*. New York: Harper and Row, 1965.

> A discussion of the dynamic in which a characteristic, image, or role is attributed to one family member by one or more others to whom such attribution is functional, the invalidation of any efforts on the part of the recipient to differentiate from the attribution, and the progressive induction of the individual into acceptance of it.

Laqueur, H. P. Mechanisms of Change in Multiple Family Therapy. In: C. J. Sager and H. S. Kaplan (Eds.), *Progress in Group and Family Therapy*. New York: Brunner/Mazel, 1972.

> The pioneer of multiple-family therapy provides a comprehensive overview of the many dynamics of change in this approach, including learning by analogy, delineating the field of interaction, identification, tuning in, trial and error, amplification and modulation of signals, and others.

Levitsky, A. and Perls, F. S. The Rules and Games of Gestalt Therapy. In: J. Fagan and I. L. Shepherd (Eds.), *Gestalt Therapy Now*. Palo Alto: Science & Behavior Books, 1970.

> After first reviewing some of the basic principles of gestalt therapy, such as staying in the present and the use of responsible and involving language, the authors define many of the specific intervention procedures common to this orientation: fantasized dialogue, playing the projection, reversal, exaggeration, rehearsal, feeding a sentence, and more.

Liberman, R. P. Behavioral Approaches to Family and Couple Therapy. In: C. J. Sager and H. S. Kaplan (Eds.), *Progress in Group and Family Therapy*. New York: Brunner/Mazel, 1972.

> The author defines concepts basic to the social learning approach and provides a detailed outline for implementing a program of behavior modification. In a step-by-step manner such tasks as making a behavioral analysis of the problem, specifying objectives, determining current base lines, mod-

eling, locating reenforcers, shaping, and intermittant reenforcement are delineated.

Liddle, H. A. and Halpin, R. J. Family Therapy Training and Supervision: A Comparative Review. *Journal of Marriage and Family Counseling,* 1978, 4, 77-98.

Observing that the literature on training and supervision is fragmented and disorganized, the authors review, categorize, and compare existing publications on the subject. Topics examined include goals, techniques, supervisor-trainee relationship, personal therapy, politics, and evaluation of outcomes. A comprehensive summary table is provided for quick access to material in the study.

Mace, D. R. Marriage Enrichment Concepts for Research. *The Family Coordinator,* 1975, 2, 171-173.

As guest editor of a special section on the emerging field of marriage enrichment, the author identifies nine areas for research if the movement is to be furthered. Relevant areas include obstacles to participation, the group process, leadership patterns, effectiveness studies, the definition of key concepts like growth and enrichment, inter-couple support and therapy, and the nature of prevention.

Menninger, K., Mayman, M. and Pruyser, P. *The Vital Balance.* New York: Viking, 1963.

A presentation of the organismic theory of personality utilizing general systems principles of adaptation, organization, interaction, homeostasis and heterostasis, steady-state maintenance, regulation, and others. The authors apply the model toward an understanding of coping mechanisms of everyday life and towards a theory of progressive dyscontrol and dysfunction. Contains implications for prevention and therapy

Miller, S., Nunnally, E. and Wackman, D. *Alive and Aware: Improving Communication in Relationships.* Minneapolis: Interpersonal Communication Programs, 1975.

The reader for a structured communications training

program for couples. Reviews and illustrates such dynamics as the awareness wheel for sorting and expressing personal information, shared meaning for checking out and feeding back the partner's messages, styles of communication, and procedures for exchanging views in ways that preserve and vouchsafe the self-esteem and separateness of each.

Minuchin, S. *Families and Family Therapy.* Cambridge: Harvard University Press, 1974.

Viewing family transactions in terms of their clarity, diffusion, or rigidity in maintaining appropriate boundaries among the many subsystems of the total system, the author expounds an approach that enables the therapist to probe, map, join, and restructure these involvements. Specifies a number of procedures suited to each of these tasks and contains several exemplary interviews and commentaries illustrating the process in motion.

Napier, A. Y. with Whitaker, C. A. *The Family Crucible: The Intense Experience of Family Therapy.* New York: Harper & Row, Publishers, 1978.

Through an exposition of their intense work with the Brices over time the authors explicate a host of family dynamics and therapeutic procedures, spanning several orientations of intervention. In Claudia, the scapegoated daughter, can be seen the system's tendency to single out one member to manifest its disturbance and to help it covertly to avoid its more primary conflicts, the mother's depression, the father's emotional inaccessibility, and the latent stress between husband and wife. Demonstrates the battle for control, the joining, the overcoming of the status quo. Richly illustrates such interventions as the use of the positive intentions of family members, the expansion and alteration of perceptions through enigmatic, sometimes seemingly absurd comments and actions. Portrays the multipersonal and intergenerational aspects of the system through conjoint sessions encompassing three generations.

Napier, A. Y. The Rejection-Intrusion Pattern: A Central Family Dynamic. *Journal of Marriage and Family Counseling*, 1978, 1, 5-12.

> Describes a pattern frequently seen in marital breakdown, in which one partner seeks closeness and the other separateness. Examines the family of origin milieu in which one partner was engulfed and the other rejected, the exquisite matching process in which the pair become involved, the covert similarities that are masked in the pattern, and the regulatory dynamics through which intuitively agreed-upon levels of distance and closeness are maintained. Implications for therapy are discussed.

O'Leary, K. D. and Turkewitz, H. Marital Therapy from a Behavioral Perspective. In: T. J. Paolino and B. S. McCrady (Eds.), *Marriage and Marital Therapy*. New York: Brunner/Mazel, 1978.

> After discussing generic features of the behavioral approach, whether operant, respondent, or cognitive, the authors explore the development of behavioral marital intervention as applied to courtship, engagement, marriage, and disengagement stages of relationship. Consideration of such processes as assessment, specification of desired behaviors, clear communication, problem-solving skills, prompting social reenforcement of outcomes, the writing of contracts, and other modalities. Consideration of outcome studies and future directions in the behavioral orientation.

Overturf, J. Marital Therapy: Toleration of Differentness. *Journal of Marriage and Family Counseling*, 1976, 3, 235-241.

> An examination of the dynamic of differentness in the marital relationship. While difference can be perceived initially as an opportunity to bring closure to a partner's unfinished individuation, the later recognition of separateness can induce stress and threat. Partners often attempt to maintain the myth of inappropriate mutuality, to inhibit separateness, but the task of therapy is to facilitate the tolerance of difference and the continued process of differentiation.

Paul, N. L. The Role of Mourning and Empathy in Conjoint Marital

Therapy. In: G. H. Zuk and I. Boszormenyi-Nagy (Eds.), *Family Therapy and Disturbed Families*. Palo Alto: Science & Behavior Books, 1967.

> An early and classic exposition of the role of unresolved grief in the creation and continuation of marital and family dysfunction. Intense incomplete experiences of loss and disappointment result in fixation points later displaced onto spouse and others and contributing to symbiotic rigidity. Presentation of the process of operational mourning through directed inquiry, associative listening, self- and cross-confrontation leading to more secure ego boundaries, improved object relations, greater reality testing, and strengthened interpersonal empathy.

Paul, N. L. Self- and Cross-Confrontation Techniques Via Audeo- and Videotape Recordings in Conjoint Family and Marital Therapy. Presentation at the American Orthopsychiatric Association Annual Meeting, 1968.

> The author describes an experiential procedure in which a family member is confronted with his or her own previously recorded material or with the playback, with permission, of excerpts from another family. Provides a means for overcoming perceptual blocks and emotional impasses in the generation and maintenance of interpersonal disharmony.

Paul, N. L. Parental Empathy. In: E. J. Anthony and T. Benedek (Eds.), *Parenthood: Its Psychology and Psychopathology*. Boston: Little, Brown and Company, 1970.

> A look at the psychodynamics of intergenerational transmission of unresolved emotionality. After defining empathy as the parent's capacity to make contact with and to experience the full range of his or her own emotionality as well as that of the child, the author demonstrates the process through which blocks and fixation points are covertly transmitted to the offspring even when the parents believe themselves to be doing otherwise. Must reading for an understanding of transgenerational diffusion.

Paul, N. L. Personal Communication, 1977.

Paul, N. L. and Paul, B. B. *A Marital Puzzle: Transgenerational Analysis in Marriage.* New York: W. W. Norton, 1975.

In a detailed presentation of verbatim transcripts and therapist commentary from seven sessions with a young professional couple, the authors reveal the full scope of their theory and practice. Their conflict, the husband's extramarital affair, and the wife's attempted suicide are disclosed as grounded in each partner's relationships with the family of origin. The dynamics of emotional fixation, displacement, diffuse ego boundries, and maladaptive object relations are seen along with such intervention procedures as directed inquiry, confrontive drawing of parallels, the use of self- and cross-confrontational recordings, and associative listening. An in-depth look at one clinician's repertoire.

Perls, F. S. Dream Seminars. In: J. Fagan and I. L. Shepherd (Eds.), *Gestalt Therapy Now: Theory, Techniques, Applications.* Palo Alto: Science & Behavior Books, 1970.

A pioneer of gestalt therapy demonstrates how to bring the dream back to life and to use it for integrating aspects of the self spontaneously revealed in it. Not so much theory as the depiction of the therapist's facilitation of the reenactment. Work on five dreams from different individuals is presented.

Polanyi, Michael. *Personal Knowledge: Towards a Post-Critical Philosophy.* Chicago: The University of Chicago Press, 1958.

A monumental study of epistemology by a distinguished physical chemist and social scientist. Scientific knowledge in particular but also knowledge in general, he demonstrates with rigorous logic, is not made up of facts gathered in a dispassionate and detached manner. Knowing is, instead, an act in which the inquirer personally participates, both in discovery and validation, and for which he is responsible. Examines the meaning of such concepts as objectivity, probablility, method, subsidiary and tacit components, commitment, and universal intent.

Polster, E. and Polster, M. *Gestalt Therapy Integrated: Countours of Theory and Practice.* New York: Vintage Books, 1973.

> A second generation of gestalt therapists formulate a concise statement of principles and practices, elaborate on them, and develop their own. Explication of such dynamics as contact functions, the integration of past and present, awareness, and experiments. Implications of gestalt beyond the individual, with couples, families, and groups. Filled with concrete examples.

Rogers, C. R. A Theory of Therapy, Personality, and Interpersonal Relationships As Developed in the Client-Centered Framework. In: S. Koch (Ed.), *Psychology: A Study of a Science, Vol. III.* New York: McGraw Hill, 1959.

> The tightest and most comprehensive statement of the theory and practice of the originator of client-centered therapy. Detailed consideration of such dynamics as conditions of worth in development, formation of self-concept, the meaning of anxiety and defensiveness, incongruity, and many more. Also explications of heavily researched conditions of therapeutic change, empathy, acceptance, reflective listening, and therapist genuineness. Overview of a therapy of considerable staying power.

Rogers, C. R. *On Becoming A Person: A Therapist's View of Psychotherapy.* Boston: Houghton Mifflin, 1961.

> A collection of the author's papers in which he begins a generalization of client-centered findings into such areas as interpersonal communication and relationships, family life, research, education, and group process. Summarizes findings and hypotheses regarding the facilitation of personal growth. A characteristic blending of personal and scientific views.

Satir, V. *Conjoint Family Therapy.* Palo Alto: Science & Behavior Books, 1967.

> A classic by one of the luminaries of family therapy. Contains her views on such dynamics as marital conflict, the

induction of the child into triadic process, the dysfunctions of communication, and the pitfalls of a pathology perspective in intervention. Extensive elaboration of the role of the therapist, the stages of intervention, and the place of the family chronology. A growth-oriented model.

Simkin, J. S. The Use of Dreams in Gestalt Therapy. In: C. J. Sager and H. S. Kaplan (Eds.), *Progress in Group and Family Therapy.* New York: Brunner/Mazel, 1978.

Viewing the dream as a wholistic representation of the client's experience, the author describes the therapeutic enactment as a means of integration and awareness. Sets forth such procedures as retelling in the present, identifying with and portraying different dream elements, staying with the foreground, the use of body language, and recollection in the group process. Case presentation of principles.

Sluzki, C. E. Marital Therapy from A Systems Perspective. In. T. J. Paolino and B. S. McCrady (Eds.), *Marriage and Marital Therapy.* New York: Brunner/Mazel, 1978.

Converging on communication systems and particularly on cybernetic interaction effects and sequences, the author reviews eighteen prescriptions for interrupting and re-directing the flow. Attention to such dynamics as speaking for self, impeding mind reading, blocking gossiping and go-between efforts, eliciting behaviors by restraining them, and more.

Steinglass, Peter. The Conceptualization of Marriage from a Systems Theory Perspective. In: T. J. Paolino and B. S. McGrady (Eds.), *Marriage and Marital Therapy.* New York: Brunner/Mazel, 1978.

An excellent clarification of the systems approach to marriage. After briefly reviewing core systems concepts of organization, control, energy, and time and space, the author then examines their relative utilization in four theories: the structural of Minuchin, the Bowen theory, the communications perspective of the Mental Research Institute, and the sociological viewpoints of structure-function and development. Provides a constructive integration of different orientations through an adaptational and life cycle focus.

Stone, P. J., Dunphy, D. C., Smith, M. S., and Ogilvie, D. M. *The General Inquirer: A Computer Approach to Content Analysis.* Cambridge: The M. I. T. Press, 1966.

The authors define content analysis as a research technique for making inferences by systematically and objectively identifying specified characteristics within text. Detailed look at such procedures as specifying categories of analysis, determining the nature of systematic investigation, locating texts and units, and the making of inferences. Considerable implications for bringing order to the clinical function of tracing couple interaction.

Tillich, P. *Theology of Culture.* New York: Oxford University Press, 1959.

A classic statement of the analogical and correlational nature and function of symbols. Exploration of symbols as representational, participatory, disclosive, transcendent and immanent, and compelling. Humanistic and philosophical dimensions of language and symbol.

Villasenor, D. *Indian Sandpainting of the Greater Southwest.* Healdsburg, California: Naturegraph Company, 1963.

A discussion with illustrations of the rites through which the healer, using sand and other natural substances, creates the ritual paintings that analogically integrate the self and restore harmony between self and environment.

Warkentin, J. and Whitaker, C. The Secret Agenda of the Therapist Doing Couples Therapy. In: G. H. Zuk and I. Boszormenyi-Nagy (Eds.), *Family Therapy and Disturbed Families.* Palo Alto: Science & Behavior Books, 1967.

Presupposing that marital therapists bring different goals, assumptions, and attitudes to the process of intervention, the authors set forth ten working principles inherent in their approach and challenge others to explicate their secret agendas as well.

Watzlawick, P., Weakland, J. and Fisch, R. *Change: Principles of Problem Formation and Problem Resolution.* New York: W. W. Norton, 1974.

Defines the nature of first order and second order change and the relative appropriateness of both. Shows how second order change is unpredictable, abrupt, apparently illogical, and reverses the premises governing the system as a whole. Analyzes the four principles of second order change: the solution as keystone of the problem, the element of paradox, focusing on effects rather than causes, and reframing the situation in a way that accounts for concrete facts or events as well or better than previously perceived but creating a new experience within it.